Advocacy and Archaeology

Advocacy and Archaeology
Urban Intersections

Edited by
Kelly M. Britt and Diane F. George

berghahn
NEW YORK · OXFORD

First published in 2023 by
Berghahn Books
www.berghahnbooks.com

© 2023, 2026 Kelly M. Britt and Diane F. George
First paperback edition published in 2026

All rights reserved. Except for the quotation of short passages
for the purposes of criticism and review, no part of this book
may be reproduced in any form or by any means, electronic or
mechanical, including photocopying, recording, or any information
storage and retrieval system now known or to be invented,
without written permission of the publisher.

Library of Congress Cataloging-in-Publication Data

Names: Britt, Kelly M., editor. | George, Diane F., editor.
Title: Advocacy and Archaeology: Urban Intersections / edited by Kelly M. Britt and Diane F. George.
Description: New York: Berghahn Books, 2023. | Includes bibliographical references and index.
Identifiers: LCCN 2023004607 (print) | LCCN 2023004608 (ebook) | ISBN 9781800739642 (hardback) | ISBN 9781800739659 (ebook)
Subjects: LCSH: Urban archaeology. | Archaeology—Social aspects. | Archaeology—Political aspects. | Social justice. | Archaeology and history.
Classification: LCC CC77.U72 A36 2023 (print) | LCC CC77.U72 (ebook) | DDC 930.1—dc23/eng/20230208
LC record available at https://lccn.loc.gov/2023004607
LC ebook record available at https://lccn.loc.gov/2023004608

British Library Cataloguing in Publication Data

A catalogue record for this book is available from the British Library

EU GPSR Authorized Representative

LOGOS EUROPE, 9 rue Nicolas Poussin, 17000, LA ROCHELLE, France
Email: Contact@logoseurope.eu

ISBN 978-1-80073-964-2 hardback
ISBN 978-1-83695-637-2 paperback
ISBN 978-1-83695-612-9 epub
ISBN 978-1-80073-965-9 web pdf

https://doi.org/10.3167/9781800739642

To all those archaeologists that have inspired us and our work,
and to future archaeologists: may you find inspiration in these pages.

Contents

List of Illustrations ix

Foreword xii
   Margaret Purser

Preface xxvii

Acknowledgments xxxiv

Part I. Preservation of Cultural Resources

Chapter 1
PANYC: The Why, the Then, and the Now 1
   Joan H. Geismar

Chapter 2
"Cursed Be He That Moves My Bones": The Archaeologist's Role in
Protecting Burial Sites in Urban Areas 14
   Elizabeth D. Meade and Douglas Mooney

Part II. Raising Public, Descendant, and Community Voices

Chapter 3
Digging Truth: Archaeology and Public Imagination in Shockoe Bottom 45
   Ana Edwards and Matthew R. Laird

Chapter 4
Seneca Village Interpretations: Bringing Collaborative Historical
Archaeology and Heritage Advocacy to the Forefront and Online 68
   Meredith B. Linn, Nan A. Rothschild, and Diana diZerega Wall

Chapter 5
Right to the City: Community-Based Urban Archaeology as
Abolitionist Heritage 98
   Kelly M. Britt

Part III. Knowledge and Power

Chapter 6
"Think Like a Historical Archaeologist": Moving Beyond the
Primary Source Document in K–12 Education 127
  Appendix 141
    Elizabeth Martin

Chapter 7
"DIVERS[]S" and the Political Legacies of an "Experience-Exhibition" 145
    María Fernanda Ugalde and O. Hugo Benavides

Chapter 8
American Apotheosis: Confronting Exceptionalism in the
(Re)Production of National Identity 169
    Diane F. George

Afterword 201
    Christopher N. Matthews

Index 215

Illustrations

Figures

1.1.	New York City's five boroughs consolidated in 1898. © Joan H. Geismar.	2
1.2.	P-A-N-Y-C as written on a blackboard at the 1980 organizational meeting of Professional Archaeologists of New York City (facsimile). © Joan H. Geismar.	3
1.3.	Sharon Wilkins and Caledonia Jones at PANYC's 2015 annual public meeting after receiving engraved Marshalltown trowels for their contribution to New York City archaeology. © Joan H. Geismar.	5
1.4.	Fort Gibson's exposed early nineteenth-century northwest defenses, now a National Park Service outdoor exhibit on Ellis Island. Courtesy of the National Park Service and Hunter Research, Inc.	7
1.5.	James Jackson's 1799 tombstone, a surprise relic of the former potter's field located in what is now New York City's Washington Square Park. © Joan H. Geismar.	9
1.6.	The PANYC button. © Joan H. Geismar.	11
2.1.	Detail of the PAF's Philadelphia Historical Burial Places Database showing the distribution of redeveloped cemeteries in a portion of Center City. © Philadelphia Archaeological Forum.	27
2.2.	Map depicting the general location of cemeteries documented in Meade 2020. © Elizabeth D. Meade.	29
2.3.	Sample map showing documented cemeteries in Lower Manhattan based on Meade 2020. © Elizabeth D. Meade.	30
3.1.	Overview of the Lumpkin's Jail excavation in the closing stages of the investigation in December 2008, view facing north. © David M. Doody, Courtesy of the City of Richmond. Significant features included the kitchen building (*center left*), cobbled courtyard and brick drain (*center right*), and inundated jail foundation (*center bottom*).	52

3.2. Altar set up at the Lumpkin's Jail site by a local cultural organization, the Elegba Folklore Society, at the start of the excavation in August 2008. A libation ceremony and offerings of food, imagery, and stones served to honor ancestors who were subjected to the slave trade in Richmond, and provided to the present-day community a tangible representation of the significance of the site and importance of the investigation in uncovering a critical element of the city's history, 2008. © Ana Edwards 62

4.1. A portion of Egbert L. Viele's 1855 "Map of lands included in the Central Park from a topographical survey" showing Seneca Village. Courtesy of Municipal Archives, City of New York. 69

4.2. The foundation wall of the Wilson house uncovered during the 2011 excavation. © Meredith B. Linn and the Institute for the Exploration of Seneca Village History. 76

4.3. Curry comb excavated from the Wilson house shown with two of the ribs that hold the teeth next to the body of the comb. A wooden handle would have attached to the arrow-shaped base, secured by the copper alloy cuff. Courtesy of the NYC Archaeological Repository: The Nan A. Rothschild Research Center, public domain. 77

4.4. Ariel Williams, descendant of Seneca Village resident, Andrew Williams, with IESVH member and Manhattan Borough Historian Emeritus Cal Jones viewing the new CPC signs interpreting Seneca Village in Central Park. Still from video produced by the Central Park Conservancy. Reproduced with permission. 83

5.1. The United Order of the Tents Eastern District #3 Headquarters, 87 MacDonough Street, Brooklyn, NY. 2019. © Kelly M. Britt. 99

5.2. The United Order of the Tents Eastern District #3 Sign. 2019. © Kelly M. Britt. 100

5.3. 227 Duffield Street, Brooklyn, NY protest. *Left:* 227 Duffield Street front facade. *Right:* Author's daughter at protest to save the building. 2019. © Kelly M. Britt. 117

5.4. Historic Hunterfly Road Houses, Weeksville Heritage Center, Brooklyn, NY. 2017. © Kelly M. Britt. 119

6.1. Examples of history lessons using primary sources, geared to the Regents test. Stanford History Education Group. Screenshot by Elizabeth Martin. 133

6.2. Historical Thinking Chart, recreated from original chart by the Stanford History Education Group. 134

7.1. Museo Nacional del Ecuador Frontside, Av. Patria, Quito, 2019. © María Fernanda Ugalde. 155

7.2.	House in Quito decorated with collage combining motifs inspired by Boticelli's *The Birth of Venus* and a Valdivia "Venus" figurine. March 2021. © María Fernanda Ugalde.	156
7.3.	Part of the exhibition showing some of the displays containing, in the front (*left section*), some of the female figures from the Formative Period. © María Fernanda Ugalde.	158
7.4.	Part of the exhibition showing some of the displays containing some of the male figures from the Regional Development Formative Period. © María Fernanda Ugalde.	158
7.5.	Part of the exhibition showing some of the displays containing some of the figures representing possible gender diversity in the past (female couples, female shapes with male dresses, etc.). © María Fernanda Ugalde.	159
8.1.	"America Declared Independent—July 4, 1776." Courtesy of Transferware Collectors Club, Pattern Number 13827.	175
8.2.	*The Apotheosis of Washington*, engraving and etching by John James Barralet, 1800–1802. Painting in the collection of the Metropolitan Museum of Art, Gift of William H. Huntington, 1883, public domain.	178
8.3.	Complete versions of two of the prints found on a jug from the Assay site. *Left:* Jefferson quote and American eagle, Metropolitan Museum of Art, "Jug 1800–1830," The Collection, The American Wing (public domain). *Right:* Ship, stock print with American flag, "Success to Trade" banner. Reproduced with permission from Division of Cultural and Community Life, National Museum of American History, Smithsonian Institution, Object ID CE.63.087, Robert H. McCauley.	185
8.4.	*Left:* Jug with stanza from Ruston, American Independency (Division of Cultural and Community Life, National Museum of American History, Smithsonian Institution, Object ID CE.63.080, Robert H. McCauley). *Right:* Sherd from jug with the same print found at the Assay site. © Diane F. George.	187
8.5.	Shell-edged pearlware soup dish with black overglaze transfer print of Columbia, from the Beekman Street site. © Diane F. George.	188
8.6.	Chinese porcelain saucer in overglaze sepia enamel and gilt with American eagle, from the Beekman Street site. © Diane F. George.	191

Table

6.1.	Unit with suggestions.	142

Foreword

Margaret Purser

The beginning ideas for this volume grew from some far-reaching conversations between its editors, Kelly M. Britt and Diane F. George, in early 2020. Mulling over the increasing use of archaeology as a platform for advocacy and social action, they began counting the various case studies they could name, just among shared friends and colleagues in American historical archaeology. In the process, they observed how many of these projects were taking place in the densely urban contexts of major metropolitan areas across the United States and elsewhere. By the first months of 2020, they had extended some initial invitations, drawn up the requisite book proposal, and found a publisher. The basic goal was to produce a volume of focused case studies in advocacy-oriented archaeology in urban spaces. The discussion would update and perhaps reframe a conversation in our field about the links between archaeological practice and social action that was at least two decades old by that point. We all began drafting chapters.

Not even the most prescient among us in those early conversations could have imagined the events that would unfold over the subsequent months of 2020 and 2021. A global pandemic shut down the routines of daily life nearly overnight, and created entirely new ones shaped by quarantine: masks, social distancing, and seemingly random shortages of basic commodities. The resulting infection and death rates exposed the brutal inequities of health care systems, wealth distribution, and living conditions across the globe. An explosive summer of mass protests for social justice triggered by the horrific murders of Black men and women by police officers began as highly localized events and grew within days to national and global scales. Monuments to Confederate generals and British slave traders became sites of transformative reinterpretation of both urban landscapes and collective memory. In the United States, these events played out amid the roiling tempest of a national election year and culminated with a mob of domestic terrorists breaching the United States Capitol Building bent on reversing the outcome of the election and ending more than two centuries of peaceful transfers of political power in the country. As the authors have revised and refined the chapters over this momentous period, it has been impossible not to take these events into account. Collectively, they have created an inescapable rupture in time, cleaving it into palpable "before" and "after" times for those who lived through the experience.

In many ways, these same events make the work the chapters of this volume explore more salient and important than ever. So much of what has happened during this consequential period has unfolded as radical encounters in the present with unresolved or unacknowledged pasts. So many moments have demonstrated the continually transformative relationships among people and place and time, especially in urban contexts.

Incorporating what we have learned since our earlier discussions brings a sharper focus to some of the emphases in our work. To begin with, many of us have designed our archaeological projects to expose and address the erasure of particular groups of people, periods of time, frames of mind, or inhabited places from present-day consciousness. The events over the past two years tell us that there really is no such thing as complete erasure: that the perceived absences or invisibility we are exploring are always only partial. Somewhere in the affected population, that lingering memory or knowledge is still palpable. And so it is really still present, in its very absence from the broader public sphere, like a negatively charged space.

In moments of encounter with radically different remembrances of these pasts or places, past acts of attempted erasure or denial themselves have become today's flashpoints: the commemorative statue, the desecrated burial ground, the demolished building, street, or neighborhood. "The Past" may appear to roll out behind us as an inexorably enumerated timeline, but the process of defining "pastness" is punctuated with radical moments of identity creation and transformation that occur in the present. Our archaeological practice is increasingly bound up in these punctuated moments, both as participants and at least occasionally as their creators, in collaboration with the community members with whom we often now work.

Another critical heightening of our archaeological focus brought on by the events of the past year centers on materiality, and the ways in which materiality, broadly construed, is integral to human action, both individual and collective. Noticing that stuff matters, and that human social life quite literally "takes place," is hardly a radical turn for archaeology in the early twenty-first century. Indeed, those notions inform a set of basic tenets for the field that we share with a wide array of disciplinary neighbors and cousins working across both past and present, from historians to geographers to folklorists, and so on. They form the core of a wide array of twenty-first century heritage practices (heritage being used in this chapter in its broader sense to encompass the fields of archaeology, historic preservation, conservation, and interpretation). But the sheer scale and drama of the role played by objects, places, and material practices over the past two years has us all searching for new vocabulary, and wider frames of reference.

In particular, look at the ways that objects and places became highly charged, multilayered symbols in an unflinchingly intentional theater of contest in nearly every public venue imaginable. Masks—and mask-wearing—reframed notions of personhood that played out in an explicitly public arena. Social distancing protocols scattered polka dot maps across the floors of public places, from post offices to grocery stores to the VIP section of inaugural seating on the steps of the US Capitol. Material targets of contestation—Civil War monuments, Black Lives Matter murals, and public streets, parks, plazas, and administrative buildings across this country (as well as similar sites in many others)—became the location/locale/locus of intensely reiterative placemaking, as each new layer of paint, each rally, each occupation, and each march drew its meaning from the explicit juxtaposition with all those that had come before. Once again, the contexts for this highly visible set of material practices were not only very performatively public, but also most often urban.

Meanwhile, the suddenly cloistered life of quarantine brought a new consciousness of the intimate surroundings of interior spaces, and of the newly familiar localized places defined by nearby streets, blocks, and neighborhoods. Archaeologists make their living parsing the material culture of the past into coherent narratives. But for those of us who do so while working in and with present-day communities to document their lives, heritage, and voices, being immersed in this year-long theater of performative materiality at a very localized, intimate scale has revealed nuances about the relationships between people, places, and things that we are only beginning to process.

Where does all this leave a group of historical archaeologists contributing to a volume called "Archaeology and Advocacy"? We are reflecting on our original work, finding a host of new questions, and if anything, renewing our commitment to this kind of archaeology conducted with communities in the present and for the future. What follows is a brief introduction to the volume's contents and some of the key concepts and questions that thread through the rest of these chapters.

Archaeology and Advocacy

What does it mean to talk about "archaeology" and "advocacy" in the same sentence? As the volume's editors discuss in the preface, advocacy approaches in historical archaeology cover an increasingly broad range of projects, partnerships, goals, and strategies. The chapters in this volume explore this diversity as a developmental trajectory over the course of the discipline's history. Moreover, this trajectory is one we share with all the historical and social sciences that seek to define the relevance of the past in the present. How historical archaeology's work connects with and contributes to that larger discourse is a key theme running through many of the volume's chapters.

The earliest approaches to advocacy in historical archaeology might be described as "advocacy for the resource." This form is embedded in the very origin story of the field and still forms a core value for its practitioners. It is also obviously one we share with all other heritage- and preservation-related practices. There are several specific disciplinary legacies that feed into our approach to the work. In the early days of historical archaeology's emergence as a field, the larger preservation world sharply privileged both the surviving documentary record and the elite architecture of the built environment over the archaeological record of the past. Archaeological data were not seen as contributing information of the same value or integrity as that of the written record in particular, so working to counter this perception became a central rationale for historical archaeologists' early research efforts. By the mid-1970s, this argument had become more nuanced: the idea that archaeological resources and research could be used to revise and expand a written record that was itself biased and incomplete became integral to the field. It is this justification, which emphasizes the power of archaeology to expose and correct historical erasures and silences, that still drives much of the historical archaeology in the United States and elsewhere.

What is new in more recent iterations of this kind of advocacy-based work, including research discussed in several chapters in this volume, is the assertion that the ultimate value of these archaeological resources and their analysis and interpretation is their ability to alter present-day society's assumptions and perceptions about the past, and thus to affect social and political change in the present. This moves the power of the objects and sites themselves from a remedial role of revising or augmenting some essentialized record of the past, to actively invoking "new" pasts as rationales for present-day change to create better—or at least alternate—futures.

Beginning as early as the 1990s, a second set of modalities linking archaeology and advocacy began to emerge. These new modalities shifted the focus of advocacy from the artifacts, sites, and archaeological resources to present-day people, and in particular, to communities that held specific connections to those archaeological resources. These new approaches grew directly out of earlier work with local communities and organizations. Over time, archaeology happening *in* communities became archaeological explorations *of* those communities, and finally, fully collaborative work *with* communities designed to achieve much more present- and future-driven goals. Examples of this latter kind of work are now innumerable, and community-based archaeology and its cousins in related disciplines have entire journals and programs devoted to it, such as the *Journal of Community Archaeology and Heritage, Heritage and Society,* and *Public Archaeology,* to name a few. There are formal organizations with ongoing programming such as the "Archaeology in the Community" organization, and many others (Jones and Pickens 2020).

In these projects, the archaeology itself may be as focused on the process of designing and doing the work as on the ultimate product of the project as a singular piece of research or final report. This is archaeology as praxis, where it is not (just) the data that matter, so much as the processes of exploration, documentation, and above all, narration. These projects are often long-term, multifaceted, and embedded in extensive ongoing partnerships with numerous community organizations, governmental agencies, or educational institutions. Perhaps more importantly, project goals can explicitly target community-driven needs and issues, such as combating gentrification, preventing crime, reducing conflict, or revitalizing economically blighted districts or neighborhoods. The urban contexts of many of these projects can also mean that "community" is construed much more broadly across scales, from a local neighborhood to the city as a whole and beyond. The issues being addressed may begin as very local ones, but almost inevitably invoke much more comprehensive issues, such as structural racism, environmental justice, or national ideological narratives of identity and origin.

Any and all of these kinds of advocacy-oriented archaeological projects can and do happen everywhere. So why focus on urban contexts, and why now in particular? If that question was relevant in early 2020, it has become even more so following the events of the rest of that fateful year. Setting those recent events aside for the moment, urban contexts have long been a focus of special research emphasis in historical archaeology in the United States and internationally, with at least two dedicated volumes in the field's flagship American journal *Historical Archaeology* (1987, 2008) and innumerable books and articles published globally. More importantly here, urban archaeology has evolved in very parallel ways to advocacy-based archaeology. It has grown from archaeological projects conducted *in* cities to increasingly complex and critical archaeologies *of* cities, city people, and city life (Mullins and Warner 2008, 1).

As a result, urban archaeology and community-based collaborative archaeology have grown up together. So, for the authors of this volume, the sheer density and ever-changing texture of urban placemaking, the dynamism and complexity of urban social life, and the frequently contested nature of urban places as sites of varying scales of both community identity and social power all help to focus and problematize key aspects of archaeology as advocacy. Cities as material places are constantly being built, demolished, and rebuilt by repeated decisions about what to keep, what to change, and what to remove. These transformations are never politically, socially, or economically neutral, and repeatedly impact the lives of generations of smaller, more marginalized neighborhoods, enclaves, and districts: erasing some places altogether, moving sectors of the population from one area to another, and shifting people's access to land, housing, and other infrastructure. The archaeological record of this fractured landscape transformation has proven to be a powerful platform for revealing those impacts, raising questions about processes of erasure and dispossession, and challenging the city's official narratives, which normalize today's distributions of power and authority (Matthews 2020, 4–9).

The different sections of this volume both reflect and amplify this longer-term intellectual history and evolutionary trajectory linking archaeology and advocacy. The first section, "Preservation of Cultural Resources," explores the earlier, foundational concept of advocacy as protection of places and resources: identifying and protecting physical sites from destruction or erasure and protecting and sharing the information generated from archaeological research as something useful and valuable in the present. The first chapter grounds the volume in the origins of the field with Joan Geismar's historical review of New York's Professional Archaeologists of New York City (PANYC). PANYC formed forty years ago when archaeologists across the city banded together to coordinate advocacy for both the preservation of places and public access to information recovered from development-driven excavation projects. Elizabeth Meade and Douglas Mooney's chapter extends this discussion of advocacy for places in the urban fabric with a focus on a particular type of urban place: burial grounds. They explore burial grounds as a category of urban site particularly vulnerable to the material consequences of being forgotten, which is the inherent characteristic of urban change over time. More importantly, they detail how destroying these places constitutes a form of loss from a city's collective memory that repeatedly impacts present-day communities already marginalized in urban contexts.

Across the chapters of this introductory section, the identities of those engaged in the advocacy efforts in question shift from exclusively professional archaeologists to include an ever-broader range of community members and organizations, which leads easily into the second major section of the book, "Raising Public, Descendant, and Community Voices." Here, the chapters focus on the developing role of archaeology as praxis: as an inclusive and collaborative platform for encouraging dialogue in the present about the past and its meaning. Ana Edwards and Matthew Laird unravel the complex interplay among place, memory, and social action that unfolded in Richmond, Virginia, when archaeological work in the city sequentially revealed a set of powerful African American sites: a slave-trading complex, a burial ground, and ultimately a set of discarded human remains at a medical college. Their chapter explores the power of both the places themselves, and the archaeological exposure of the places, to validate social memory and provide a launching point for social commentary and action in the Richmond community. Meredith B. Linn, Nan A. Rothschild, and Diana diZerega Wall use the twenty-year history of the Seneca Village Project in New York's Central Park to reflect on the realities of crafting genuinely collaborative interpretations of places and pasts that are charged with powerful but complex and diverse meanings for many different communities in the present day. Their work also explores both the challenge and the potential of digital media for extending this collaboration into new social dimensions. Britt's chapter closes out the section by circling back to advocacy as the protection of community-valued places but employs this traditional disciplinary strategy in new ways. Her work with Brooklyn's United Order of the Tents leverages the heritage values of the organization's headquarters building to empower the local neighborhood in its struggle to own and use everyday community places in today's ongoing contests over who controls urban spaces.

The narratives being constructed in and through these projects are not just about restoring lost or misrepresented voices from the past, but about articulating how those past voices inform and challenge today's issues and experiences. Even more powerfully, the discourses unfolding in these projects specifically unpack how today's dominant perceptions of the past are used to justify and rationalize continuing exclusion, erasure, and disenfranchisement. The authors do so by recognizing and privileging the voices of descendants and community members living today.

The book's final section, "Knowledge and Power," contextualizes these efforts in ways that extend well beyond the material immediacy of specific urban places and communities to the scope and scale of national identity construction. The essays are unified in seeing archaeological research and thought as an enduring challenge to any singular, essentialized historical narrative of a single national identity. Elizabeth Martin discusses the power of an archaeological approach to teaching about the past to dismantle the singular and inevitable narratives embedded in kindergarten (K) through grade 12 social sciences curriculum covering American history. In particular, she leverages archaeological thinking to give both a historical place and an intellectual voice to high school students who are not "inculcated into white-middle-class American culture at a young age, with no interruptions in their education and a home that is not food-insecure," and so find themselves written out of the historical narrative in even the most progressive textbooks or curriculum standards. María Fernanda Ugalde and O. Hugo Benevides reflect on their exhibit in the National Museum of Ecuador, which documented gender plurality in that country's Precolumbian history as an intentionally designed encounter with the constructed nature of Ecuadorian national identity. Weaving their own personal lived experience into the exhibit's design, they explain how the exhibition, as experienced by viewers, challenged the carefully constructed nationalist narrative by exposing the colonialist violence that links today's homophobia and transphobia with the rise of the key religious and political institutions of that modern nation-state. George continues this theme with a discussion of the transformative work that can be accomplished when archaeological documentation of the commercially produced material symbolism of early post-Revolutionary America's "imagined community" is juxtaposed with the nostalgic invocation of that very same symbolism and iconography by today's nativist political groups. The constructed myth embodied in "Washington's Apotheosis" British transfer prints provides a deeply ironic challenge to the claims to a "true" American identity made by wearers of red MAGA hats manufactured in China.

Perhaps even most importantly in the culminating chapters of this volume, these authors emphasize archaeological perspective as much as methodology. They define the archaeological habits of mind that empower archaeology as advocacy. Their language ranges from Martin's charge to "think like a historical archaeologist," to Ugalde and Benevides' efforts "to look again and look differently," to George's belief in the potential of archaeologically informed "knowledge and education" to challenge today's increasingly dark nationalist and nativist political trends. And likewise, these articles clearly reframe what is meant by advocacy itself, moving well beyond the preservation of artifacts and sites to conceptualize archaeological praxis as a tool for social change. Taken together, these chapters give us an idea of where advocacy-based archaeology will go from here. They charge the practitioners of this approach with reconfiguring the nature of knowledge construction itself—materially, socially, and politically. That new process of knowledge construction is inherently multivocal, experiential, and collaborative.

Concepts Explored

While they are organized into separate sections, the chapters of this volume are best seen as a conversation among the different authors, being elaborated upon across these categories. In fact, many of the papers could have fit easily into more than one section. Three key concepts emerge from the authors' discussion, which could be labeled authority, mobility, and plurality. These are concepts archaeologists have been discussing for decades, in all manner of historical and cultural contexts. But shifting the focus to advocacy for specific communities in the present means that these familiar ideas take on new meanings.

By 2022, it is already something of a truism in archaeology and a wide array of other heritage-related fields that professional experts are not and should not be the only people to wield the power of deciding which objects, buildings, or places are important and to whom. In practice, however, in any given urban context, this authority is shared across myriad official government agencies and political bodies, defined by a range of policy frameworks from federal to municipal, and negotiated between and among a wide variety of community organizations: historical societies, advisory boards, commercial organizations, neighborhood associations, and so on. These entities all debate how to define attributes like authenticity, accuracy, singularity, beauty, condition, value, and significance. They negotiate how these attributes will inform decisions about what will happen to some part of the urban fabric and why.

Advocacy-oriented archaeology projects are often designed to create platforms that enable community members or groups who do not have direct access to this kind of decision-making authority to assert an alternative authority based on the documented results of the project. These results tend to highlight local knowledge and local narratives of value and significance, with conventional archaeological data and research woven into other works such as oral history, folklore, and ethnography. In many cases, the existence of the archaeological project itself leverages broader community participation in the decision-making process.

In other, nonurban contexts, these kinds of community-based projects can often assume an explicit connection between the past occupants of a place, represented by their remaining archaeological record, and contemporary occupants living in the area or nearby. Modern urban contexts can make this assumption extremely problematic. Today's urban populations are highly mobile, physically as well as economically and socially. People's connections to both past and place are nonlinear and fractal in complexity: associations with cultural institutions such as churches, schools, or cemeteries can map out widely across a given city's neighborhoods, as generations shift and relocate over time. Conversely, the physical neighborhoods traditionally identified with immigrant populations can retain that identity over decades, but the specific immigrant groups living in those neighborhoods can change radically over the same period. Last but by no means least, urban contexts have always seen significantly higher proportions of their populations who rent rather than own their residences. Even more broadly, the urban fabric itself creates an enduring material framework that shapes where and how successive generations live and work in its built environment. As a result, most urban residents inhabit places created and controlled by someone else. And while each generation modifies and remakes these places, they do so in a continuously reiterative interaction with the inherited palimpsest of that evolving framework.

How then do advocacy-oriented archaeology projects identify either the people or the places relevant to their work? What other forms of community affinity, identity, and place attachment need to be identified and documented as critical parts of these projects? And finally, what is the value of places that, through archaeological project work, become essentially new or renewed sites of collective memory: places where the assumed past connections between some specific "place" and "community" yield to a more future-oriented, collaborative designation of a documented place as a site for ongoing interpretation, reflection, or pilgrimage?

Identifying such places and documenting the people who have lived there throughout any given city's past means encountering a diverse array of past occupants, land uses, and histories. That is the fundamental nature of cities as forms of human settlement anywhere in the world and at any time. In any North American context, as well as in many other colonialist contexts around the world, that settlement history begins well before the arrival of European urban settlement systems. Much of historical archaeology's disciplinary story has been about opening up a more inclusive narrative of place to encompass these complex histories.

In the advocacy-oriented cases in this volume, this pluralist approach is extended in several ways. These projects both document and facilitate the connection of diverse groups to their sites and places. The interpretive programs described here focus on including multiple voices and the collaborative development of diverse and complex narratives. But beyond this, these projects create both places and processes that encourage the telling of more than one story, which is not just a way to generate new or different facts for richer narrative content. These projects aspire to be inclusive, transdisciplinary, and open-ended as a form of practice. They do not just document multiple stories but teach plurality as a mode of knowledge construction.

Questions Raised

What happens when archaeology is practiced as advocacy? What is gained, or accomplished, and for whom? How does it change the archaeology? How does it change the situation of the moment? How does it change people's perceptions of past and present, going forward? The authors in this volume are participants in a much broader dialogue exploring the meaning and relevancy of our field in the twenty-first century. Their work here opens up at least two distinct paths for continuing that dialogue.

The first would be to delve into what might be called archaeological habits of mind. Many of these projects—and others like them—do not necessarily involve large-scale excavations and analysis of those recovered materials. Even when they do, this work is only one component of a much larger collaborative project. Perhaps even more importantly, these projects are often designed to continue long after any excavation has been completed, particularly in terms of fostering collaborative engagement among different community members and organizations. This model is not a particularly new part of our larger discipline. It is standard practice in projects conducted under the domain of contemporary archaeology, where archaeological methods and conceptual frameworks provide powerful new insights into present-day issues such as homelessness (Zimmerman et al. 2010) or migration (De Leon 2013). In fact, the distinction between "contemporary" and "historical" archaeology is increasingly blurred, as practitioners of the latter undertake more projects that explore the very recent past, such as the impact of 1960s freeway construction and urban renewal (Matthews 2020; Mullins 2006).

But still, a certain intellectual vertigo can come with trying to explain the ways in which one is an archaeologist without reference to our discipline's hallmark methodology. Yet we still think like archaeologists, and like historical archaeologists for that matter, as the chapters in the final section here so cogently reveal. So what does that mean, exactly? And how does it matter? The projects discussed in these chapters suggest that the answer goes beyond any contribution of our scholarly experience with either materiality or constructs of pastness, although these important elements underlie and inform the rest. Instead, this work suggests that what may be the most powerful contribution that archaeologists make in these deeply collaborative projects is perspective. Our role is less as authorities in either methodology or content, and more as people trained to analyze how and why current narratives of the past read the way they do, and how all the disparate sources of new information produced by these new kinds of projects amplify, challenge, expand, or change those narratives.

A less conventional but potentially more important part of what we bring to these urban situations of advocacy and activism can be found in the ways that doing this kind of work has transformed our own professional practice and the meaning of "doing archaeology." This is particularly true for the growth of a more collaborative, inclusive archaeological praxis referred to earlier and its role in reframing notions of authority and knowledge construction. In ways that we are just beginning to understand, the performative, iterative nature of this new kind of praxis, and the shift of focus from the products of archaeology as research to the processes of archaeology as a practice, has become what we bring to the moment.

The second path winding through these chapters follows the ways in which the particular advocacies of which these projects are a part are taking place within a larger reconfiguring of the nexus among people, places, and the past. We study this as archaeologists, but we are also living it in our everyday lives. Part of this reconfiguring is driven by the increasingly complex patterns of human mobility in the early twenty-first century, as discussed earlier. Climate change, economic and political destabilization, and human conflict drive ever-greater waves of migrants and refugees. Tens of millions of people globally are currently displaced from their homes, on the move across international boundaries or temporarily sheltered in refugee camps. Millions more have settled somewhat more permanently in new locations far from former homes and communities.

For these people, past connections to both place and heritage have been severed, and new ones are being built. Once again, this global reality is intensified in urban contexts, where higher population densities and a more mobile resident population combine with historical identities as destination sites for migrants, both internal and external. How will the older pasts of a city become meaningful to these new residents, if at all? How will those same cities recognize and make room for the kinds of placemaking that new residents will need to engage in to create their own connections to their new communities? It is in this context that advocacy-based archaeological practice becomes a platform for dialogue around these kinds of issues. Sites interpreted in these projects tell the complex stories of a city's places in ways that invite more stories to be told. They also elevate the visibility of the city's layered and continually evolving landscape, contextualizing today's placemaking in what has come before.

At the same time, some urban places have become localized sites of transformative reckoning with unacknowledged and unresolved elements of much larger national and global pasts. Almost by definition, many of these sites were originally created as intentionally public, official statements of what, or who, deserved remembering and commemorating. Today, these places act as living theaters of contested narratives, not just about the past, but about the meaning of the past in the present. They act as material manifestations both of today's unbalanced power relations, and of how these are connected to enduring legacies of colonialism, racism, and inequality. In the terms discussed here, they also make visible what places and stories have been erased or ignored from the authoritative, official narrative. Pulling down a monument or layering it with spray-painted messages that assert a very different memory and commemoration transforms the way people see and use that place. What was once an unchallenged display of authoritative statements meant to instruct a passive public becomes a multivocal and ongoing public forum of engagement and debate.

This shift creates an environment in which people go to such places not only to learn about or remember the past but also to actively evaluate the meaning of that past in the present. And they do so not just once, but repeatedly, in the context of the ongoing flow of current events. In such an environment, advocacy-based archaeological projects like the ones discussed in this volume are increasingly engaged in helping to create and recreate such places and using them to foster this ongoing dialogue. Advocacy-based archaeology further complicates and reframes the commemorative landscape by undertaking this work at sites that are often not on any official list of landmarks. It documents and interprets "missing" places that can speak to the very erased or forgotten pasts whose absence is now the defining feature of that official list. This kind of work also makes more visible the connections that such local places and events have to similar sites in other places. In the process, notions of whose pasts are relevant and what communities are being defined by these histories begin to expand in scale, from local to regional, national, and beyond.

Final Thoughts

In 2007, Lonnie Bunch, then director of the National Museum of African American History and Culture, wrote of a concept he called "usable pasts" and its value in conceptualizing the role of historical museums in contemporary society (2007, 46). He explained that history in general, but particularly those histories that people do not want to remember or seek to erase, can provide "useful tools and lessons that help one navigate contemporary life" (Bunch 2007, 46). The power and value of these tools in the present make the argument that those histories must be remembered and those erasures restored. But they also suggest that the way people in the future may need to use these tools, to navigate the present of their own time, may not be the same as today. This notion of the past, or at least knowledge of the past, as a dynamic, adaptive set of resources for navigating futures to come resonates powerfully in a world freshly aware of both the uncertainty of the future and the inevitability of change.

Advocacy-driven archaeology creates usable pasts intended to take this notion one step further, to affect some kind of change in the present that will in turn impact those futures. As such, it joins a growing body of work in the larger field of archaeology as well as several neighboring disciplines that is exploring such "future-oriented" pasts (Rosenzweig 2020, 287). Preserving the past for the future is hardly a new idea, of course: it is the often-implicit assumption that lies at the heart of all heritage legislation and organizational development of the past century, all over the world. But in recent years, practitioners working across numerous heritage-related fields have increasingly challenged us to articulate these assumptions. They reject the older version of this logic, which envisioned the preserved past as a set of material and cultural monuments that spoke to future generations as an authorized and inherently didactic narrative, giving evidence for and bearing witness to a largely fixed and static story of what happened. Instead, many are now exploring how to recast the active selecting, remembering, and preserving work all people do in defining their heritage through time as "a series of activities that are intimately concerned with assembling, building and designing future worlds" (Harrison et al. 2020. 4). Moreover, these activities are ongoing, dynamic, contested, and multivocal, making heritage "a processual and discursive, as well as material, legacy" (Harrison et al. 2020, 5). Echoing Bunch's discussion of how museums can help make the broadest and most inclusive range of "usable pasts" accessible, the role of those working in heritage fields is to develop processes that make such public discourse accessible, especially to those usually marginalized or disenfranchised from it. The authors in this volume use their own work to lay out a range of possibilities for what that kind of archaeology might look like, going forward.

Margaret Purser is a historical archaeologist who received her doctorate in anthropology from the University of California, Berkeley in 1987. She taught courses in archaeology, material culture studies, and cultural landscape studies at Sonoma State University from 1989 to 2020. She has worked on community-based cultural landscape projects on Nevada ranching, Sierra Nevada goldmining, maritime landscapes in California's Sacramento River Delta and the Sonoma County coast, and sugar plantations in Pacific coastal Guatemala since the mid-1980s. From 2000 to 2010, she conducted a community mapping project in the historical Pacific port town of Levuka, Fiji, as part of its nomination to the UNESCO World Heritage List. Her current project is the Santa Rosa Neighborhood Heritage Mapping Project, which documents that small California city's many diverse and vibrant neighborhoods in the context of today's rapid social, economic, and environmental transformations.

References

Bunch, Lonnie. 2007. "Embracing Ambiguity: The Challenge of Interpreting African American History in Museums." *Museums and Social Issues* 2 (1), 45–56.
De Leon, Jason. 2013. "Undocumented Migration, Use Wear, and the Materiality of Habitual Suffering in the Sonoran Desert." *Journal of Material Culture* 18 (2), 321–45.
Harrison, Rodney, Caitlin DeSilvey, Cornelius Holtorf, and Sharon Macdonald. 2020. "'For Ever, for Everyone . . . '" In Rodney Harrison, Caitlin DeSilvey, Cornelius Holtorf, Sharon Macdonald, Nadia Bartolini, Esther Breithoff, Harald Fredheim, Antony Lyons, Sarah May, Jennie Morgan and Sefryn Penrose (eds.), *Heritage Futures: Comparative Approaches to Natural and Cultural Heritage Practices*, 3–19. London: University College London Press.
Jones, Alexandra, and Sydney Pickens. 2020. "The Power of Community Archaeologists in Uncertain Times." *Journal of Community Archaeology and Heritage* 7 (3), 155–57.
Matthews, Christopher. 2020. "Urban Erasures: Historical and Contemporary Archaeologies." *Journal for the Anthropology of North America* 23 (1), 4–11.
Mullins, Paul. 2006. "Racializing the Commonplace Landscape: An Archaeology of Urban Renewal along the Color Line." *World Archaeology* 8 (1), 60–71.
Mullins, Paul, and Mark Warner. 2008. "Revisiting Living in Cities." *Historical Archaeology* 42 (1), 1–4.
Rosenzweig, Melissa. 2020. "Confronting the Present: Archaeology in 2019." *American Anthropologist* 122 (2), 284–305.
Zimmerman, Larry J., Courtney Singleton, and Jessica Welch. 2010. "Activism and Creating a Translational Archaeology of Homelessness." *World Archaeology* 42 (3), 443–54.

Preface
Thoughts on Urban Pasts, Presents, and Futures

Beginnings

In September 1991, workers excavating for a new federal office building in Lower Manhattan just north of City Hall uncovered the remains of approximately eleven human beings at the location of what was marked on an eighteenth-century map as the "Negro's Burial Ground." The bodies were removed and sent to Lehman College for analysis while work at the site continued. Although archaeologists from a private firm had been retained to ensure compliance with section 106 of the National Historic Preservation Act (NHPA) during the project, they had no research plan for such a contingency. All of the archaeologists were white. The General Services Administration (GSA), the federal agency responsible for the project, hoped to move on from this discovery quietly and quickly. Excavation for the new building continued.

When news of the find became public, Black New Yorkers, spiritual, cultural, and perhaps literal descendants of those interred in the burial ground—the "descendant community" (Blakey 2010, 63)—swiftly organized. Using vigils, protests, petitions, letters, and lobbying, activists formed a groundswell of opposition among both politicians and the public. Journalists, artists, religious leaders, and "activist scholars" joined in (Mack and Blakey 2004, 14–15). This grassroots movement led to the involvement of Mayor David Dinkins, the city's first Black mayor, city councilors such as Mary Pinkett of Brooklyn, and various Congresspeople such as Representative Gus Savage of Illinois. State Senator (and later governor) David Paterson formed an oversight task force to raise awareness and ensure proper treatment and memorialization of the remains. At first, the opposition elicited only vague promises from the GSA not to destroy the site and to have the archaeologists excavate the burials, despite their lack of expertise or connection to those whose remains were located there and the absence of an appropriate research plan. Excavation continued.

In February 1992, more bones appeared—in the bucket of a backhoe. Daniel Pagano, the archaeologist for the New York City Landmarks Preservation Commission (LPC), stated that the remains—arm, leg, and jaw bones—of as many as twenty individuals had been disturbed (Dunlap 1992). Pagano was denied entry to the site, and a GSA official reiterated the agency's commitment to "dignified removal" of the remains (Dunlap 1992). Excavation continued.

In July 1992, ten months after the first burials had been exhumed, Mayor Dinkins wrote to the GSA demanding that they stop work. The GSA regional administrator refused. The House Subcommittee on Buildings and Grounds held a hearing on the matter at which Dinkins testified. Activists and politicians continued to speak out. Less than one week later, on 29 July 1992, the head of the GSA reversed its earlier decision after "discussions on Capitol Hill" (Finder 1992). The agency agreed to suspend work in the area where most of the burials had been found. One day later, excavation permanently stopped.

The African Burial Ground (ABG), as it came to be known, marks a major shift in how archaeology is done in the United States. The idea of "public archaeology" became part of the discipline's lexicon in the 1970s along with the rise in Cultural Resources Management (CRM). When not used to refer to CRM archaeology itself, public archaeology generally meant top-down education of the public, largely in order to protect resources through legislation and pressure for archaeological involvement in new projects. As an example of the expansion of public archaeology, in 1980, Dickens and Bowen (1980, 55) advocated for broadening the definition to include "public participation and education." During their work on the Metropolitan Atlanta Rapid Transit Authority (MARTA) project, they implemented a "program of public lectures, responsible press coverage, and unsensational TV news reports" to foster public interest in the archaeology being conducted. Nevertheless, much "public archaeology" through the early 1980s seems to have been performed in support of the work of (white) archaeologists—to grow interest in the field rather than to relinquish the right to control knowledge of the past.

By the time of the ABG project, archaeologists had thus certainly thought about and engaged in "public archaeology" in the sense of bringing archaeological findings to the community, but the ABG brought the community to the archaeology. In a sense, the ABG created a model of what might be called *participatory* archaeology in which the interested public drove the research agenda and had control over the remains and the memorialization of the site. Michael Blakey, the director of the team of scientists from Howard University and the Smithsonian Institution who studied the remains, characterized the most important "product" of the ABG campaign as "the expanding international commitment to the right of descendant communities to determine the disposition of the dead and their participation as clients in the formulation of research questions and interpretations of many kinds of historic sites. The watershed of public engagement and the plural democratization of science was successfully demonstrated in New York City" (2020, S190). The ABG and its legacy is at the heart of this volume.

Urban Spaces from the Northeastern United States to Ecuador

Most of this book focuses on case studies located in the urban northeast of the United States, with the exception of a contributing chapter from Ecuador. Why the primary focus on the American northeast, and why this disjuncture to the Global South? As you will soon read, many of the chapters pay homage to the Lower Manhattan African Burial Ground site either explicitly or as descendants, so to speak, of the significant shift in the discipline provoked by this project. The impact of that site—changing the narrative not only of how to do archaeology but also of who should have a say in the decision-making—rippled outward, particularly to other northeast urban spaces in the United States. These communities had similar sacred sites below their sidewalks and similar preservation policies that impacted the who, what, where, and why these sites were excavated. Therefore, while the impact of this shift is extensive and global, we chose to focus on the northeast and the legacy of the ABG in the major urban centers there.

As we put together this volume, however, we felt it was incomplete. The implications of this shift in paradigm is that archaeology must address the past and present but also look to the future. While all of the authors have addressed this concern in some way—by providing resources for future advocacy work, by providing support for the futures of local communities, by addressing the education of future generations, or through efforts to challenge and shift historical narratives for the future—it seemed appropriate to look outward geographically and conceptually as well as temporally. A final case study, from Ecuador, illustrates how urban space itself influences public interaction with the products of archaeology (material culture) in a context that is wholly transgressive of existing narratives and cultural structures. This final case study shifts the meaning of urban archaeology and provides a glimpse into how archaeological advocacy might expand even further.

Specters of a Just Society

Over the past thirty years, since the success of the African Burial Ground, advocacy in archaeology has been discussed and practiced in various and evolving ways. More recently, a number of scholars have begun to talk about *activist* archaeology (e.g., Atalay et al. 2014; Barton 2021). We believe using and practicing archaeology in a way that actively advocates for social justice is the crucial piece for advocacy in our field in the sense of an archaeological praxis that works actively to better the world. From Britt's work with the United Order of Tents, to Elizabeth D. Meade and Douglas Mooney's creation of digital databases to protect the dead, to Martin's work on K–12 pedagogy, and George's excavation of the genealogies of exceptionalist American narratives, all of the chapters in this volume illustrate different ways of using and practicing archaeology as what we believe are active advocates for social justice.

As Margaret Purser explores in the foreword to this volume, we find ourselves in unsettling and unsettled times. Expanding on Purser's discussion of the impact of COVID-19, this collection of writings and case studies on archaeological advocacy is the result of several concerns. Toward the end of the previous (45th) presidency, but before COVID, the editors came together to create a forum for discussing what we called "The Age of (Un)Reason." Worn down by the increasing attacks on faculty teaching from a justice and equity perspective, with some faculty even experiencing threats to their and their family's lives, we came together to vent, commiserate, share experiences, and talk strategies and best practices. Since that first meeting in 2018, matters have only gotten worse.

Over the past seven years, the world has shifted—although such processes always have deeper roots in the past. The "culture wars," "identity politics," and "contract with America" of the 1990s has become the crusade against "Critical Race Theory," anti-"wokeness," and "Make America Great Again" of the 2010s and 2020s. About one-third of Americans believe that the US Presidential election of 2020 was stolen through massive fraud. Citizens stormed the US Capitol trying to stop Congress from certifying that election, seemingly encouraged by members of Congress and the president. Black Lives Matter forced a reckoning with the murder of Black people by law enforcement; but those protesting this outrage have been marginalized by the right as terrorists and agitators. Similarly, the #MeToo movement has been pushed out of the frame by counternarratives of angry, man-hating women and falsely accused men.

Of course, culture change most often happens this way and, thus, these dialectical threads are not unusual or wholly unexpected. It is perhaps the confluence of so many weighty narratives—including the recent Russian invasion of Ukraine and the horrific stories and images coming out of that embattled country—and the excesses of late capitalist absurdity, infused by the stress and anxiety of the global pandemic and increasingly dire news about climate change that create the feeling of extreme times.

Derrida (1994) wrote that the past is always present in the form of a specter—a haunting. Marxism did not disappear with the fall of the Soviet Union; rather, that particular version of Marxism died, but the specter of Marx remained as a future potentiality, haunting the neoliberal present. In the same way, the specter of a just and equitable society haunts this era of late capitalism. Social justice has never been realized in the Global North, but there have been times when it has been pushed close to the surface, such as during the civil rights era in the United States. Its specter, and the potentiality of a world in which it is fully realized, haunts this volume. We hope to show that archaeology can and should be a way to bring this specter to life.

What Is Advocacy?

While writing and researching for this volume, one point became clear—the definition for advocacy and what constitutes advocacy, particularly in the field of archaeology, is not fixed. For purposes of this volume, we define advocacy in its broadest sense, to be as all-encompassing as possible. Therefore, our vision of advocacy emphasizes the goal rather than the actions themselves. We define it as any work involving archaeological resources or praxis that aims to make the world a more just place. This broad-based definition refers to both direct and indirect advocacy in the sense that the archaeologist's work can be a form of direct action or a step—or more removed, such as providing resources for those engaged in direct action. Advocacy can include:

- Forming an organization, group, or not-for-profit.
- Creating a resource for activists/archaeologists to use.
- Exposing genealogies of power and providing alternative narratives based on archaeological data that can enter present-day discourses and make room for different, more just futures.
- Facilitating, promoting, and collaborating in community engagement, activities, and empowerment.
- Developing curriculum in various educational spaces including K–12, higher education, and venues for the general public. Creating alternative avenues of knowledge production.

- Democratizing how, where, and by whom/for whom archaeological work is conducted.
- More traditionally, advocating for resources through laws, funding, and raising awareness.

This conceptualization of advocacy guides this volume's authors in presenting their work. The case studies represent various approaches to advocacy but all are united by the common goal of realizing changes that move the world toward equity, equality, and justice.

New Beginnings

As some of the following chapters show, advocacy and activism within archaeology is not new. This is particularly true in urban spaces due to the destructive/reconstructive nature of urbanization and the impact it has on historical sites and present-day communities, which necessitate an engaged approach to archaeology. However, over the past two decades, discussions on a praxis that incorporates a more activist framework, an "engaged" approach, have gained momentum within archaeology. This sphere can be situated within the larger discipline of anthropology, which has seen the same shift within the last thirty years (Low and Merry 2010). As Ortner (2019) discusses, this "engaged turn" in anthropology focuses on research projects expressly intended to participate in larger societal discourses, particularly ones focused on critiques of power, a diversity of methodologies, and creative writing and presentation strategies.

While archaeology is usually slower to follow disciplinary shifts, as discussed in the foreword and volume, we have long since moved away from simple descriptions of past cultures and have incorporated anthropological theory and concepts. "Anthropological" archaeology, at least in historical archaeology, is somewhat redundant in 2022. While archaeologists are increasingly utilizing an engaged approach (e.g., Little and Shackel 2007, 2014; Atalay 2012; Bollwerk et al. 2015; Matthews 2020; Hays-Gilpin et al. 2021; Barton 2021), there is still resistance to embracing a fully "engaged turn." But given the social/economic/political contexts as touched on above, how can archaeology not be engaged with the lived experiences of those most marginalized and threatened by things such as global capitalism, climate change, gentrification, racism, homophobia and transphobia, and so much more.

Although the ABG was now thirty years ago, archaeology still has a long way to go. It is questionable whether we can ever truly escape our colonial history, one that we share with anthropology. But employing our skills and knowledge as advocates rather than as controllers of knowledge/definers of the past/authors of history is a necessary step in trying to do so. The chapters in this volume continue the discussion around an engaged practice in the discipline with a sense of urgency, advocating for advocacy itself, and using archaeology as a tool to make the world a better place.

References

Atalay, Sonya. 2012. *Community-Based Archaeology: Research with, by, and for Indigenous and Local Communities*. Berkeley: University of California Press.

Atalay, Sonya, Lee Rains Clauss, Randall H. McGuire, and John R. Welch, editors. 2014. *Transforming Archaeology: Activist Practices and Prospects*. Walnut Creek, CA: Left Coast Press.

Barton, Christopher P., ed. 2021. *Trowels in the Trenches: Archaeology as Social Activism*. Gainesville: University Press of Florida.

Blakey, Michael L. 2010. "African Burial Ground Project: Paradigm for Cooperation?" *Museum* No. 245–246, 65(1–2): 61–68.

———. 2020. "Archaeology Under the Blinding Light of Race." *Current Anthropology* 61 (S22), S183–S197.

Bollwerk, Elizabeth, Robert Connolly, and Carol McDavid. 2015. "Co-Creation and Public Archaeology." *Advances in Archaeological Practice* 3 (3), 178–87.

Derrida, Jacques. 1994. *Specters of Marx: The State of the Debt, the Work of Mourning and the New International*. Translated by Peggy Kamuf. New York: Routledge.

Dickens, Roy S., Jr., and William R. Bowen. 1980. "Problems and Promises in Urban Historical Archaeology: The MARTA Project." *Historical Archaeology* 14, 42–57.

Dunlap, David W. 1992. "Mistake Disturbs Graves at Black Burial Ground." *New York Times*, 21 February 1992. Gale OneFile. link.gale.com/apps/doc/A174789471/STND?u=nysl_me_fordham&sid=bookmark-STND&xid=b7dc17ef.

Finder, Alan. 1992. "US Suspends Digging at Site of Cemetery." *New York Times*, 30 July 1992. Gale OneFile.link.gale.com/apps/doc/A174903451/STND?u=nysl_me_fordham&sid=bookmark-STND&xid=f70a1418.

Hays-Gilpin, Kelley A. Sarah A. Herr, and Patrick D. Lyons, editors. 2021. *Engaged Archaeology in the Southwestern United States and Northwestern Mexico*. Louisville: University of Press of Colorado.

Little, Barbara, and Paul Shackel, editors. 2007. *Archaeology as a Tool of Civic Engagement*. Lanham, MD: AltaMira Press.

———. 2016. *Archaeology, Heritage, and Civic Engagement: Working Toward the Public Good*. New York: Routledge.

Low, Setha, and Sall Engle Merry. 2010. "Engaged Anthropology: Diversity and Dilemmas An Introduction to Supplement 2." *Current Anthropology* 51 (2), S203–S226.

Mack, Mark E., and Michael L. Blakey. 2004. "The New York African Burial Ground Project: Past Biases, Current Dilemmas, and Future Research Opportunities." *Historical Archaeology* 38 (1), 10–17.

Matthews, Christopher. 2020. "A People's Preservation: Urban Erasures in Essex County, NJ." *Journal for the Anthropology of North America* 23 (1), 47–66.

Ortner, Sherry. 2019. "Practicing Engaged Anthropology." *Anthropology of This Century* 25. http://aotcpress.com/articles/practicing-engaged-anthropology/.

Acknowledgments

We would like to thank our editor, Caryn Berg, for being so understanding and patient as we brought this labor of love to completion in the middle of a pandemic. To all the contributors to this volume and the community members they work in collaboration with for their ongoing efforts to use the knowledge of the past to advocate for social justice causes. To Jneyde "Nehemiah" Williams for her creative and symbolic artwork for the cover. And last, but not least, our family and close friends, who provided support and love through the making of this volume.

Chapter 1

PANYC
The Why, the Then, and the Now

Joan H. Geismar

Introduction

Just over four decades ago, during the winter of 1980, a unique urban archaeological advocacy group was formed in New York City. It was "born" on a bitter cold Saturday afternoon when seventeen local archaeologists met in an unheated New York University classroom to create a new organization. This was the inception of Professional Archaeologists of New York City, or PANYC. What follows is a brief look at why PANYC was created all those years ago, its history, and where it is today. Although it is based on fact, this story incorporates my recollections—those of someone privileged to be there from the beginning.

While the chapters in this volume discuss many forms of advocacy in urban archaeology, in the early days of the field we were just beginning to explore its potential. Coming together as a professional organization to advocate for the city's buried resources was a novel idea. This chapter is meant as a reminder of our origins and a contribution to our collective memory of the discipline. It is an anecdotal tale about a single place, New York City, but the events and ideas resonate beyond the tale's narrative focus. Hopefully, it is also a good story.

The Early Days of PANYC

Professional Archaeologists of New York City is a volunteer, not-for-profit, grassroots organization. Among its missions is to protect what was,

---

Notes for this chapter begin on page 12.

Figure 1.1. New York City's five boroughs consolidated in 1898. © Joan H. Geismar.

at its inception, New York City's newly revealed archaeological potential and to ensure those correct investigatory procedures were followed. Another component of the mission was to make city agencies and the general public aware of New York's rich archaeological potential—to many, a mind-bending concept. At the time, this was especially so for Manhattan, the most developed of New York City's five boroughs (the others being Brooklyn, Queens, Staten Island, and The Bronx [Figure 1.1]). How could one of the world's most urbanized tracts of land, one that had been built and rebuilt over time, possibly include an archaeological component?

PANYC was among the first, if not the first, advocacy group to foster urban archaeology in a major American city. To be sure, prior to the inception of PANYC, Alexandria, Virginia, had begun conducting archaeological investigations in the city and had created the position of City Archaeologist. But PANYC differs in that it was not then, nor is it now, directly involved in any actual archaeological undertaking. While PANYC members may work in—and even for—the city, their work is independent of PANYC. In other words, PANYC does not "do" archaeology, instead, we make sure that archaeology is done. Nor is PANYC municipally sponsored. At its inception, PANYC was an independent advocacy group with

Figure 1.2. P-A-N-Y-C as written on a blackboard at the 1980 organizational meeting of Professional Archaeologists of New York City (facsimile). © Joan H. Geismar.

a mandate to protect and promote New York City archaeology; and so it remains.

PANYC's organizers were two local university archaeology professors: Bert Salwen of New York University and Ralph Solecki of Columbia University. Salwen, a trained engineer, became an archaeologist in a second career and is considered by many the "Father" of Urban Archaeology (Rothschild 1990). Solecki, forever associated with his Neanderthal discoveries at Shanidar Cave in Iraq, became involved in archaeology as a teenager growing up on Long Island. At the time of that Saturday afternoon meeting, he had conducted several large New York City cultural resource projects. As for the participants, they included the late Jerry Jacobson, a former student of Bert who taught at City College and excavated and documented the Burial Ridge site on Staten Island, the largest known prehistoric burial site in the New York Metropolitan area. Also in attendance were several anthropology/archaeology graduate students (Diana Wall, Sydne Marshall, and me, among them) and newly minted PhDs Nan Rothschild and Anne-Marie Cantwell.

The organization's acronym, PANYC, was Jerry's brainchild. On that fateful Saturday, in a surprise move, he walked to the front of the classroom where we were meeting, picked up a piece of chalk, and, without saying a word, wrote P-A-N-Y-C on the blackboard (Figure 1.2). Thus, did the organizational name follow the acronym rather than the other way around. That day, and at that moment, Professional Archaeologists of New York City, with its perfect acronym, was created.

What had brought us to that day was the introduction in 1977 of New York City's local environmental laws, specifically Executive Order Number 91, fashioned after New York State's Environmental Quality Review Act, or SEQRA. While the state law was SEQRA with an "S," the city law was CEQR with a "C" (City Environmental Quality Review). Under this new mandate, city projects subject to discretionary actions, such as permits or waivers, were subject to CEQR review, which included addressing archaeological resources.

With the law in place, what galvanized PANYC's creation were the excavations directed by Nan Rothschild and Diana Wall on the Goldman Sachs site at Broad and Pearl streets in Lower Manhattan—better known as the Stadt Huys (or State House) Block. It was here, on the edge of what had been Lower Manhattan's original East River shore (that is until mid-eighteenth and early-nineteenth-century land reclamation extended the landmass three blocks into the river) that New York City's first large urban dig was initiated. Beginning in October 1979, excavation with backhoe and trowel uncovered long-buried eighteenth- and nineteenth-century foundations as well as the features that have become the hallmark of urban American digs such as privies and cisterns with their often-mendable ceramics, glass, and other detritus. There also was an eighteenth-century well that was looted before it could be fully explored, an unfortunate downside of an urban dig (see Loper 1981 for a vivid newspaper account of the dig). The investigation, under the auspices of the New York City Landmarks Preservation Commission (LPC), unequivocally demonstrated that archaeology was indeed among the city's environmental issues, and PANYC's goal was to make sure it was properly addressed.

At our first official meeting on 21 May 1980, Ralph Solecki, who passed away in 2019 at the age of 101, was elected PANYC's president. In that capacity, Ralph issued a letter to city agencies and politicians among others, stating:

> Professional Archaeologists of New York City (PANYC) is a new organization of local archaeologists dedicated to the preservation and interpretation of the archaeological and historical heritage of our great city. We are a volunteer, nonprofit group concerned with the protection and proper treatment of archaeological resources here . . . Our guiding principle is to ensure that sites already under protective jurisdiction stay protected, while we direct our attention to sites that are immediately threatened. PANYC needs to establish a preservation atmosphere through its own activities in this city.

Miraculously, and to our delight, the letter elicited numerous positive responses. It was an exciting time. And since PANYC was open not only to professional archaeologists but also to those in allied fields, among its members were (and are) archaeological practitioners, academics, agency archaeologists, and, initially, an environmental lawyer who provided help-

Figure 1.3. Sharon Wilkins and Caledonia Jones at PANYC's 2015 annual public meeting after receiving engraved Marshalltown trowels for their contribution to New York City archaeology. © Joan H. Geismar.

ful advice (we currently have an archaeologist/lawyer among our forty-four members). Together, this somewhat diverse group fostered an awareness of the archaeological resources that can and do survive in one of the world's most intensely developed urban environments.

In addition to letter writing and a flurry of issues addressed by PANYC's Action Committee (early on, in one four-month period, the committee dealt with as many as seventeen local archaeological issues), PANYC began organizing an annual public program. For this, we reached out to the Museum of the City of New York, which graciously agreed to co-sponsor and provide a venue for these programs. These programs, like the rest of the world, came to a halt during the world's devastating COVID-19 pandemic, but when life will again be "normal," PANYC will hold its fortieth public program at the museum. We have been pleased over the years to offer two awards: one, a monetary award for a student paper, the other a "special" award (an engraved Marshalltown trowel) for a non-archaeologist who has fostered New York City archaeology. For example, in 2015, Sharon Wilkins and Caledonia Jones received engraved PANYC trowels to commemorate their efforts associated with the archaeological exploration of the mid-nineteenth-century community of Seneca Village in what is now Manhattan's Central Park (Figure 1.3).

PANYC Comes of Age

In 1997, again in conjunction with the Museum of the City of New York, PANYC organized and mounted a comprehensive exhibit about the organization that proved to be extremely popular. "We Dig New York" ran for five months and, in retrospect, I marvel at what was accomplished. It highlighted PANYC's role in the city's archaeology and documented its successes as well as some of its disappointments. It also reflected the support the New York City Landmarks Preservation Commission had bestowed on PANYC in the early years. Beginning in 1978, the commission had taken it upon itself to nurture New York City archaeology and review city archaeological projects. This effort began with the above-mentioned Goldman Sachs/State House block and was almost immediately followed by several major private development projects. These were entire, or almost entire, city blocks, such as Seven Hanover Square, and the Telco and 175 Water Street development projects, the last two in or associated with the landmarked South Street Seaport Historic District.

Even before the museum exhibit, however, PANYC had established itself as a champion of New York City archaeology. This commitment was brought home in 1992 when, as president of PANYC, I received a call from Ian Burrows of Hunter Research who was winding down an archaeological project on Ellis Island. The purpose of the call was to ask PANYC to intercede before the National Park Service reburied Fort Gibson's exposed early-nineteenth-century northwestern defenses that helped define Ellis Island before it was extended by landfill (Figure 1.4). Anne-Marie Cantwell, PANYC's vice president, and I rushed out to the island and made a case for leaving the wall exposed to serve as an example of the island's physical evolution. Miraculously, we were successful, with the help of the National Park Service's Chief Historical Architect, who was on-site and listened to our plea. Not only was the excavation left exposed, but the National Park Service also installed an accompanying exhibit. Also in the 1990s, PANYC was deeply concerned with the proper handling of the African Burial Ground site in Lower Manhattan, the resting place of New York's enslaved and free Africans for most of the eighteenth century. Located east of Broadway and north of Chambers Street, it is identified on at least one mid-eighteenth-century map as the "Negroes Burial Ground" (Maershalck 1763). And so it remained until, with the city's expansion, it was closed in 1795.

Fast forward to 1991, when commercial buildings with deep basements were razed in anticipation of the construction of a new General Services Administration (GSA) office building. With federal money involved, the site was subject to review under Section 106 of the National Historic Preservation Act (NHPA), which requires consideration of historic proper-

Figure 1.4. Fort Gibson's exposed early nineteenth-century northwest defenses, now a National Park Service outdoor exhibit on Ellis Island. Courtesy of the National Park Service and Hunter Research, Inc.

ties in federal undertakings. An archaeological assessment was initiated. Much to everyone's surprise, testing revealed that despite the site's long construction history, and undoubtedly because the site was a gully prior to filling and grading, burials remained;[1] thus the need to "handle" the situation arose.

The GSA was determined to clear the site, while the local African American community (really multiple communities) wanted it saved. Under the 106 process, many meetings were held but they were contentious and tempers were high. In essence, the GSA paid lip service to the process while being dismissive of community concerns. PANYC attended many meetings, wrote many letters, and actively worked to help right this wrong. Ultimately, the GSA abandoned part of the site to create a memorial, but not before what proved to be over four hundred burials were removed. All recovered human and nonhuman material was analyzed at Howard University and, in 2003, the human remains were reinterred on the grounds of the African Burial Ground memorial.[2]

The Present and Future of PANYC

Of course, over PANYC's more than forty years, much has changed. For example, we are long past what those of us who "do" local archaeology call the "Golden Years of New York City Archaeology." This was in the

1980s and early 1990s, when archaeological work was part of one large-scale private excavation after another in Lower Manhattan's historical South Street Seaport and Wall Street districts. The projects, which came under environmental review due to special permits or other discretionary actions, kept coming—and so did major discoveries. These included landfill features uncovered and documented at the Telco (Rockman et al. 1982) and 175 Water Street (Geismar 1983) sites (at 175 Water Street, these included a 100-foot- [30.5-meter-] long derelict merchant vessel incorporated into the cribbing to hold the landfill in place and keep the East River out), the findings at the aforementioned Stadt Huys site, and the Broad Street (Grossman 1983) and Seven Hanover Square (Rothschild and Pickman 1990) sites, each with Dutch components.

These were among PANYC's successes, and certainly, there were others. But there were, and are, disappointments. To bring PANYC into the present, while LPC continues to review archaeological reports and formally considers the archaeological potential of eighteenth-century (or earlier) landmarked properties, this consideration currently does not extend to the nineteenth century. PANYC's appeals to the commission to include these archaeological resources among the agency's institutional concerns have not succeeded. To be sure, the agency assesses all archaeological potential under city environmental review and often addresses nineteenth-century archaeology in landmarked districts on a case-by-case basis, but it does not follow an institutionalized protocol to consider such properties. But we have not given up yet. PANYC continues to advocate for LPC's institutionalized recognition of the significance of nineteenth-century archaeological resources on privately owned landmarked properties.

Now, more often than not, rather than with large-scale private development, archaeology is conducted in connection with public infrastructure projects, usually under the auspices of city agencies, such as the Department of Design and Construction (DDC), or the Economic Development Corporation (EDC), or the Department of Parks and Recreation (Parks), but other city-sponsored projects can raise archaeological issues. And many investigations are in parks located throughout the city's five boroughs. In some cases, these park projects have LPC oversight, and in others, oversight comes from within the Parks Department, often, however, in concert with Landmarks, a "partnership" that has a history of PANYC's input but that came about slowly.

Following the requirements of regulatory review, the focus of investigation in these park projects as well as in others is not necessarily where research indicates a possible archaeological issue, but rather is limited to where direct construction impacts will occur, that is, the area of potential effect (APE). While this concern inhibits archaeological discovery

Figure 1.5. James Jackson's 1799 tombstone, a surprise relic of the former potter's field located in what is now New York City's Washington Square Park. © Joan H. Geismar.

and can be frustrating, there is no doubt that it preserves potential and unknown sites from the disturbance that archaeological investigation itself causes. Further, despite these research limitations, it is amazing what spectacular finds are made, such as the unanticipated discovery of James Jackson's tombstone found during excavations for a catch basin in Washington Square Park in Greenwich Village (Geismar 2012) (Figure 1.5). The tombstone, from 1799, and the research it engendered changed the very concept of the late-eighteenth- and early-nineteenth-century Potter's Field once located in what is now the park.

So, with the exception of the sought-after formalized protocol for considering nineteenth-century archaeological resources on privately owned landmarked property, archaeology in New York City is now a recognized issue and does not usually require quite the same vigilance from PANYC that it once did. However, we address what needs consideration and remain focused on raising the awareness of New Yorkers to the fact that all five boroughs have an archaeological past. In this regard, the aforementioned annual PANYC public program is a major event on our calendar, one that continues to attract a substantial and enthusiastic audience. PA-

NYC also sponsors or co-sponsors and organizes special symposia. One program on the archaeological potential of urban landfill was a partnership with Columbia University. Another, on education, was co-sponsored with the New York Archaeological Council (NYAC). PANYC also occasionally co-sponsors programs with the Metropolitan Chapter of the New York State Archaeological Association, including one in 2019 that explored the research value of construction materials such as brick and mortar.

As time has passed, and archaeological awareness and concerns have changed, PANYC has evolved. There is little question that recognition of the city's archaeological potential has grown. The environmental laws that affect archaeology are long-established, albeit not always graciously accepted, and local newspapers and online outlets often report on New York City's archaeological discoveries and happenings, frequently involving PANYC members. Perhaps like the flea that demands the drawbridge be raised as it floats by, we at PANYC believe we have contributed to this awareness. PANYC has also made inroads into some of the city's preservation groups, such as the venerable Municipal Arts Society, which opted more than a decade ago to include an archaeologist as a member of the society's Preservation Committee.

PANYC still seeks ways to keep New York City archaeology at the forefront and continues to get involved when archaeological missteps occur. Our annual program and other outreach continue to engage and educate the public while our letters communicate with officials who hold sway over the city's archaeological heritage. Occasionally, we even venture beyond New York City, if there is a far-reaching adverse effect on archaeology (a relatively recent example is a PANYC letter in protest of misguided precedent-setting archaeological protocols under consideration in the Arizona Senate, unfortunately not a PANYC success). And where PANYC once stood alone, archaeological advocacy has taken root in other American cities. For example, since 1998, the Philadelphia Archaeological Forum (PAF) has served a somewhat similar advocacy function in historical Philadelphia, although with expanded procedures (see Meade and Mooney, this volume). Now the importance of urban archaeology in documenting the history and life of a city is often recognized and promoted by historians and preservationists as well as archaeologists (for example, the Municipal Art Society's Preservation Committee supported PANYC's quest for the LPC to institutionally address nineteenth-century archaeological resources on privately owned landmarked properties).

Successes aside, in some instances, environmental laws do not apply or might be circumvented, and PANYC will step in. A case in point was the planned as-of-right construction of a twenty-two-story hotel with archaeological potential on Manhattan's Bowery. Lacking a mandate for an

Figure 1.6. The PANYC button. © Joan H. Geismar.

archaeological review, PANYC was among those who reached out to the owners who proved willing to listen. An archaeological investigation by Chrysalis Archaeological Consultants not only revealed evidence of the Atlantic Garden, a popular nineteenth-century "German biergarten and concert hall" (Rueb 2016), but also provided a wealth of archaeological material now on display in a museum setting on the hotel's second floor. Here, successful advocacy not only protected valuable archaeological resources but also helped create a forum for moving archaeology into the public sphere.

Conclusion

This brings us back to PANYC's beginning. I, for one, believe that what prompted those seventeen New York City archaeologists to meet in an unheated New York University classroom on that cold Saturday afternoon more than forty years ago endures. I know I am not alone in believing that what came out of that meeting all those years ago remains relevant and valid. Hopefully, our story and the continued importance of this professional organization will provide inspiration for archaeologists in other urban settings.

I trust that PANYC will continue to advocate for archaeology in New York City for as long as necessary. As we move forward and even reexamine our practices and goals, we have a new adjunct logo, one that appropriately incorporates a PANYC button to "push" should archaeological resources require our attention and protection (Figure 1.6).

Just a word: this is a story about the inception of a movement that proved to be at the forefront of urban archaeological activism. It is not a "how to" or "how not to," but rather a chronicle of something that was in the right place at the right time with the right people behind it. Perhaps the takeaway could be, if it is worth doing, it is worth trying. It is a matter of having all your ducks in a row, so to speak, combined with determination and—yes—excitement and enthusiasm.

Acknowledgments

I thank Kelly M. Britt and Diane F. George for including my contribution in this volume and for their wonderfully helpful and wise input. My thanks also to Nan Rothschild, Linda Stone, and Amanda Sutphin for kindly reading earlier drafts.

Joan H. Geismar, an archaeological consultant in the New York metropolitan area, received her doctorate in Anthropology from Columbia University. A founding member of Professional Archaeologists of New York City (PANYC), she recently completed her seventh nonconsecutive term as president and has served on the executive board since 1984. She is the recipient of several preservation awards and, in 1999, was designated a Centennial Historian of the City of New York. Among her research interests are community studies and the development of the urban condition.

Notes

1. A myth has been perpetuated that construction workers found the burials when, in fact, they were first encountered during the testing phase of the mandated archaeological review.
2. The extensive African Burial Ground Project reports can be accessed online: https://core.tdar.org/project/4859/the-archaeology-of-african-burial-ground-national-monument-new-york.

References

Geismar, Joan H. 1983. *The Archaeological Investigation of the 175 Water Street Block, New York City*. Prepared for HRO International. Prepared by Professional Services Industries, Soils Systems Division, Joan H. Geismar, Principal Investigator.

———. 2012. *Washington Square Park, Greenwich Village, New York, Phase 2 Construction Field Testing Report*. NYS Site Designation: Washington Square Park Potter's Field; NYS Site No.: USN A06101.01695. Prepared for the New York City Department of Parks and Recreation. Prepared through Tucci Equipment Rental Corporation. Prepared by Joan H. Geismar, Ph.D., LLC.

Grossman, Joel. 1983. *Broad Street Plaza Site Phase 1 Report and Mitigation*. Report for the Broad Street Plaza Site, New York, N.Y. Area 1 Lots 12–14. Greenhouse Consultants, Incorporated. Prepared for Fox and Fowle, Architects., P.C.

Lorber, Claudia. 1981. "Digging Up Our Urban Past." *The New York Times Magazine*, 12 April 1981. Section 6, 55. https://www.nytimes.com/1981/04/12/magazine/digging-up-our-urban-past.html?smid=em-share.

Maershalck, Francis W. 1763. *A Plan of the City of New York*. Reduced from an Actual Survey. I. N. P. Collection of Historical Prints. P. 1754-B-50. M. A. Roque, London. Miriam and Ira Wallach Division of Art, Prints, and Photographs. Print Collection. NYPL. https://digitalcollections.nypl.org/items/510d47d9–7ac7-a3d9-e040-e00a 18064a99.

Rockman [Wall], Diana, Wendy Harris, and Jed Levin. 1982. *The Archaeological Investigation of the Telco Block, South Street Seaport Historic District, New York, New York*. Prepared by Diana Rockman [Wall], Wendy Harris, and Jed Levin for Jack Resnick and Sons, Inc. Professional Services Industries, Soils Systems Division.

Rothschild, Nan A. 1990. "Bert Salwen, 1920–1988." *Historical Archaeology* 24 (1): 104–9. http://www.jstor.org/stable/25615763.

Rothschild, Nan A., and Arnold Pickman. 1990. *The Archaeological Evaluation of the Seven Hanover Square Block A*. Final Report. NYS Museum No. 624. Submitted to the LPC December.

Rueb, Emily S. 2016. "Awakening the Bowery's Ghosts." *The New York Times,* 12 February 2016. https://www.nytimes.com/2016/02/14/nyregion/awakening-the-bowerys-ghosts.html.

Solecki, Ralph. 1980. Letter. PANYC Newsletter NO. 1. August 1980, 6. https://www.panyc archaeology.org/newsletters/PANYC-Newsletter-001.pdf.

Chapter 2

"Cursed Be He That Moves My Bones"
The Archaeologist's Role in Protecting Burial Sites in Urban Areas

Elizabeth D. Meade and Douglas Mooney

> Good friend for Jesus' sake forebear; To dig the dust enclosed here; Blessed be the man that spares these stones; And *cursed be he that moves my bones.*
> —Epitaph on the grave of William Shakespeare

Introduction

For centuries, the pace of development in urban areas within the northeastern United States resulted in the frequent obliteration of cemetery sites. As populations swelled and areas of urban development expanded, many burial locations transformed from sacred sites—at least to some—into valuable property ripe for development. As a result of loopholes in environmental review laws that would otherwise require developers to complete archaeological investigations, gaps in social memory and the documentary record, and governmental inaction or apathy, sites containing human remains have been repeatedly disturbed by construction activities. Using case studies from New York City and Philadelphia, this chapter examines how archaeologists have documented and are working to document the changing landscape of historic period cemeteries in urban areas. Furthermore, it explores how such documentation is used by archaeologists to advocate for the protection of human remains during the

---
Notes for this chapter begin on page 40.

seemingly non-stop redevelopment efforts that occur as cities shape and reform their identities directly through the materiality of the urban fabric.

A Long History of Gruesome Discovery

The unexpected discovery of human remains during construction work and home renovation projects has long fascinated members of the general public. Historically, these encounters with skeletal remains resulted in extensive newspaper coverage, sometimes repeated over days or weeks as attempts were made to reunite bones with identities. Press coverage was often sensationalized, laden with extensive detail about ghastly and morbid discoveries and interviews with the individuals who made them. Following the disinterment of graves in what is now believed to be a family cemetery in Brooklyn Heights (Meade 2020), the *Brooklyn Daily Eagle* reported that neighborhood boys seized the box of remains from the construction site, using skulls as footballs and having a "saturnalia with the bones" (*Brooklyn Daily Eagle* 1885, 4). Upon the discovery of a former burial ground for enslaved people during road work in northern Manhattan in 1903, the *New-York Tribune* published an image of a decorative pyramid of recently excavated human remains (*New-York Tribune* 1903, A3). In more recent examples, following the disturbance of the early nineteenth-century burial vaults of the Spring Street Presbyterian Church in 2006, the *New York Post* featured a picture of disturbed remains within the construction excavation under the headline "Skeleton Crew" (Weiss et al. 2006).

In Philadelphia, the discovery of unmarked human burials were, likewise, the subject of much public fascination, the reporting on which has enjoyed a conspicuously long history of its own. There, the earliest known news coverage of such an unexpected finding appeared in an edition of Benjamin Franklin's *Pennsylvania Gazette* in 1743 and documented the uncovering of the "Bones of a human Body of about 5-foot Stature in a Garden in Walnut-street" (*Pennsylvania Gazette* 1743, 2). The later decades of the nineteenth century proved to be the true heyday of Philadelphia cemetery–related reporting as multiple burial grounds were impacted by an explosion of construction throughout the city. The local newspapers responded to these discoveries with ever-more-colorful chronicling, such as the following lead-in to one story from 1889 (*Philadelphia Inquirer* 1889, 3):

"PLAYING WITH BONES

Ghastly Toys for Children at Twelfth
and Carpenter Streets

OVER FIFTY SKELETONS EXHUMED

The Neighbors Indignant at the Careless Manner in Which the Remains Are Handled by the Laborers—Intestinal Disorders May Result"

As late as 2009, the *Inquirer* was still coming up with snappy leads to their stories about the discovery of human remains, in this case related to the exposure of intact burials during the renovation of a basement in the Franklinville section of the city, only this time it also managed to accurately capture the larger gravity of the situation: "Philadelphia: City of Forgotten Burial Grounds" (Gambardello 2009).

While these discoveries can seem dramatic to current and modern newspaper publishers and neighborhood residents alike, archaeologists recognize them as something altogether different: preventable occurrences. The nature of cemeteries in urban settings has changed dramatically over time, as small burial places in densely concentrated urban neighborhoods were replaced by large "rural" cemeteries in peripheral areas beginning in the first half of the nineteenth century (Sloane 1991). Changing land use and development/redevelopment patterns resulted in the disappearance of urban cemetery sites from both the landscape and social memory. However, the redevelopment of such sites did not always include the disinterment of human remains, either partially or in full. As human remains continue to be impacted by construction projects taking place where no archaeological analysis is required before work begins, there are often insufficient legal protections for human remains in abandoned or obliterated burial places until after such remains are exhumed. Sometimes, even after the discovery of forgotten burials, adequate protections are inexplicably lacking, as the *Inquirer* once again called out following the disturbance of burials from the former First Baptist Church cemetery in 2016, "Old bones found—and nobody's in charge" (Salisbury 2016).

There is a clear need for the identification of sites that are sensitive for human remains in cities that have seen dense and rapid development to ensure that such remains can be protected or exhumed prior to any anticipated redevelopment efforts. Archaeologists and archaeological advocacy groups are in a unique position to help prevent such desecration and to ensure that unmarked cemetery sites are properly identified and—where necessary—tested, and that any preserved human remains are documented, protected, or respectfully relocated as appropriate. This form of advocacy can occur in either indirect and direct action, through both documentation of and education about cemetery sites *before* potential development as well as more active archaeological investigations and traditional community advocacy strategies during and after development. Given the complexities of the role of cemeteries in the changing landscape of cities, the identification of burial sites can be similarly complex. The mere identification of burial sites is therefore critical to an archaeologist's advocacy efforts, for if we are not aware of the locations of lost or forgotten burial sites, how can we best advocate for their protection? The complete and proper identification of redeveloped burial sites in urban areas requires intensive research to understand how past residents from various backgrounds—including ethnicity/geographic origin and socioeconomic status—used space for burials and how burial sites associated with different groups were either protected in perpetuity or redeveloped. Through this important work, archaeologists can serve as proxies for the dead by not only identifying their burial places, but also advocating for the protection or disinterment of their remains before disturbance or destruction can occur.

In recent years, two large-scale, intensive analyses were completed by local archaeological organizations and independent archaeologists to increase public awareness of such sites. The ultimate goal of these projects was to ensure that no human remains are disturbed by future construction. More than five hundred cemeteries in New York City were identified and mapped as part of Elizabeth D. Meade's doctoral dissertation on the role of cemeteries in the deathscape of the five boroughs (Meade 2020).[1] In Philadelphia, more than three hundred cemeteries were identified and mapped by the Philadelphia Archaeological Forum ("PAF") as part of the group's ongoing advocacy efforts in that city, and the map continues to grow.[2] Identifying sites that are potentially sensitive for skeletal material is the first step in the critical role of protecting human remains from further disturbance and advocating for more uniform and widespread laws protecting burial sites.

Legal Protections for Human Remains

For decades, archaeologists around the world have debated the ethics of the study and documentation of the skeletal remains of burial populations and whether archaeologists have the right to do so (e.g., Bahn 1984; Zimmerman 1994; Bruning 2006; Scarre 2013; Anthony 2016). The quest for scientific knowledge by the living can be at odds with the beliefs of the deceased, who, without stakeholders to advocate for them, lack the power to prevent the disturbance of their graves or the study of their remains. As stated by Joyce and Crossland (2015), "as bodies are revealed, so are the hidden and often incommensurate understandings of the body after death held by different participants" (3). This chapter does not specifically address the ethical issues of the archaeological disturbance of burial sites, nor does it necessarily advocate for the archaeological excavation of human remains, except where such investigation may be the only available means of protecting remains from disturbance. Rather, this chapter explores archaeologists' unique ability to advocate for the protection of human remains in specific locations from being disturbed by *others*, particularly in situations where no legal or financial mechanisms are in place to do so or when other stakeholders or descendant communities are absent or unaware of the presence of burial places of potential cultural importance.

A significant barrier to an archaeologist's ability to be an advocate is the lack of explicit legal protections for human remains on former cemetery sites that have been redeveloped, even those for which human remains were never disinterred. While protections may be in place for active cemeteries or those preserved either privately or as a result of local, state, or federal actions (e.g., landmarking or listing on the National Register of Historic Places), almost no clearly defined protections specifically address human remains on obliterated cemetery sites that are no longer actively used for burials or no longer visibly recognized as burial places. Protections that do exist are frequently unrecognized, willfully unenforced, or outright ignored by public officials who have the legal, ethical, and moral authority to enforce them. Unfortunately, this lack of understanding of legal protection—or even of the basic processes that must be followed when human remains are encountered—far too often apply to many of the professional archaeologists who might be asked to consult on these matters.

Legal protections given to former cemetery sites tend to differ by locality and are often tied to environmental review laws that govern development projects. There are therefore few protections for documented burial places outside of the realm of environmental review. Some federal legislation exists to protect archaeological sites that by default includes cemetery locations, such as the National Historic Preservation Act of 1966. Other federal legislation addresses protections for burial places associated with specific cultural groups. The Native American Graves Protection and Repatriation Act (NAGPRA) was passed in 1990 in an attempt to address and correct systemic problems associated with the archaeological exhumation of burials of Indigenous persons from precontact sites across the United States. Though revolutionary in its time for providing one of the first pathways toward the systematic repatriation of Indigenous human remains and cultural property, NAGPRA is not without its limitations. The legislation has been criticized for its role in pitting religion against science and forcing Indigenous groups to assess the value of their cultural property (Cryne

2009), has suffered from undetermined or disputed claims of cultural affiliation (Schillaci and Bustard 2010), and, despite having been enacted decades ago, has not successfully ensured the repatriation of remains and other objects of cultural heritage in many places across the United States (Orona and Esquivido 2020).

NAGPRA legislation was passed around the same time that conflicts arose over archaeological investigation of the African Burial Ground in New York City (Blakey 2020), which foregrounded the need for greater protection of burial places associated with enslaved persons of African descent, both from development-related disturbance and from archaeological investigations with research designs that lack a focus on the historical injustices of enslavement, the African diaspora, and revolutions in the bioarchaeological study of geographic origin (Blakey 2020). Recent legislative efforts were initiated with the goal of protecting burial places of people of African descent, in particular those who were enslaved, including the US African American Burial Grounds Network Act (S.2827), which was introduced to the US Senate in March 2020.[3] The bill would allow for the creation of a network to identify and preserve burial places associated with African American populations and to promote public education about enslavement and the historical segregation of many cemeteries, but only with the consent of the property owner.

Legal Protections for Human Remains in New York City/New York State

In New York City, archaeological resources are protected under city,[4] state,[5] and federal law.[6] The state's cemetery laws provide guidance for the maintenance of abandoned cemeteries, but do not include regulations for former cemeteries that have since been redeveloped.[7] A recent bill in the New York State legislature acknowledges the lack of legal protections for unmarked burials across the state,[8] stating that "the sanctity of human burial sites is an intrinsic and paramount value among all cultural and religious traditions which practice the custom of burying the dead" (NY Senate Bill S4422 §2). While the bill would be among the first in the country to provide protection for human remains and funerary objects in redeveloped burial grounds, it stipulates that such protections would begin only after human remains are encountered during construction or episodes of vandalism or looting. There are no provisions for protecting known burial ground sites before ground-disturbing activities commence.

As with the federal laws described above, the oversight of these laws and agencies typically only applies to sites and projects that involve funding or permitting actions that trigger environmental review laws. Projects that are not subject to environmental review legislation, referred to as "as-of-right" efforts,[9] can occur on sites known to be sensitive for human remains with no legal requirements to complete archaeological investigations prior to the start of construction. Contractors are still legally required to call 911 to notify the New York City Office of the Chief Medical Examiner if they uncover human remains on a site, but only *after* they have been impacted. However, neither the medical examiner nor the Landmarks Preservation Commission (LPC) has the legal authority to halt an as-of-right project to ensure that archaeological analyses are completed; they can only ensure that the required New York City Department of Health (NYCDOH) permits are obtained to allow for a funeral director to exhume and relocate any recovered remains.

Legal Protections for Human Remains in Philadelphia/Pennsylvania

In Philadelphia, archaeological resources are protected, at least on paper, under the city's Historic Preservation Ordinance,[10] administered under the purview of the Philadelphia Historical Commission (PHC),[11] and at the state level by the Pennsylvania History Code,[12] as overseen by the Pennsylvania Historical and Museum Commission (PHMC).[13] Projects that involved state environmental permitting were, once upon a time, required to consider potential impacts to archaeological resources and to conduct archaeological investigations in advance of construction; however, a 1995 amendment to the State History Code effectively put an end to those efforts.[14] Backed by the Pennsylvania Homebuilders Association, this amendment shifted financial responsibility for performing archaeological assessments from the permit applicant to the PHMC and placed greatly compressed time limits on the completion of those studies. Subsequent reductions of necessary state funding for these investigations served the final blow (PAF 2020).

At the city level, the Historical Commission is empowered to identify potentially significant archaeological sites in conjunction with the review of construction permit applications, to list sites in the Philadelphia Register of Historic Places and provide for their protection, and to require the conduct of archaeological investigations in advance of construction. Unfortunately, an archaeologist has never been appointed to the full commission, and the commission staff, which carries out the majority of day-to-day operations, has not employed a professional archaeologist, or anyone with a broad understanding of archaeological preservation, since the late 1980s. As a result, little consistent effort is made to consider possible construction impacts to archaeological resources. On top of that, Philadelphia's Historic Preservation Ordinance contains no formalized process for the conduct and review of archaeological investigations.

At the state level, numerous Pennsylvania laws and statutes govern a variety of issues pertaining to cemeteries and the disposition of human remains. For the most part, these laws are antiquated, having been enacted in the nineteenth or early twentieth century, are spread throughout multiple sections of the Pennsylvania Consolidated Statutes,[15] and create a perception of ambiguity by not directly addressing the specific issue of unmarked or redeveloped cemeteries. These statutes do, however, cover a wide range of specific circumstances (such as the maintenance and operation of cemeteries and the taking or use of cemetery ground for the construction of roads) and establish processes involved in the removal and relocation of burial remains, markers/monuments, and other cemetery objects in these cases. The protection of historic burial grounds is specifically addressed in the Historic Burial Places Preservation Act of 1994,[16] which defines such a site as a "tract of land that has been in existence as a burial ground for more than 100 years, in which there have been no burials for at least 50 years and wherein there will be no future burials or is listed in or eligible for the National Register of Historic Places as determined by the PHMC." Several statues additionally establish penalties for the disturbance of burials and other cemetery features, but these mainly pertain to individual acts of vandalism.

Even if existing Pennsylvania laws seem ill-suited to address the specific circumstances surrounding unmarked or redeveloped burial grounds, it does not mean that there are no laws that can be successfully applied in these cases. When extant statutes are taken collectively, they establish several key principles that have a direct bearing on the ability to protect unmarked burial grounds. First, and most importantly, these statutes unequivocally vest ultimate jurisdiction over the disposition and treatment of burial remains with the courts, typically the various county Courts of Common Pleas, and make it a crime to disturb or remove remains without prior court authorization. Second, these statutes make it clear that while land used for the interment of the dead can be bought and sold, the remains of individuals buried in that land cannot. The existence of burials in a tract of land is always an exception to clear title. The disposition of a deceased individual's physical remains vests in the next of kin, or, where no heirs can be identified, in the courts.[17] So not only is it impermissible for the purchasers of land containing unmarked burials to own those remains, but they additionally cannot take actions that might affect their continued preservation. Last, although Pennsylvania's existing cemetery laws are typically interpreted as applying primarily to active or marked burial grounds, no statute has explicit language that prevents them from also being applied to abandoned or unmarked cemeteries. Pennsylvania law generally describes a cemetery as "a place for the disposal or burial of deceased human beings, by cremation or in a grave, mausoleum, vault, columbarium or other receptacle."[18] This definition does not include or infer an expiration date for the life of a burial ground or require the presence of visible markers, so a reasonable interpretation is that a property formerly used as a cemetery continues to be a cemetery, subject to all applicable Pennsylvania state laws, authorities, and penalties, so long as human burials continue to be contained within it.

In Philadelphia, while no separate local ordinances protect unmarked or abandoned cemeteries, the main problem is not an absence of available legal protections but a lack of enforcement of and willful indifference to applicable state laws. Despite the frequency with which unmarked cemeteries are impacted by construction projects in the city, local officials react each time as if it was the first occasion where such a thing has happened and exhibit an all too predictable reaction consisting of a combination of feigned confusion, wide-eyed incredulity, and resolute denial of knowing what to do next. This reaction is inevitably followed by protestations that there are no laws allowing the city to intervene, that various city agencies have no jurisdiction in the matter, and that no actions can be taken because the construction is being carried out by a private individual or corporation on privately owned land (Chernick 2017). This response, in turn, requires the maddeningly endless re-litigation of the issues in the court of public opinion and actual city courts—like something out of the film *Groundhog Day*.

Despite the disingenuous protestations of city officials, there is a process to be followed in instances where human remains are found at construction sites. The County Code requires notification of the police and Medical Examiner's Office to determine whether the remains are historical in nature or associated with recent criminal activity.[19] If those remains are determined to be historical, and likely associated with an unmarked burial site, then, in an ideal situation, the property owner should obtain a permit to exhume and respectfully relocate those remains. Unfortunately, the medical examiner or coroner is not required to report their findings to other government agencies, nor is the landowner or developer required to take any action. Moreover, no city agency or administrative body has been given explicit oversight responsibility in these cases and no ordinance spells out the precise process to be followed when abandoned graves or unmarked cemeteries are impacted by construction. This lack of clear procedure and oversight responsibility results in the desecration of burials and the violation of descendants' legal rights.

The PAF has argued, however, that the jurisdictional authority for the city to intercede on behalf of unmarked burial grounds and to stop the disturbance of human remains already exists. Developers in the city are required to conduct due diligence background research for planned construction projects in order to obtain building permits from the Department of Licenses and Inspections (L&I). While these investigations generally address environmental and safety issues, they could very easily include searches for potential prior burial/cemetery use. Given that L&I does not have the legal authority under existing Pennsylvania law to approve actions that could impact human burials, the agency should deny construction applications that could result in the disturbance of remains, require archaeological investigations in advance of construction, or temporarily halt active projects that do impact human remains. Unfortunately, the department has so far officially refused to acknowledge that it has any statutory means of interjecting itself into such cases.

Archaeology and Advocacy Efforts for Cemetery Sites

Given the issues with legal and institutional protections, the role of archaeologists in advocacy efforts aimed at documenting and protecting burial sites or the human remains interred within becomes more critical (see Edwards and Laird, this volume). An archaeologist's ability to protect burial locations requires the identification of known burial places through intensive research. This research is benefited by mapping cemeteries not only to document their locations, but also to allow the archaeologist to understand the role of different types of burial places within the urban landscape. Even those archaeological investigations completed under the oversight of strict environmental review legislation can misidentify cemetery locations if incorrect research methodology is applied (e.g., researching only the sites of known churches for evidence of cemeteries or not closely examining property records). The creation of the wide-ranging databases of the cemeteries of Philadelphia and New York City has been a substantial effort to provide consistent resources for archaeologists dealing with these issues.

The Documentation of Philadelphia's Cemeteries

In Philadelphia, the most outspoken and leading advocate for the protection of abandoned and unmarked burial sites is the PAF, an all-volunteer 501c(3) organization founded in 1998 and dedicated to promoting public knowledge of and appreciation for the city's incredible archaeological heritage. Its members are drawn from the ranks of local professional archaeologists, preservationists, university professors and students, tour guides, and others with a deep interest in Philadelphia's history. In addition to sharing information about the many archaeological discoveries over the past sixty years, since the dawn of historical archaeology as a recognized field of study, the organization works to ensure that identified sites are properly documented. It also actively advocates for improved protections for archaeological resources by advising local, state, and federal agencies, and by serving as a consulting party in ongoing investigations and projects.

The PAF has long recognized the importance of Philadelphia's forgotten and abandoned burial grounds and their potential value as irreplaceable archaeological resources in their own right. For more than ten years, several PAF members have worked to document the city's many burial grounds. One of these efforts involved trying to determine just how often unmarked cemeteries had been disturbed by various construction projects in the past by scouring through the searchable online newspaper archives and quantifying the findings. That effort, which is still being periodically updated, employed a series of simple key word and phrase searches to identify published accounts of burial disturbances in the city. The results are truly mind boggling and serve to make local officials' repeated inaction, denial, and opposition to reform even less comprehensible.

The PAF research has found evidence of scores of prior cemetery disturbances that were recorded in the popular press. In all, at least fifty-three burial sites have been impacted to varying degrees from the year 1800 to the present. Moreover, at least seventeen of those cemeteries were impacted on multiple occasions, with the least fortunate among them—typically the various abandoned city potter's fields—disturbed on half a dozen or more separate instances. The burial ground that has been impacted perhaps most frequently is the Odd Fellows Cemetery in north Philadelphia, which was officially relocated in the early 1950s, and where the discovery of burial remains since then has occurred so often, no one is able to determine an accurate total. When individual episodes of disturbance are tallied for all impacted cemeteries, the data show that burial site disturbances have been reported at least eighty-six times over the past 220 years. Since 1985 alone, the year the city revised its Historic Preservation Ordinance, twenty different burial grounds were disturbed by construction activities—an average of approximately one every 1.75 years. Given this shocking frequency, the city's failure to establish clear procedures to protect its many unmarked burial sites and unwillingness to even acknowledge that it has a legal, ethical, and moral obligation to take responsibility whenever these sites are encountered are simply indefensible.

While these numbers are in and of themselves stunning, in point of fact the actual number of cemetery impacts is certainly several orders of magnitude greater. We can be confident in this assertion because the local news outlets occasionally report instances in which developers or construction crews get caught trying to hide the evidence. In 2003, one of the city's local television news channels aired a story under the lead-in "Some Bones From Unearthed Cemetery End Up In Trash: Human Skulls, Bones Found In Construction Trash Container" (NBC 10 News 2003). The report indicated that the remains were initially found at a construction site in the Logan section of north Philadelphia but were subsequently traced by police back to another site near the intersection of 6th and Catharine Streets in south Philadelphia, where work crews had disturbed parts of the abandoned St. Paul's Methodist Episcopal Church graveyard during the building of new housing units.

Additional indications of previously unreported and sometimes long-ago impacts have been frequently documented when archaeologists have been called in to exhume remains from unmarked and abandoned cemeteries in the city. For instance, the archaeological relocation of burials from the former Second Presbyterian Church burial ground (ca. 1752 to 1864) on Arch Street, conducted in conjunction with the larger investigations of the National Constitution Center Site in Independence Mall, found evidence that multiple previously intact burials had been entirely or partially disturbed by numerous forms of historical construction episodes within the cemetery ground. Most of these impacts occurred after the cemetery was abandoned by the congregation, but others likely occurred while it was still in active use, and resulted from the construction of new buildings, the construction of brick-lined privies, the widening of an adjacent street, and the installation of public utilities in the nineteenth century.

Another primary focus of the PAF's research is the identification and accurate mapping of all cemetery sites that have ever existed in Philadelphia. Central to this effort has been the research of archaeologist Kimberly Morrell, who took the information compiled by earlier chroniclers of the city's burial grounds (Barker 1940–49; Torres 1997) and combined it with her own findings to create a detailed static AutoCAD map of some two hundred or so cemeteries across the entire metropolitan area. In more recent years, Morrell's data were transformed and expanded upon by PAF members into an interactive and publicly accessible geospatial ("GIS") database managed with QGIS, an open-source software application. The database prioritizes abandoned and unmarked cemetery locations but includes the many extant historic burial sites across the city. It also attempts to document the likely locations of former private family burial grounds, many of which were never accurately documented on published maps of Philadelphia. Future improvements to the database will contain separate data points associated with past discoveries of Revolutionary War burials from both sides in the Battle of Germantown, the locations of uncertain or unexplained discoveries of human remains and known secondary burial sites created by the past disturbance and unauthorized disposal of burial remains. Specific historical data associated with each specific burial site is in the process of being added, and include such information as religious and ethnic affiliation, dates of operation, historic map references, current land use, data regarding past efforts at relocation, and evidence of impacts indicating the continued presence of burial remains. The database will also eventually contain identified historical documentation derived from newspaper articles and other sources, both published and unpublished.

The publicly accessible version of the PAF's cemetery research is called the Historic Philadelphia Burial Places Map and Database, launched in February 2018 (Salisbury 2018b). Currently documenting the location and historic boundaries (where known or indicated on historic maps) of more than three hundred burial sites throughout the city, this resource was made available to the public with the explicit intent of serving as a tool for preventing the future disturbance of abandoned and unmarked cemeteries (Figure 2.1). Shortly after its initial release, the database was linked to the online map collection maintained by the Athenaeum of Philadelphia via its Greater Philadelphia GeoHistory Network website, and in March 2018, the PAF was awarded a Petersen Fellowship by the Athenaeum to be used for continued cemetery research and documentation, and to create a more robust and readily interactive GIS-based version of the database. Work on the improved version is currently ongoing.

The basic premise behind the burial places database and the research it contains is to avoid the worst possible—but up to now most common— outcome for abandoned and unmarked cemeteries in Philadelphia: the discovery of burial remains during an active construction project. When a discovery of this nature happens, the preservation of burial remains in place is often no longer possible, potential options for moving the project forward become limited, construction schedules are thrown into disarray, and unanticipated costs can begin to skyrocket. By making it easier for private developers, city agencies, and others to identify the locations of former burial places in advance of construction, it is hoped that appropriate steps can be taken to avoid impacts to those sites. If that is not possible, the alternative is to allow time for the establishment and implementation of appropriate measures, such as archaeological exploration and the exhumation of remains, which will ensure any burials and associated arti-

Figure 2.1. Detail of the PAF's Philadelphia Historical Burial Places Database showing the distribution of redeveloped cemeteries in a portion of Center City. © Philadelphia Archaeological Forum.

facts can be respectfully moved out of harm's way and reinterred in a new resting place. All parties should see the process of identifying unmarked burial sites in advance of construction as a benefit that could eliminate the potential of unforeseen disaster, unwanted lawsuits, and damning public recrimination.

The particular and driving impetus behind the decision to launch the online map and database was the very public, slow-motion debacle that had unfolded at one of the city's oldest established burial grounds: the First Baptist Church cemetery (ca. 1707–1859) near the corner of 2nd and Arch Streets in the Old City neighborhood. Between September 2016 and September 2017, during the construction of a new residential complex, the developer and site contractors repeatedly exposed and impacted hundreds of intact burials in a series of incidents intensively documented in the press (e.g., Salisbury 2016; Stewart 2017; Gordon 2017a; Gordon 2017b). Throughout this entire saga, Philadelphia's Law Department maintained that the city had no legal jurisdiction in this matter because the work was being conducted by a private developer on privately owned land. L&I claimed to have no cause to intervene in the work as the construction permit had already been approved. The Medical Examiner's Office argued that it had no authority to compel the developer to take action and the PHC asserted that its hands were also tied, even though the site was located in the Old City Historic District. Even the PHMC declared that it had no ability to intercede because state laws, including the Historic Burial Places Preservation Act, did not apply in this situation (Salisbury 2016; Stewart 2017).

Ultimately, the persistent advocacy of the PAF, the incessant public humiliation of the developer and city officials in the press, and the outrage expressed by other concerned citizens compelled the Department of Licenses and Inspection to urge the developer to petition the Orphans' Court for permission to relocate burial remains from the site. It was also the legal arguments put forth by Mark R. Zecca, the PAF's attorney during Orphans' Court proceedings, that refuted persistent assertions by the city and developer that the court has no authority in this matter.[20] Finally, the affirmation by the Orphans' Court that it did have undeniable legal jurisdiction over the burials at this site compelled the developer to hire a qualified archaeological firm to respectfully exhume the remains in preparation for their eventual reburial elsewhere (AECOM 2017).[21]

In the end, it was the egregious manner in which this saga unfolded, along with the failure of all parties who had legal, institutional, and moral authority to intervene in these events but repeatedly refused to do so, that pushed the PAF to act quickly and make its burial places database publicly available. In June 2017, the PAF, in conjunction with the PHMC, organized a public meeting to discuss in detail the legal, ethical, and practical issues associated with burial ground preservation in Philadelphia, and to formally announce the impending launch of the cemetery database. The PAF additionally outlined the broad elements of a plan by which, with the use of the database, avoidable future impacts to the city's abandoned and unmarked burial sites could be eliminated, or at least minimized (Salisbury 2017).

The Documentation of New York City's Cemeteries

The database of New York City's cemeteries was compiled by Elizabeth D. Meade as part of her 2020 doctoral dissertation at the Graduate Center of the City University of New York (CUNY). More than 520 cemeteries in the five boroughs—the Bronx, Brooklyn, Manhattan, Queens, and Staten Island—were researched and mapped as part of the project (see Figures 2.2 and 2.3). The cemetery sites were identified through years of documentary research, using various sources including property records/land convey-

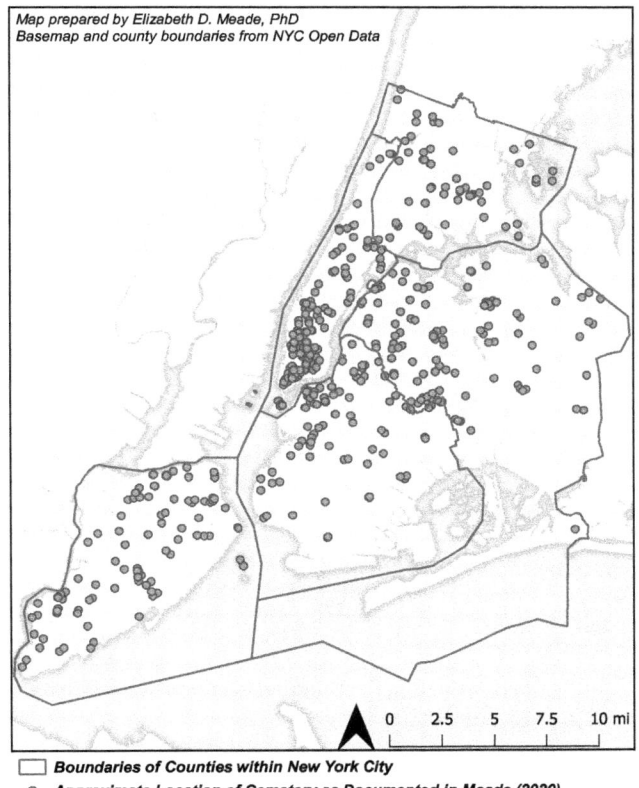

Figure 2.2. Map depicting the general location of cemeteries documented in Meade 2020. © Elizabeth D. Meade.

ances, historical maps, church/religious records, cemetery records, local histories, newspaper articles (including those reporting the accidental discovery of human remains during earlier construction efforts), and other primary and secondary source materials documenting human burials during historic-period New York City. Where possible, the original boundaries of each burial place were documented and mapped in a GIS database.

The study's methodology was tailored specifically to identify cemetery sites using specific data sets and research methods. As such, it resulted in the identification of cemeteries even in areas that had previously been the subject of archaeological investigations, but where historical cemeteries were not identified given limitations in the research methodologies. Furthermore, the methodologies Meade's study employed allowed for the

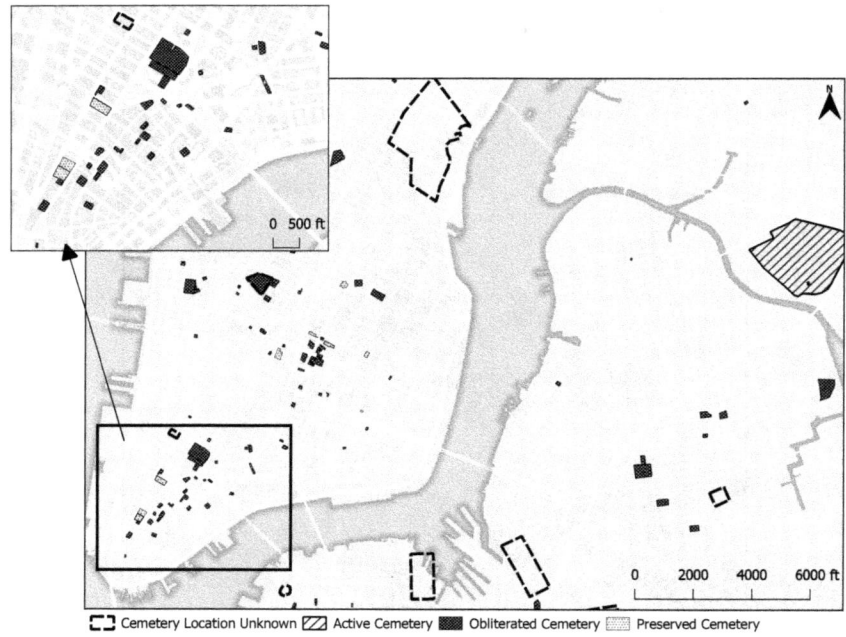

Figure 2.3. Sample map showing documented cemeteries in Lower Manhattan based on Meade 2020. © Elizabeth D. Meade.

confirmation of the boundaries of certain burial grounds that previous archaeological assessments were unable to confirm. For example, more than one dozen previous archaeological assessments (including those written by the author) had attempted to document the former municipally operated potter's fields that were situated on Randalls Island between 1843 and 1851, and later on adjacent Wards Island between 1851 and 1868. Despite intensive research, studies had failed to confirm the exact years of use or specific boundaries of the potter's fields. The 2020 documentation of New York's cemeteries, however, combined an intensive review of property conveyances and historical property maps with map georeferencing to document the burial ground's exact boundaries.

To understand the role of burial places within both the urban landscape and the broader deathscape of New York City, the data were compared and contrasted according to a number of different variables relating to the groups that established each site (e.g., religious groups, municipal organizations, private families, etc.); the dates of establishment and years of use for each burial places; and each cemetery's current status (e.g., active, preserved, or obliterated). To make the data accessible to the public, a web map version of the GIS database was created. The study concluded that approximately 60 percent of the documented burial places that had been established in New York City since the seventeenth century were obliterated/redeveloped. In the context of the study, *obliteration* was defined as a change in the land use of a burial place (e.g., conversion to a park, redevelopment, etc.) such that the site is no longer in use or recognized as a burial place, but does not indicate that the remains interred within were exhumed (Meade 2020). Partial or full exhumation could not be documented in approximately 40 percent of those cemeteries that were categorized as obliterated (Meade 2020). The database therefore identifies locations in all five boroughs where human remains are potentially still extant on sites that could be developed in the future. The study also identified those types of burial places that were more likely to have been redeveloped. These included municipally controlled burial places, in particular those associated with the indigent (such as potter's fields and military or hospital cemeteries), segregated burial places for enslaved Africans and individuals of African descent, which are believed to have been underrepresented in the study as a result of a lack of historical documentation, and small family or homestead burial places.

One of the goals of the study was to document and map these locations so that the database could be used by review agencies (e.g., LPC and New York State Office of Parks, Recreation, and Historic Preservation, also known as OPRHP), archaeologists, and the general public to protect these sites during any development that may occur in the future (Meade 2020). The database is currently available as a webmap and has been shared with reviewing agencies (including LPC and OPRHP), local archaeological firms, and local residents/laypersons. The easy access to the database has been intended to promote broader awareness among the general public and to introduce new research techniques to archaeologists and historians to allow them to better identify and document historical cemeteries when completing research on new sites.

Successful Use of the Databases in Advocacy Efforts in Philadelphia

Since the public launch of its Historic Philadelphia Burial Places database in 2018, the PAF has continued to track proposed construction projects throughout the city, to the extent possible, and has been able to successfully employ that tool to avoid or mitigate potential burial impacts to unmarked burial sites associated with several properties and undertakings. The first such effort occurred in 2018, shortly after the database launch, and involved the city's ambitious "Rebuild Philadelphia" program.[22] This initiative will use funding generated by a new beverage tax on sugary drink products to invest millions of dollars in the rejuvenation and physical improvement of aging public parks, recreation centers, and library facilities at more than four hundred sites across the metropolitan area. The PAF utilized an interactive map of proposed rebuild sites in conjunction with the burial places database in order to identify more than a dozen locations where proposed renovations had the potential to disturb abandoned and unmarked historic burials. This list was shared with the Rebuild staff and, to date, at least one upcoming renovation project—the Capitolo Playground at 10th and Federal Streets in South Philadelphia—has undergone historical review based on the PAF's information that the location was formerly the site of the Lafayette Cemetery. An archaeological consultant was contracted to provide oversight.

A second use of the database resulted in both regrettable and joyous results involving a newly discovered burial ground only brought to the PAFs attention in late 2017. Located on the 4100 block of Chestnut Street in West Philadelphia, this burial site was previously depicted in just a handful of late nineteenth-century historic maps and required considerable research to positively determine its identity and community association. The result of those efforts, performed initially by the PAF, and subsequently by Dr. Donna J. Rilling, professor of history at the State University of New York (SUNY) at Stony Brook,[23] found that this cemetery was created by an African American mutual aid society known as the African Friends to Harmony in 1826, and likely represented the oldest known Black burial site in West Philadelphia (Rilling 2018; Salisbury 2018a; Doyle 2018). Subsequent research discovered that the African Friends to Harmony cemetery (also known as Harmonia Burial Ground) was likely established by members of the two oldest Black congregations in the area—the African Baptist Church of Blockley (now Monumental Baptist Church) and the Mount Pisgah African Methodist Episcopal Church (Rilling 2018).

At the time of its discovery, the former cemetery parcel was divided in two, with the western part occupied by an at-grade car wash and facing impending redevelopment into a six-story modular apartment complex and the eastern portion lying beneath a parking lot owned by the University of Pennsylvania (Goulding 2018a). In an effort to ensure a thorough archaeological assessment of the future apartment site, the PAF reached out to the Philadelphia Civic Design Review Committee, the Department of Licenses and Inspections, and Councilwoman Jannie Blackwell, in whose district the site was located.[24] Unfortunately, these efforts amounted to naught, as the Department of Licenses and Inspections continued to maintain that it had no jurisdiction in the matter and no authority to interrupt construction or require archaeological investigations. As a result, the apartment building was constructed, reportedly with the assistance of "environmental and soil specialists," but not archaeologists, and a pledge from the developer not to disrespect any burials that might be present (Saakashvili 2018). Unsurprisingly, no burials were reported to have been found during construction, and it may never be known with certainty if any evidence of burials was identified at all.

Following this episode and the extensive negative press it generated, the PAF was contacted by University of Pennsylvania representatives for advice related to that portion of the former cemetery that fell within property it owned. Although the university had no immediate plans to redevelop its land, that outcome was a possibility in the distant future, and it sought information regarding the legal process that should be followed in that event as well as any other recommendations or guidance the organization could offer. PAF representatives shared the information about this cemetery thus far incorporated into the burial places database and outlined the process for petitioning the Orphans' Court for permission to exhume and relocate intact burials. PAF also advised the university of the value of public transparency in all matters related to this site and the need to request the services of a local archaeological firm experienced in cemetery relocations. Finally, the organization urged the university to reach out to the descendant Monumental Baptist and Mount Pisgah AME congregations, along with other West Philadelphia officials, to solicit their input regarding the appropriate treatment and ultimate disposition of any remains yet preserved within the former burial ground. To its enduring credit, the university accepted this advice and, in conjunction with the descendant church communities, decided to move ahead with archaeological explorations of their part of the site even though impending disturbances were not immediately forthcoming (Goulding 2018b). These initial investigations were completed in early 2019 and confirmed the presence of multiple preserved burials (Shaw 2019). All parties subsequently decided to move forward with the immediate exhumation of remains and reburial in a more fitting and respectful location, and obtained a relocation permit from the Philadelphia Orphans' Court.[25] An on-site commemoration of those interred in this ground was held in February 2020, with the relocation work completed shortly thereafter. On Palm Sunday, 5 April 2020, the remains of the 161 individuals exhumed from Penn's portion of the African Friends to Harmony Burial Ground were formally reinterred in a new grave site at the historic Eden African American Cemetery in Collingsdale, Delaware County, Pennsylvania (Belefanti 2020).

More recently, the PAF again utilized its database to help protect a poorly documented burial site in West Philadelphia, adjacent to the 30th

Street Railroad Station, where a large surface parking lot was to be redeveloped for the construction of a sizable office, residential, and commercial complex. The PAF learned of this proposal, the Schuylkill Yards project, in the spring of 2019 and immediately contacted the Philadelphia Planning Commission to inform them that the Historic Philadelphia Burial Places database identified this site as located in the vicinity of one or possibly two late-seventeenth century cemeteries and had been used for more than 150 years as Quaker burial grounds and city-owned potter's fields. The PAF also shared newspaper accounts documenting the discovery of human remains and intact burials at or near this location over several decades in the twentieth century. While Planning Commission representatives initially claimed that there was little that they could do to intervene in this matter, they did quickly contact the developer to inform them of the PAF's assertions and concerns. Being keenly aware of the tragic events that had recently transpired with the First Baptist Church Cemetery, the developer commissioned a historical assessment of the property and convened a subsequent meeting with interested parties to discuss the issue of potential historic burials. This meeting included representatives from the PAF, the PHMC, the PHC, and the Philadelphia Society of Friends Yearly Meeting. It resulted in a recommendation that a professional archaeological firm be contracted to further investigate the site and develop a plan of action for addressing the potential discovery of burials remains (Salisbury 2019a; 2019c).

Following the meeting, the PAF was asked to serve as an official advisor to this project and a local archaeological firm with experience in documenting historic cemeteries was brought under contract to draft Archaeological Monitoring Protocol and to begin conducting limited subsurface testing in accessible areas at the periphery of the property (Richard Grubb & Associates 2019). This testing quickly resulted in the discovery of a number of previously disturbed human skeletal remains (Salisbury 2019b) and prompted the petitioning of the Philadelphia Orphans' Court for permission to implement procedures outlined in the Monitoring Protocol when construction at the site commenced and to relocate any recovered remains from the site to the nearby Woodlands Cemetery. The developer entered into a memorandum of understanding (MOU) with the cemetery formalizing an agreement for the future reinterment of remains at that site. They also entered into a declaration of trust with a staff member of the University of Pennsylvania Museum of Archaeology and Anthropology who agreed to serve as trustee Ad Litem for any recovered remains until such time as they have been reburied.[26] In this case, the project developer acted proactively and assertively to enact measures designed to protect and respectfully treat any human remains, intact or otherwise, contained within the Schuylkill Yards development site. As of 2022, construction work at the site remains temporarily on hold and no further explorations of the property have occurred, so no additional discoveries of human remains have been made.

Despite these successes and the Historic Philadelphia Burial Places database's public availability, to date, widespread independent use of this tool by developers or city agencies has been somewhat disappointing. However, there have been some recent indications that this situation might finally be changing. In February 2020, the PAF received a request from the Philadelphia Water Department to incorporate the burial places map data into its own GIS database for use in conducting project-specific historical background reviews (Mary Ellen McCarty, email communication from the Philadelphia Water Department to the Philadelphia Archaeological Forum, 5 February 2020). These data were subsequently shared with the department, and in January 2021, the city issued a request for proposals ("RFP") for the planning and design of a variety of new Green Stormwater Infrastructure facilities. One of the tasks required of the implementation of this planning process was to conduct historic background research to determine previous site usage and identify potential limiting factors that might affect the placement or design of stormwater facilities. The liberal use of the PAF's burial place data will hopefully play a key role in selecting appropriate sites for these features, as previous stormwater mitigation measures have been proposed in extremely close proximity to at least one known historic cemetery. In 2018, PWD announced plans to install tree trench features in the sidewalk adjacent to the extant Palmer Cemetery in the Fishtown neighborhood. In that case, the PAF argued that the boundaries of that historic burial ground likely originally extended to the curb line. As a result, the PAF was able to convince the department to put the construction of that specific greening initiative on hold pending further review.

Using the PAF Model to Promote Advocacy in New York City

The New York City database is more recent and has not yet been utilized for advocacy in the same manner as the PAF Philadelphia database. It is hoped that archaeologists and reviewing agencies in New York, with the PAF as a model, can use the NYC database in a similar manner. The database appears to have already had a positive result in increasing awareness of redeveloped cemetery sites and is therefore accomplishing its goals as an example of indirect advocacy. In terms of environmental review, former cemetery sites are being flagged for archaeological analysis, even in areas where previous archaeological assessments failed to document the presence of cemeteries. Furthermore, the database appears to be successful in generating broader general public interest in abandoned cemetery sites in certain neighborhoods and within specific communities.

New York City has professional archaeological societies (the Professional Archaeologists of New York City [PANYC]) devoted to the active advocacy of archaeological resources in general (see Joan Geismar's history of PANYC in Chapter 1 of this volume). However, none has specifically made it part of its mission to document and protect cemetery sites around the city in the same manner as PAF. Similarly, there are few examples of indirect advocacy efforts beyond studies of known or active cemeteries or the locations of graves of well-known New Yorkers. However, community-driven advocacy for former burial sites outside the specific realm of archaeology was successful in the past, resulting in the completion of archaeological analyses on known cemetery sites long in advance of proposed development. As discussed in Chapter 3 of this volume (Edwards and Laird), the archaeological investigation of the African Burial Ground in Lower Manhattan remains a critical turning point in the inclusion of descendant communities and stakeholders in the archaeology of cemetery sites in New York City and across the United States (LaRoche and Blakey 1997; Orser 2007; LPC 2018). Since then, community advocacy for and involvement in archaeological investigations of former burial grounds has changed.

One example of a successful advocacy campaign is the archaeological investigation of the Harlem African Burial Ground that was completed by the environmental, planning, and engineering consultant firm Allee, King, Rosen, and Fleming now known as AKRF, Inc., in 2016. The investigation was the result of years of research and advocacy on the part of the Harlem African Burial Ground Task Force, a group of local residents, religious leaders, politicians, and historians formed in 2009 to bring attention to the site's history and call for its further investigation and memorialization.[27] After many episodes of redevelopment, the cemetery was sealed beneath the foundation of a municipal bus depot in the first half of the twentieth century. Working with the Task Force and the New York City Economic Development Corporation, AKRF completed initial testing to confirm the presence of human remains on the site, the first step in what will eventually be the site's redevelopment and eventual commemoration.

Since the foundation of the Harlem African Burial Ground Task force, other such groups have been formed in communities around New York City dedicated to preserving and memorializing burial places. Similar task forces and community groups have formed to advocate for the protection and preservation of cemetery sites associated with the enslaved individuals whose stolen labor was critical to the growth and resilience of New York

City. Many of these groups have called for archaeological investigations or worked closely with archaeologists to uncover information about the burial populations that is absent in the documentary record. Similar groups include the PS 90 Task Force,[28] which was assembled in response to proposed redevelopment of a former school site that includes a portion of a burial place known as the Flatbush African Burial Ground. A community-based group of local residents and politicians was involved in the rededication of a New York City Park in the East New York neighborhood of Brooklyn as Sankofa Park African Burial Ground to recognize the site's historical use as a burial place for free and enslaved individuals of African descent between the sixteenth and nineteenth centuries (Ajamu 2019). The park is in the process of being redesigned both to provide green space to the local community and to honor those individuals interred on the site, including recently reburied remains initially exhumed as a result of new archaeological investigations (Richling 2021). The Elmhurst History and Cemeteries Preservation Society was formed to document the history of what was historically the small settlement of Newtown, Queens.[29] The group has made recognition and preservation of the neighborhood's cemeteries part of its mission, including a local burial place now known as the Elmhurst African Burial Ground, a site repeatedly threatened by development in recent decades.

Since the conflict over the archaeological investigation of African Burial Ground, the role of descendant community groups and local stakeholders has grown increasingly strong in New York City. Additional advocacy work is being completed by historical societies and preservation groups. Therefore, despite New York City's more stringent environmental review laws compared to those of Philadelphia, the impact of both direct and indirect community advocacy is critical to ensuring the protection of cemetery sites. It is the hope that the New York City cemeteries database will help these groups in their active and vocal advocacy efforts and will inspire the creation of additional task forces with similar missions for a larger number of obliterated burial sites throughout the five boroughs that still contain human remains. Through the collaboration of archaeologists, community groups, local politicians, and city agencies, it may be possible to reduce the number of known burial sites that are disturbed as a result of redevelopment.

Conclusions

The Philadelphia and New York City burial databases represent years of documentary research, mapping, and collaboration that resulted in the documentation of hundreds of forgotten burial places in two of the largest and most densely populated cities in the United States. The documentation of burial places requires intensive research following highly specialized methodologies specifically designed to reveal the locations of long-lost burial places, even when those burial places lack visibility in both the landscape and the documentary record. Archaeological investigations of cemetery sites in cities including New York and Philadelphia have proven that the specific needs of urban populations can lead to the creation of an astonishing number of cemetery sites over time and that, as demographics shift and cities grow, cemeteries will either be either preserved or destroyed by redevelopment as a city remakes itself. Though the cultural forces driving such transitions may vary, the result is usually the same: cities typically have a large number of undocumented or poorly documented sites that contain human remains and are vulnerable to redevelopment. The documentation and recognition of these sites is therefore a critical component of any cemetery advocacy effort that lays the groundwork for actively protecting human remains and burial sites in the future.

In launching its burial places database, the PAF initially thought that efforts to protect forgotten and unmarked cemeteries would result in fairly rapid success, and that the enactment of fundamental and necessary public policy changes within city government related to the preservation of these sites would meet with little opposition. Sadly, that has not been the case, and today, institutional indifference, intransigence, and apathy regarding the respectful treatment of the physical remains of our ancestors and forbears remains seemingly as entrenched as ever. This situation should remind us all that bringing about meaningful historical preservation reforms and improvements is never easy and can only be achieved through the continued vocal advocacy of not just the public, but also the members of the archaeological community who know these resources best (See Geismar in this volume).

In New York City, cemetery sites have a greater amount of protection when environmental review laws are involved but are still highly vulnerable to redevelopment. A combination of community advocacy and archaeological advocacy is therefore critical to the protection of burial sites in New York City. However, these issues are not unique to these two cities, and these models for advocacy can be applied to most modern large cities in the United States and beyond. Using these case studies as examples, archaeologists in other cities can and should begin to create similar databases of lost cemetery sites or even other types of archaeological resources that may require professional attention. For example, a similar project in Richmond, Virginia, could build on the work being completed by the Sacred Ground Project (see Edwards and Laird, Chapter 3 of this volume) and expand awareness of other redeveloped or forgotten burial places in that city, as well as map the spatial connections between historical sites associated with enslavement in Richmond. With increased awareness of these types of sites and the efforts required to document and protect them, archaeologists in different cities can complete similar mapping and research efforts. An increase in such indirect advocacy nation-wide can, in turn, give archaeologists an advantage in more active advocacy efforts, potentially to the point where more effective and uniform legislation can be passed to protect burial sites from construction-related disturbance.

By training, qualified historical archaeologists typically have expertise in combining an understanding of landscapes with historical documentary research in order to determine a site's sensitivity for human remains. Many archaeologists also have extensive experience working with descendant communities to ensure the protection and respectful treatment of human remains on sites threatened by development. Such consultation has only increased following the implementation of legislation including NAGPRA and earlier, initially disastrous collaborations between archaeologists and descendant community groups, such as the beginnings of the excavation of the African Burial Ground in Manhattan. This experience puts the archaeological community in a strategic position to serve as advocates for the dead—at least those members who are committed to the protection of burial sites, who are willing to stand up to avaricious developers or unwilling politicians, and who share a desire for meaningful collaborations with descendant populations and community groups. Despite the fact that cemeteries are a type of resource that can stir intense public passions, in cases where legal protections are lacking, archaeologists and advocacy groups may be the only thing standing between known burial places and bulldozers.

Elizabeth D. Meade, PhD, is a senior technical director and archaeologist at AKRF, Inc., an environmental consulting and engineering firm in New York City. She holds a bachelor's degree in anthropology from NYU, a master's degree in anthropology from Hunter College, and a PhD in anthropology at the CUNY Graduate Center. Elizabeth has been conducting archaeological investigations in New York City and the surrounding region for nearly twenty years and her work has included a wide variety of sites including historic period cemeteries, nineteenth-century households, and colonial-era ships.

Douglas Mooney is a professional archaeologist with more than thirty years' experience in cultural resource management. He has BA in anthropology from West Virginia University and a master's degree in anthropology from Penn State University. Douglas has primarily worked in the City of Philadelphia since 1999, including at the National Constitution Center and President's House Sites in Independence Mall, the Bethel Burial Ground at Weccacoe Playground, the I-95/Girard Avenue Improvement Project in the city's Old City, Northern Liberties, Kensington-Fishtown, and Port Richmond neighborhoods. He has served as the president of the PAF since 2007.

Notes

1. For more information and to view the database, visit: www.cemeteriesofnyc.com.
2. For more information and to view the database, visit: https://www.phillyarchaeology.net/paf-activities/burial-places-forum/.
3. US African American Burial Grounds Network Act, S.2827, 116th Cong. (2020), https://www.congress.gov/bill/116th-congress/senate-bill/2827.
4. New York City Environmental Quality Review [CEQR] as overseen by the New York City Landmarks Preservation Commission (LPC).
5. New York State Historic Preservation Act of 1978 as overseen by the New York State Office of Parks, Recreation, and Historic Preservation (OPRHP).
6. Section 106 of the National Historic Preservation Act, as overseen by OPRHP operating as the New York State Historic Preservation Office (SHPO).
7. https://www.dos.ny.gov/cmty/CEMETERYpercent20LAWpercent20MANUALpercent2005-09-18.pdf.
8. "Unmarked Burial Site Protection Act" in 2019 (2019 NY Senate-Assembly Bill S4422, A5298) Assembly Bill A5298 and Senate Bill S4422); https://www.nysenate.gov/legislation/bills/2019/s4422.
9. Defined as those projects that "compl[y] with all applicable zoning regulations and [do] not require discretionary action by a government agency and [are] not receiving government funding" (LPC 2018, 16).
10. Section 14–1000 of the Philadelphia Zoning Code.
11. The PHC is also responsible for review and oversight of federally involved projects. under the Certified Local Government program.
12. Pennsylvania Consolidated Statutes, Title 37, Historical and Museums (37 Pa.C.S.).
13. The PHMC also serves as the Pennsylvania SHPO for federally funded or permitted projects.
14. 1995, P.L. 647, No. 70.
15. These laws include 9 Pa.C.S., Burial Grounds; 20 Pa.C.S.,Decedents, Estates and Fiduciaries; and 28 Pa.C.S., Health and Safety)² and Unconsolidated Statutes (e.g., Supplementary Act, Burial Grounds Act, 1887, P.L. 96, No. 47; Cemeteries and Graveyards Protected Act, 1894, P.L. 397, No. 296; Burial Grounds and Conveyance Act, 1913, P.L. 551, No. 354. A complete, in-depth discussion of every Pennsylvania law that addresses or relates to cemeteries and burial grounds is beyond the scope of the present chapter.
16. 9 Pa.C.S. § 211-215.
17. 20 Pa. C.S. § 305.
18. 9 Pa. C.S. § 101; https://codes.findlaw.com/pa/title-9-pacsa-burial-grounds/pa-csa-sect-9-101.html.
19. The County Code Act, 1955, P.L. 323, No. 130.

20. Mark R. Zecca. 2017. Memorandum of Law and Proposed Decree Submitted by Mark R. Zecca Pursuant to the Direction of this Court, August 3, 2017. Court of Common Pleas of Philadelphia County, Pennsylvania, Orphans' Court Division, Case No. 972 of 2017.
21. Court of Common Pleas of Philadelphia County, Orphans' Court Division. Human Remains at 218 Arch Street, Philadelphia. Case No. 972 of 2017. Preliminary Decree, 14 August 2017.
22. https://www.phila.gov/programs/rebuild/.
23. This research was part of a nomination to the Philadelphia Register of Historic Places (officially listed November 2018).
24. Philadelphia Archaeological Forum (PAF). Letter to the Philadelphia Civic Design Review Committee. 19 January 2018.
Philadelphia Archaeological Forum (PAF). Letter to the Philadelphia Department of Licenses and Inspections. 19 January 2018.
Philadelphia Archaeological Forum (PAF). Letter to Councilwoman Jannie Blackwell. 24 January 2018.
25. Court of Common Pleas of Philadelphia County, Orphans' Court Division. Human Remains at 4111-4123 Chestnut Street Philadelphia, Case No. 1222 of 2019 (Control # 194424). Final Decree 26 November 2020.
26. Jerry Sweeney and Doug Mooney. 2019. Memorandum update to Schuylkill Yards consulting parties. 16 August 2019.
27. https://www.habgtaskforce.org/home.
28. https://ps90taskforce.nyc/.
29. https://www.elmhursthistoryandcemeteries.org/.

References

AECOM. 2017. *218 Arch Street/First Baptist Church of Philadelphia Cemetery Relocation Project, Philadelphia, Pennsylvania*. Report prepared for PMC Property Group, 26 October 2017.

Ajamu, Amadi. 2019. "Celebration and Re-Interment of Our Ancestors." *New York Amsterdam News*, 1 August 2019. http://amsterdamnews.com/news/2019/aug/01/celebration-and-re-internment-our-ancestors/.

Anthony, Sian. 2016. "Questions Raised in Excavating the Recent Dead." In *Archaeologists and the Dead: Mortuary Archaeology in Contemporary Society*, edited by Howard Williams and Melanie Giles, 21–37. Oxford: Oxford University Press.

Bahn, Paul G. 1984. "Do Not Disturb? Archaeology and the Rights of the Dead." *Oxford Journal of Archaeology* 3 (1): 127–39.

Barker, Charles R. 1940–49. *Charles R. Barker Register of Burying Grounds in Philadelphia*. Manuscript database maintained by the Genealogical Society of Pennsylvania. https://genpa.org/2015/12/charles-barker-register-of-philadelphia-burying-grounds.

Belefanti, Chantale. 2020. "Monument." *Philadelphia Tribune*, 2 December 2020. https://www.phillytrib.com/monument/article_e423b8fb-c05a-517d-9e34-e553b056949c.html.

Blakey, Michael. 2020. "Archaeology Under the Blinding Light of Race." *Current Anthropology* 61 (22): 183–97.

Brooklyn Daily Eagle. 1885. "Gothic Hall's Mystery: Some Facts About the Skeletons Found in Adams Street," 20 September 1885, 4.

Bruning, Susan B. 2006. "Complex Legal Legacies: The Native American Graves Protection and Repatriation Act, Scientific Study, and Kennewick Man." *American Antiquity* 71 (3): 501–21.

Chernick, Karen. 2017. "Philadelphia Plans for Future Density Require Dealing With Historic Sites." *Next City*, 25 October 2017. https://nextcity.org/daily/entry/philadelphia-plans-for-future-density-require-dealing-with-historic-sites.

Cryne, Julia A. 2009. "NAGPRA Revisited: A Twenty-Year Review of Repatriation Efforts." *American Indian Law Review* 34 (1): 99–122.

Doyle, Chris. 2018. "City Designates African American Cemetery under Penn Parking Lot as Historic." *The Daily Pennsylvanian*, 10 November 2018. https://www.thedp.com/article/2018/11/philadelphia-historical-commission-penn-upenn-african-american-burial-ground.

Gambardello, Joseph A. 2009. "Philadelphia: City of forgotten burial grounds." *Philadelphia Inquirer*, 15 December, 2009. https://www.inquirer.com/philly/news/breaking/20091215_Philadelphia__City_of_forgotten_burial_grounds.html.

Gordon, Elana. 2017a. "Unearthing Stories Hidden in the Bones of a Forgotten Burial Ground." *WHYY News*, 24 April 2017. https://whyy.org/segments/unearthing-stories-hidden-in-the-bones-of-a-forgotten-burial-ground.

———. 2017b. "Archaeologist claims hundreds of eighteenth-century Philly remains may have been dumped in landfill." *WHYY News*, 30 October 2017. https://whyy.org/articles/archaeologist-claims-hundreds-eighteenth-century-philly-remains-dumped-landfill.

Goulding, Alice. 2018a. "Beneath Penn Property Could Lie the Remains of West Philadelphia's Earliest Black Residents." *The Daily Pennsylvanian*, 1 March 2018. https://www.thedp.com/article/2018/03/african-american-cemetery-black-history-penn-campus-upenn-philadelphia.

———. 2018b. "U. Will Enlist Expert to Investigate African American Burial Ground Found under Penn Property." *The Daily Pennsylvanian*, 18 April 2018. https://www.thedp.com/article/2018/04/african-american-burial-ground-west-philadelphia-upenn-penn-expert-university-philadelphia.

Joyce, Rosemary, and Zoe Crossland. 2015. "Anthropological Perspectives in Disturbing Bodies: An Introduction." *Disturbing Bodies: Perspectives on Forensic Anthropology*, edited by Zoe Crossland and Rosemary A. Joyce, 169–84. Santa Fe, NM: School for Advanced Research Press.

LaRoche, Cheryl J., and Michael L. Blakey. 1997. "Seizing Intellectual Power: The Dialogue at the New York African Burial Ground." *Historical Archaeology* 31 (3): 84–106.

LPC (New York City Landmarks Preservation Commission). 2018. *Guidelines for Archaeological Work in New York City*. New York: Landmarks Preservation Commission.

Meade, Elizabeth D. 2020. "'Prepare for Death and Follow Me:' An Archaeological Survey of the Historic Period Cemeteries of New York City." PhD diss., City University of New York.

NBC 10 News. 2003. "Two Ancient Burying Grounds of New York City—One to Be Preserved, The Other Wholly Obliterated," 27 October 2003.

New-York Tribune. 1903. "Two Ancient Burying Grounds of New York City—One to Be Preserved, the Other Wholly Obliterated," 2 April 1903, A3.

Orona, Brittani, and Vanessa Esquivido. 2020. "Continued Disembodiment." *Humboldt Journal of Social Relations* 42 (42): 50–68.

Orser, Charles E. 2007. *The Archaeology of Race and Racialization in Historic America*. Gainesville: University of Florida Press.

Pennsylvania Gazette. 1743. Untitled, 10 March 1743, 2.

Philadelphia Archaeological Forum (PAF). 2020. "Protecting Archaeology." https://www.phillyarchaeology.net/philly-archaeology/archaeological-protections-in-the-city-of-philadelphia-and-its-environs.

Philadelphia Historical Commission. 2015. *The Minutes of the 637th Stated Meeting of the Philadelphia Historical Commission*, 11 September 2015: 7–9. https://document-archive.phila.gov/#/Historical_Commission/Meeting_Minutes.

Philadelphia Inquirer. 1889. "Playing with Bones, Ghastly Toys for Children at Twelfth and Carpenter Streets," 17 August 1889, 3.

Richard Grubb & Associates. 2019. *Archaeological Monitoring Protocol.* Report submitted to Penoni, 12 June 2019.

Richling, Billy. 2021. "Sankofa Park and African Burial Ground Square in East New York To Get A Fresh Look." *Bkylner,* 3 February 2021. https://bklyner.com/sankofa-park-and-african-burial-ground-square-in-east-new-york-to-get-a-fresh-look.

Rilling, Donna J. 2018. *African Friend to Harmony Burial Ground Historic Places Nomination.* Philadelphia Historical Commission. https://www.phila.gov/media/20190401093121/4111–23-Chestnut-St-nomination.pdf.

Saakashvili, Eduard. 2018. "Company Building Apartments Atop Former Graveyard Consider Hiring Consultants." *West Philadelphia Local,* 29 January 2018. http://www.westphillylocal.com/2018/01/29/company-building-apartments-atop-former-graveyard-considers-hiring-consultants.

Salisbury, Stephan. 2016. "Old Bones Found–and Nobody's in Charge." *Philadelphia Inquirer,* 4 November 2016. https://www.inquirer.com/philly/entertainment/20161102_Old_bones_turn_up_during_construction__regulatory_agencies_shrug.html.

Salisbury, Stephan. 2017. "Proposal Made to Solve a Philly Riddle: What to Do When You Dig up Old Bones." *Philadelphia Inquirer,* 2 June 2017. https://www.inquirer.com/philly/entertainment/arts/proposal-made-to-solve-a-philly-riddle-what-to-do-when-you-dig-up-old-bones-20170602.html.

Salisbury, Stephan. 2018a. "Oldest African American Graveyard in West Philadelphia Lies Beneath Proposed Apartments." *Philadelphia Inquirer,* 25 January 2018. https://www.inquirer.com/philly/news/pennsylvania/philadelphia/oldest-african-american-graveyard-in-west-philadelphia-lies-beneath-proposed-apartments-20180125.html.

———. 2018b. "New Online Map Points to the Unmarked Graveyards of Philly's Dead." *Philadelphia Inquirer,* 27 February 2018.

Salisbury, Stephan. 2019a. "Graves Beneath Schuylkill Yards? Developer Meets with Experts–and Quakers–to Discuss What to Do." *Philadelphia Inquirer,* 21 May 2019. https://www.inquirer.com/arts/brandywine-realtyschuylkill-yards-quaker-cemetery-philadelphia-20190521.html.

———. 2019b. "Human Remains Discovered at Schuylkill Yards, but Developer Has a Plan." *Philadelphia Inquirer,* 23 August 2019. https://www.inquirer.com/arts/brandywine-realty-schuylkill-yards-quaker-cemetery-bones-discovered-20190823.html.

———. 2019c. "Schuylkill Yards Development May Rest on the Quaker Dead." *Philadelphia Inquirer,* 2 May 2019. https://www.inquirer.com/arts/schuylkill-yards-quaker-cemeteries-philadelphia-history-brandywine-drexel-20190502.html.

Scarre, Geoffrey. 2003. "Sapient Trouble-Tombs?" In *The Oxford Handbook of the Archaeology of Death and Burial,* edited by Liv Nilsson Stutz and Sarah Tarlow, 665–76. Oxford: Oxford University Press.

Schillaci, Michael A., and Wendy J. Bustard. 2010. "Controversy and Conflict: NAGPRA and the Role of Biological Anthropology in Determining Cultural Affiliation." *Political and Legal Anthropology Review* 33 (2): 352–73.

Shaw, Gwyneth K. 2019. "Testing Finds Signs of African-American Burial Ground Beneath Chestnut Street Property." *Penn Today,* 7 February 2019. https://penntoday.upenn.edu/news/testing-finds-signs-african-american-burial-ground-beneath-chestnut-street-property.

Sloane, David Charles. 1991. *The Last Great Necessity: Cemeteries in American History.* Baltimore, MD: Johns Hopkins University Press.

Stewart, Tamara Jager. 2017. "Whistling Past the Historic Graveyard." *American Archaeology* 21(4). https://www.archaeologicalconservancy.org/whistling-past-historic-graveyard/.

Torres, Rene L.C. 1997. "Cemetery Landscapes of Philadelphia." Master's thesis, University of Pennsylvania, Philadelphia, PA. https://repository.upenn.edu/cgi/viewcontent.cgi?article=1494&context=hp_theses.

Weiss, Murray, Jamie Schram, and Dan Kadison. 2006. "Skeleton Crew: Building at Trump Tower Halted After Bones Found." *New York Post*, 13 December 2006.

Zimmerman, Robert. 1994. "Human Bones as Symbols of Power: Aboriginal American Belief Systems Toward Bones and 'Grave-Robbing' Archaeologists." In *Conflict in the Archaeology of Living Traditions*, edited by R. Layton, 211–16. London: Routledge.

Chapter 3

Digging Truth
Archaeology and Public Imagination in Shockoe Bottom

Ana Edwards and Matthew R. Laird

Introduction

Traditionally, advocacy for historically significant African American sites has been a grassroots affair. Individuals, clubs, families, and church groups champion preservation of sites of local meaning such as homes, schools, parks and playgrounds, churches, and cemeteries. These places represent the institutional building blocks of neighborhoods and communities established after emancipation (Cep 2020). Projects like these are fortunate when scientific research affirms their historical significance to a wider audience, but only recently have fields such as archaeology been put in service of historic preservation of African American sites as a way to insert their narratives back into the national American story, as a way of acknowledging and righting wrongs. Advocates for these projects have begun to find allies in scientists much as they have done with scholars.

Archaeologists have occupied a large space in the public imagination through popular culture (film and literature) or museums (science or natural history). Those who dig a little deeper into the history of the field inevitably encounter the well-documented, uncomfortable truth of its use as a tool of cultural imperialism, principally through the exploitation of non-European peoples' cultural resources (Blakey 2020a, S184). Their bodies—living and dead—have been a special target of the prurient curiosity of European patrons, publics, and scholars (Blakey 2020b). And yet, when

---

Notes for this chapter begin on page 65.

the question and the trowel are wielded by different hands with different intentions, the results can be stunningly humane and progressive, even if rarely without struggle.

Archaeologists and other anthropologists have become two of the most important members of this new group of allies, finding and identifying the material, explaining how humans interact with the material, and locating the stories of people and historic preservationists whose advocacy protects our resources from demolition—or at least total obscurity. The additional importance of these allies is that they have looked back on the practices in their own histories and have matured. They know—or are more open to learning—how to be allies in work that may only have existed in the individual practitioner's imagination. The creation of the Professional Archaeologists of New York City (see Geismar, this volume, Chapter 1) allowed this group to advocate for urban archaeology in the 1980s and to endorse the value of descendant communities as authentic stakeholders in the case of the New York African Burial Ground (1991). Archaeology in the Community, in Washington, DC, which promotes public understanding of archaeology through hands-on engagement, is part of a growing trend of collaborations with African American community projects. Over time, similar cases, in particular those of cemeteries, have demonstrated how powerful the yields can be of a more sociologically and "ethnically" expansive practice (Meade, this volume, Chapter 2).

While there is no single Black public imagination, Black people carry sets of beliefs with the capacity to coalesce into a collective response when faced with affronts to human decency or dignity. When bio-anthropologist Michael Blakey coined the term "descendant community," he was describing a framework that derived from and resonated with the Black people of New York (and beyond) who saw themselves as proudly carrying the responsibility of standing in for their ancestors, distant family members who could not act for themselves (LaRoche and Blakey 1997). When these New Yorkers witnessed (directly or indirectly) the remains of their ancestors being dug up, related by blood or not, their collective response was at least dismay, if not outright grief. This response was a sufficient foundation for community voices to rise united, calling for some correction. This response also represented the assertion of a new set of questions to be considered, which has since triggered the broadening, and even reordering, of urban development and land reclamation priorities to include what historical sites mean in the context of present-day stakeholders and their right to contribute to the future urban landscape.

This chapter presents a discussion about the use and impact of archaeology while drawing on the observations of those others without whose work much of the meaning of reclaimed African American sites would have been diminished or minimized. Public recognition of heretofore neglected or incompletely researched African American historical sites will be examined for its contribution to the perfect storm of social realizations forcing urban development decision-makers into the same rooms as social justice activists, paying particular attention to the role that archaeologists can have in illuminating and correcting past interpretive narratives. In Richmond, Virginia, the public response to the use of archaeology at three nineteenth-century sites, arising in the wake and context of the community struggle for and realization of the New York African Burial Ground National Monument, stands as an example. Richmond's African Burial Ground, the Robert Lumpkin slave-trading complex (Devil's Half Acre), and the East Marshall Street Well each embodies and takes to task meanings ascribed to decisions made by the powerful over the traditionally powerless.

Further, the evidentiary discoveries in the sites to be discussed have substantiated what Black people have long understood about themselves within the American story but struggled to make palatable to a society infected with (or tolerant of) racial hatred and white supremacism—that they know themselves, their roles in and contributions to American society, and have affected its landscapes accordingly (Rothman 2004). This evidence has begun to be transformed into curricular material for educators—significantly, in direct contradiction to the powerful influences of organizations like the United Daughters of the Confederacy during the formative years of public education. And, in general, for all the reticence *some* whites have for their children to learn about something as awful as America's slavery and segregationist past, *more* of them want their children to know a more complete truth.

Attaining such completeness of historical understanding is important and apt to change in response to social need. During segregation, the lesser facilities and supplies provided to Black schools, and the lower wages to Black school teachers rendered an equal education unlikely. However, education was immensely important to post-emancipation Black people precisely because it was forbidden during slavery even as they knew it gave them tools to live in and navigate a world in which they were hated and which could turn on them—individually and collectively—at any moment. Education was a defensive and offensive weapon. Black educators needed to teach their students how their Black world could work within the confines of a white world and keep their psyches strong and optimistic enough to persevere and thrive, and for many, to lead the next phase of struggle for civil rights and social equity (Jackson 1942; Painter 1976; Green 2016). All of this exists in the minds of Black people as they are faced with small and large assaults on their humanity and sense of self. Now, in this post–civil rights, desegregated "Black Lives Matter" moment, transferring what has been in Black minds all this time into America's public psyche has become the order of the day. Archaeology, by producing the material evidence of these historical realities and being wielded by the appropriate practitioners, has proved it has a role to play in this transference.

The Sites

The Devil's Half Acre (Robert Lumpkin's slave-trading business) and the African Burial Ground are neighboring sites in the capital city's founding district, Shockoe Bottom. They are separated by a single street, East Broad Street, between what were once 15th and 16th Streets, and are now, respectively, Interstate 95 and the elevated tracks of CSX Railroad. The African Burial Ground, north of Broad, was used from 1799 through 1816. The Devil's Half Acre was in business from 1844 through 1865. One is post–Revolutionary War and the other antebellum through the Civil War. One was a municipal cemetery and the other a commercial enterprise. Both had vanished from the urban landscape by the end of the nineteenth century. The Devil's Half Acre's archaeological journey has been extensive. And it is possible that no archaeology will ever be conducted at Richmond's African Burial Ground.

The East Marshall Street Well is a medical trash pit containing the human bones, tools, and other detritus of medical students' coursework in anatomy, sealed up and covered over in 1859. Yet the Well's rediscovery in 1994 elicited an entirely different response than did the New York City African Burial Ground (ABG) just three years before. When the public's engagement with ABG changed the place of Black life in scientific inquiry, the Well and its contents vanished from the public eye (and the institution of higher learning that brought them to their fate) for another fifteen years. What the two projects shared was the spectacle of discovery coupled with horror at the mishandling of our ancestors yet *again*, and the unforeseen revelations about Black life in Richmond and New York made through reclamation and redirection that continue to ripple outward, intersecting every discipline (Ellis 2019). The ABG represents a motherlode of findings and lessons learned, of "isms" unpacked and repacked again, of success and compromise. The Well Project is still on its journey.

New York City's Colonial-Era African Burial Ground

Urban archaeology tends to be done to facilitate development and is not typically convenient to scrutiny by the unqualified public. When archaeology is encountered at street level, the activity tends to warrant only momentary engagement. Big holes and heavy machinery make for cool lunchtime gawking, not social awakening. That changed with the New York African Burial Ground. In 1991, just north of the Wall Street district in Lower Manhattan, the city's seventeenth-century African Burial Ground was rediscovered through the unearthing of skeletal remains which tumbled, none-too-discreetly, from a bulldozer's bucket (Blakey 2010). The highly vocal and underestimated public response led to an up-ending of standard archaeology practices, now including community engagement, the imperative of culturally sensitive expertise, and the public's perception of the profession as a potential ally in social justice. "African diasporic archaeologists and biological anthropologists broke the Enlightenment mold at the African Burial Ground to innovate publicly engaged archaeology in the activist and interdisciplinary vein begun by Equiano (1794) and explicitly framed by Douglass (1950 [1854]) to confront slavery's justifications with fact" (Blakey 2020a, S186).

The knowledge that the remains were likely all those of enslaved Africans initially provoked outrage and launched responses from the Black community, media, government officials, and scholars. The problem stemmed from the procedures undertaken by the archaeological contractors of the General Services Administration, who were without the expertise to understand the material they were handling. They simply did not know enough about African burial practices to recognize that which was significant from that which was not. Therefore the risk of loss at the very moment of discovery was profound. Over the next two months, the eight uncovered sets of remains grew to more than ninety, with at least seventy more anticipated. In the end, 421 sets of remains were carefully unearthed, recorded, and shipped to Howard University for care and research under the direction of Michael L. Blakey.

Decisions about what to do with the remains—from research and preservation to interpretation and re-internment—were debated in public as much as possible because the Black public demanded it, and the social and political conditions for discussion within the city turned out to be right for this cemetery's "arrival." Blakey and colleague Cheryl LaRoche wrote a piece called "Seizing Intellectual Power" in 1993, one of several essays that "celebrates" in a most serious manner an insidious and opportunistic truth: "The project at once has informed and has been informed by the ever-watchful African Americans and New York public. It is a public that understands that the hypothetical and theoretical constructs that guide research are not value-free and are often, in fact, politically charged" (LaRoche and Blakey 1997, 84). New York City's politics, usually charged against Black interests, were, at this moment in the early 1990s, squarely in the hands of a Black community with the moral high ground.

Race and racism were top of mind in a city with its first Black mayor, David L. Dinkins, who had been in office just about two years when the burial ground was uncovered. And impacts of racism and racist municipal systems were prevalent in other urban spaces. The next year, in 1992, the "Los Angeles riots" broke out because the four police captured on video mercilessly beating the unarmed Rodney King were acquitted of assault (Schuppe 2016). The righteous confidence of the descendant community determined to act on their ancestors' behalf was no small foundation to its success. The media also captured the swift and persistent emotional response by New York City's Black community. Gus Savage, a Chicago-based member of the House of Representatives for twelve years, headed the House Subcommittee on Public Buildings and Grounds, leveraging his own political clout to stop the construction and change the destiny of the burial ground (Finder 1992). The world was finally paying attention and beginning to understand that the collective nature of the grief over these remains represented something much deeper than anyone had bothered to imagine.

Analysis of the bones of the 421 people whose remains had been excavated have since yielded unprecedented biological and anthropological information about Africans brought to the Dutch and British colony of Manhattan in the seventeenth and eighteenth centuries, a body of knowledge that had until then been unavailable for study. The fields that experienced true turning points in their practices and priorities included biology, anthropology, archaeology, history, historic preservation, genealogy, and genetics. Though the real point is that the fields of study ultimately affected by this site's material had never really identified colonial-era enslaved or free African people to have the potential to yield information of value. Yes, Black people were there, but they were slaves, a category of person not capable of contributing to the national narrative. The community demanded that Black scientists be in charge of the care and analysis of the bones of their Black ancestors. This did not mean every single individual on the various teams had to be Black, but that *Black experts* would select team members according to their judgment on which archaeologists, anthropologists, biologists, historians, economists, attorneys had the skills and experience to meet the needs of the project (LaRoche and Blakey 1997, 106). This was an application of public accountability and collaboration between science and social justice activism, and as such became both model and measure for other African American sites containing human remains whose stewardship was affected by racist policies, past and present.

Richmond's African Burial Ground

On 10 October 1800, a twenty-four-year-old enslaved blacksmith named Gabriel and two companions were hanged on the town gallows that were said to have been installed on the Burial Ground for Negroes. Gabriel had been a leader in an exceptionally large-scale and well-organized insurrection plan against slaveholders and slavery that had been betrayed at the last minute by frightened participants and a massive rainstorm. He was among the last of twenty-six Black men convicted and executed by the state for their roles in attempting to end slavery in Virginia that year. The event and its repercussions were big news, reaching national and international readers, affecting Thomas Jefferson's campaign for the presidency against John Adams, and temporarily lowering the price of what buyers considered the risk of uncooperative laborers from Virginia (Nicholls 2012). For enslaved and free Black people, there was increased suspicion, violence, and more stringent controls on mobility and gatherings of more than three people. A new law took effect on 1 May 1806, requiring any newly freed Black person to leave the state or risk re-enslavement. While apparently considered impractical on the ground, this law proved a useful threat to curtailing some from seeking freedom and leaving family members behind.

There is no record of where Gabriel was buried, and these authors join those historians who do not believe that contemporary authorities would have interred such a well-known representative of the controversy so close to the center of town. Nonetheless, the burial ground site was a centerpiece of Black life in early Richmond's landscape. As the first municipal cemetery, it was the first public space designated for Black use. It was no lovely park. The site was highly problematic—a woodsy hillside abutting a creek that flooded its lower regions routinely. However, the ritual internment of loved ones was one of the few gatherings permitted to Black people during slavery, and as the permitted repository, the burial ground served as a sacred place. The city closed the site in 1816, and it gradually disappeared to fill and development. The subsequent municipal cemetery, the Shockoe Hill African Burying Ground, was established as two one-acre plots but grew to more than thirty-one acres and more than twenty-two thousand burials before it was closed in 1879.

In 2002, a small group of social justice activists were introduced to the work of Elizabeth Cann Kambourian, a local historian who, while researching the geographical landmarks of Gabriel's Rebellion around Richmond, had proved the existence of the old burial ground by comparing old surveys and maps to the contemporary landscape. In December 2004, the group launched a public campaign called the Sacred Ground Historical Reclamation Project with the purpose of reclaiming the burial ground site from its use as a privately owned parking lot. Kambourian had identified the site on a planning map of Richmond made by the city surveyor in 1809 (Young 1809). The surveyor's label, "Burial Ground for Negroes,"

Figure 3.1. Overview of the Lumpkin's Jail excavation in the closing stages of the investigation in December 2008, view facing north. © David M. Doody, Courtesy of the City of Richmond. Significant features included the kitchen building (*center left*), cobbled courtyard and brick drain (*center right*), and inundated jail foundation (*center bottom*).

marked the spot in a low-lying area along Shockoe Creek in the valley of the same name, overshadowed by what was later known as Capitol Hill. No boundaries delineated the site on the map from adjacent properties but there was one structure drawn in—a "Magazine"—and reference to a "Gallows" in the legend. On 10 October 2004, the group unveiled a state historic highway marker overlooking the site of the burial ground, substantiated by the submission of the Kambourian's research and documentation provided by Philip Schwarz, professor emeritus of history from VCU, member of the city's Slave Trail Commission, and a scholar of Virginia slavery and Gabriel's Rebellion.

The initial goals of the Sacred Ground Project were to learn and share as much as possible about the burial ground as a site of significance to Black history in a city that rarely if ever acknowledged the influence of Black life on its evolution, except as raw labor. Archaeological research seemed the logical next method to follow the paper trail completed by Kambourian and others, but between 2005 and 2015 the focus of the Sacred Ground Project's work shifted to a community-driven preservation effort in the face of large-scale urban development plans. In addition, the physical conditions of the old burial ground had thus far precluded excavation. If most of the site is below the water table and in a floodplain, which it is, and the rest is under Interstate 95, preservation and interpretation of this site will be driven not by what has been lost, but—as it has been to this point—by what was once there. This place of memory is to be honored by transformation into a powerful place, engineered to manage the seasonal movements of Shockoe Valley's waters and to facilitate contemplation.

As helpful as archaeology might have been, and may yet be, for understanding the burial practices of Richmond's earlier African residents, that kind of examination remains an item on a to-do list. A great deal of archival re-examination and re-evaluation has been performed in light of recent interest; however, discussions about exhumation of remains for research purposes, should they be recoverable, have not yet yielded consensus. Feelings run from powerfully opposed to clinically intrigued while the objective opportunity may remain entirely impractical. In the meantime, the use of archaeology that featured more prominently in adjacent (and more physically cooperative) sites over the same period has helped to make the corroborative case for the burial ground's presence and value to the civil landscape today.

Robert Lumpkin's Operation at the Devil's Half Acre

On a stiflingly hot August day in 2008, the sounds of heavy construction equipment in a parking lot in downtown Richmond, Virginia, blended with the monotonous hum of traffic overhead on Interstate 95 and the low rumble of freight trains pulling into Main Street Station. The archaeologists busily directing the removal of layers of asphalt and gravel stepped over the trodden remnants of the previous day's ground-breaking ceremony, including wilted flowers soaked in puddles from the previous night's rain. They were finally beginning the excavation of the "Devil's Half Acre," the former Lumpkin's Slave Jail complex in the heart of Richmond's Shockoe Bottom commercial district, where fortunes were once made from the sale of enslaved men, women, and children. Two years of intensive documentary research and preliminary investigations had led to this day, and expectations were high. It appeared possible, even likely, that remnants of the antebellum slave jail compound survived intact beneath many feet of later fill soil and rubble, waiting to be exposed.

As partner and senior researcher with the James River Institute for Archaeology, Inc. (JRIA),[1] Dr. Matthew R. Laird had been preoccupied for months with the logistical challenges inherent in mounting a large-scale, open-area archaeological excavation in an urban setting. It would have been easy enough to focus on this project as a purely technical undertaking. Yet, from the very outset, Laird was impressed—overwhelmed, frankly—by the outpouring of interest, encouragement, and emotion from Richmonders eager to see this history unearthed. It was clear that this project would mean far more than just exposed brick foundations and boxes of artifacts.

Richmond's central location as a port and railroad hub had made it a booming industrial and transportation center by the 1850s. However, the city's greatest export was not agricultural produce or manufactured goods, but rather enslaved African Americans. Broader economic and political trends throughout the South underpinned the prolific and profitable slave trade that emerged in Richmond's Shockoe Valley in the antebellum period. Every state but South Carolina had prohibited the importation of enslaved Africans by 1803 and, in 1808, Congress enacted the African Slave Trade Act, which effectively ended the legal importation of slaves into the United States. At the same time, a profound economic shift was occurring in the agricultural economies of the Southern states. In upper South states such as Virginia, Maryland, and North Carolina, tobacco was giving way to grain crops such as corn and wheat, which required considerably less labor. Plantation owners soon found themselves with far more workers than they needed, while the enslaved population continued to grow through natural increase. Meanwhile, the rapid expansion of the cotton economy throughout the lower South—including Louisiana, Mississippi, Alabama, and later Texas—created an almost insatiable demand for labor. This confluence of supply and demand created what has been termed the "interstate slave trade." During its peak years between 1820 and 1860, there was a massive relocation of African Americans from the upper to the lower South, with an estimated 350,000 or more enslaved Virginians leaving the state (Gudmestad 1993, 8; Chen and Collins 2007, 1).

Plantation owners and their agents began traveling north to purchase additional laborers, and Richmond became the favored destination for both purchasers and speculators alike. By the 1830s and 1840s, Virginia's capital city was well on its way to becoming one of the nation's largest markets for enslaved people. An array of businesses dedicated to serving this lucrative commerce soon sprang up, including auction houses, hotels to accommodate buyers and sellers, and specialized facilities known as "slave jails," equipped to house enslaved African Americans passing through the city for sale and transportation southward (Gudmestad 1993, 11–12, 14; Chen and Collins 2007, 3–6; McInnis 2011, 65–66).

Richmond's profitable and unsavory commerce in human beings was confined to a relatively limited quarter of the city's Shockoe Valley, a low-lying area drained by the open and noxious Shockoe Creek, which emptied into the nearby James River. The heart of this mixed commercial and residential district was Wall Street, familiarly known as "Lumpkin's Alley," a narrow urban lane lined with auction houses and slave jails, including the premises operated by Robert Lumpkin.

The slave jail owned by Lumpkin from the 1840s through end of the Civil War was hardly unique, yet it became one of the most notorious landmarks of Richmond's slave trade. No doubt this was partly due to the jail's longevity in a business marked by transience, but its notoriety was attributable even more so to its fearsome reputation as the "Devil's Half Acre," where enslaved African men, women, and children were held temporarily, subjected to degrading and dehumanizing treatment, and sold off to an uncertain fate. Lumpkin was not the first to operate this facility; the documentary evidence suggests that it had been developed in the 1830s during the tenure of a previous slave dealer. So, when the thirty-six-year-old Lumpkin purchased the three thirty-foot-wide lots of Wall Street, it already included the built improvements uniquely suited to his business (Laird 2010, 7–11). As detailed in an 1876 account:

> This establishment, which has often been spoken of as the "old slave pen," was situated near Shockoe Creek, in "Lumpkin's bottom." The four principal buildings were of brick. One was used by the proprietor of the establishment as his residence and his office. Another was used as a boarding house for the accommodation of those who came to sell their slaves, or to buy. A third served as a bar-room and a kitchen. "The old jail" stood in a field a few rods from the other buildings. It was forty-one feet long, eighteen feet wide, and two stories in height, with a piazza to both stories, on one side of the building. Here men and women were lodged for safe keeping [sic] until they were disposed of at private or public sale. (Corey 1876, 4–5)

Relatively little is known about Lumpkin himself. Contemporary accounts claim that he began his career as an itinerant trader, before settling down in Richmond. Depicted as fat and cruel, he had a reputation for sexually exploiting the young African American women in his charge. One of these may have been a light-skinned woman named Mary, whom he eventually married. The extensive research conducted by the late Dr. Philip J. Schwarz, professor emeritus of history at Virginia Commonwealth University, revealed that Robert and Mary Lumpkin had at least five children together, including Martha, Anna, Robert, Richard, and John. At the height of his business, Lumpkin sent them to northern boarding schools, where ostensibly they would be protected from sale in the case of bankruptcy (Corey 1895, 48; Schwarz 2006, 1–2; Laird 2010, 11–12).

Exactly how many enslaved people passed through Lumpkin's Jail, or who they were, remains unknown. His accounts, Lumpkin later claimed, had been destroyed in a flood of Shockoe Creek. However, an incomplete ledger held by the Valentine Richmond History Center records five separate shipments of "negroes sent south" by Lumpkin between January 1849 and March 1850. Among the seventy-seven individuals listed were fifty men and women, and twenty-seven children. A number of these were mothers accompanied by as many as four of their children. For the most part, they were referred to only by their given names, but we know the full names of a few, including Susan Dillard, John Johnston, and Henry Grigsby. Lumpkin's ledger suggests the enormous investment of capital embodied in the interstate slave trade. His total costs for purchasing these seventy-seven individuals amounted to $29,622. He sold them for $37,595, a gross profit of $7,973 in that single year. To put these figures in perspective, all of the buildings on Lumpkin's property at that time, including his house, hotel, kitchen, and jail, were collectively valued at $6,000 (Lumpkin 1848–50; City of Richmond Land Book 1850).

The most compelling description of conditions at the jail was provided by its best-known inmate, a Virginian named Anthony Burns. Burns had escaped from slavery in 1854 and made his way to Boston. Tried under the Fugitive Slave Law of 1850, he was returned to Richmond and confined for four months in a cramped and stifling upper-story room of Lumpkin's Jail. The story of his harrowing ordeal was published by abolitionist Charles Emory Stevens in 1856, and vividly recounts the suffering he endured and witnessed there before his eventual release (Stevens 1856, 186–93).

The arrival of Union troops in Richmond in April 1865 brought a sudden and dramatic end to Lumpkin's slave-trading business. As the Southern troops abandoned the city on the night of April 2, Lumpkin was said to have tried to board the last departing train—which happened to be carrying Confederate President Jefferson Davis—with a recently acquired shipment of enslaved people. Turned away by armed guards, Lumpkin marched the group back to the jail and locked them up for what would be their last night of captivity. When Federal forces entered the city the next day, an exuberant crowd of African Americans gathered on Broad Street near Lumpkin's Jail. "Slavery chain done broke at last!" they chanted, "Broke at last! Broke at last! Slavery chain done broke at last! Gonna praise God till I die!" As they were freed, these last prisoners tearfully thanked God and "master Abe" (Litwack 1979, 167–68).

The next chapter in the story of Lumpkin's Slave Jail was its most remarkable. Mary Lumpkin inherited the property at her husband's death in 1866. After a chance encounter on the street in May 1867, she leased the former jail complex to Reverend Nathaniel Colver, a Baptist missionary and representative of the National Theological Institute, who had recently arrived in Richmond to establish a school to train African Americans for the ministry. The bars were removed from its windows, a whipping ring from the floor, and the former jail building served as the classroom of the Colver Institute for the next three years. The school soon outgrew these makeshift quarters and relocated several times, ultimately merging with the Wayland Seminary in 1899 to become Virginia Union University, which continues to thrive today as a premier historically Black institution of higher education in Richmond (Corey 1922, 10; Rosenberger 1922, 100).

In the early 1890s, the antebellum buildings were razed, and the property was filled and leveled to accommodate construction of the Richmond Iron Works foundry. This large, brick industrial building was demolished in the early twentieth century and, in its place, the Seaboard Air Line Railway erected a large freight depot, part of which sat directly atop the former jail site. In the late 1950s, the western part of the former Lumpkin lots was buried during construction of the Richmond and Petersburg Turnpike, which later became Interstate 95. Most recently, the site has been covered by a city-owned parking lot, leased by Virginia Commonwealth University, and located behind Main Street Station.

Virtually no physical reminders of this once densely populated antebellum slave-trading district survive in Shockoe Bottom today. "Here an atomic bomb could hardly have made a more complete clearance of the past," wrote the early Richmond preservationist, Mary Wingfield Scott, in 1950 (Scott 1950, 121). And this was before I-95 cut a broad swathe through the Shockoe Valley, running directly over the former Wall Street.

In late 2005, JRIA initiated a preliminary historical and archaeological investigation of the Lumpkin's Slave Jail Site.[2] The project was a voluntary research effort directed and funded by Richmond City Council's Slave Trail Commission in partnership with the Virginia Department of Historic Resources (DHR) and the Alliance to Conserve Old Richmond Neighborhoods (ACORN). Through painstaking documentary research using city land records, historic maps, and photographs, JRIA re-established the location of the former slave jail complex within a modern urban landscape that would have been virtually unrecognizable to Robert Lumpkin and his contemporaries.

The results of preliminary archaeological test trenching were promising. Although the western portion of the property, including the house and hotel, were covered by the highway, it appeared that a substantial portion of the site, including the notorious jail building itself, remained accessible beneath the parking lot. At depths ranging between eight and eleven feet below the modern ground surface, JRIA archaeologists encountered a well-preserved section of cobble paving and other historic features. Encouraged by these findings, the Slave Trail Commission agreed that a full-scale archaeological excavation of the site was warranted. Once the necessary funding was secured, the second phase of the investigation began in August 2008. This time the testing area was significantly larger, measuring roughly 160 feet long by 80 feet wide. For the first several weeks, archaeologists worked with heavy equipment operators to painstakingly dig through the fill layers covering the site, removing thousands of cubic yards of soil and debris. The remains of the Seaboard Air Line Railway freight depot and the Richmond Iron Works foundry were identified, documented, and removed. As the excavation continued deeper, an array of intact features associated with the Lumpkin's Jail complex began to be revealed.

The first major find was a large area of cobble paving that represented the central courtyard of the slave jail complex described in historical accounts. Running along its eastern edge was a brick drain that still effectively channeled water after more than 150 years. Adjacent to the courtyard was the brick foundation of the kitchen building, measuring twenty-eight feet long by eighteen feet wide. One completely unexpected feature, which initially proved baffling, was a massive brick retaining wall which ran north-south across the lots. Evidently the original lots had sloped considerably eastward toward Shockoe Creek, and construction of the retaining wall created more usable space on the lots. Yet it also served to divide the site into two distinct levels: the upper, "public" sphere of Lumpkin and his clientele, and a lower, sunken area, nearest Shockoe Creek, occupied by the enslaved people who passed through this forbidding place. This plain brick wall served a practical purpose on a sloping site, but it also formed an imposing physical and psychological barrier to those held against their will at the "Devil's Half Acre." This spatial arrangement appears to have been typical of Southern cities, in which slave buildings were situated "down and at the back" of urban lots, reinforcing their inferior status (Wade 1964, 59–60; Vlach 1997, 151–53).

In the latter weeks of the excavation, JRIA archaeologists finally found tantalizing evidence of the jail building, buried fifteen feet beneath the modern ground level. Frustratingly, this deepest part of the site was prone to persistent ground-water seepage and flooding, and only limited testing could be conducted without damaging the sensitive historic features. Despite these challenging conditions, archaeologists identified another well-preserved section of cobble paving and brick drain. They also found two building foundations situated exactly eighteen feet apart in the location predicted from the historic photographs. An 1876 account had described the building as measuring eighteen feet wide, confirming that this must have been the footprint of the infamous jail.

The excavation phase of the project was completed in December 2008, and early the following year the site was carefully reburied to protect it from continued exposure to the elements. Although the site and its compelling features had once again been covered over, in many ways, the larger project was only beginning.

Throughout the roughly five-month excavation, the project generated considerable interest from the media. Local and national news outlets picked up on Richmond's efforts to delve into its past, and the March 2009 issue of *Smithsonian* magazine featured an extensive article about the project (Tucker 2009, 20–22). Dr. Laird and his JRIA colleagues also had the opportunity to share the results of the investigation with a large number of visitors to the site, including elected officials, scholars, historic preservation advocates, students, and members of the interested public. Having seen the tangible evidence in the ground, and even standing on the cobblestones of the antebellum courtyard, many remarked that they had been profoundly moved by the experience, and came away with a visceral sense of a history they felt had long been neglected.

In the years following the archaeological excavation, Dr. Laird had the opportunity to present the results to diverse groups at events hosted by Virginia Union University, the Black History and Cultural Museum of Virginia, the Jewish Community Center of Richmond, and Richmond's Civil War and Emancipation Day celebrations, among many others. He has also met with community groups and students in each of Richmond's public high schools. He found that telling the unique story of Lumpkin's Slave Jail, framed in the context of the compelling archaeological findings, was a particularly effective way to begin a broader discussion about Richmond's history and how its most complicated and painful aspects have historically been paved over.

All archaeological sites have the potential to yield information about the past, and the tangible results—features, artifacts, and landscapes—provide an opportunity to engage the public directly with the history of their community. The Lumpkin's Slave Jail site, in particular, embodies how Richmond's post–Civil War "progress" too often involved burying those places the dominant culture chose to forget, while simultaneously erecting monuments to a more comfortably imagined past. By searching for Lumpkin's Jail, the City of Richmond deliberately sought to challenge its own "authorized heritage discourse," a concept established by Laurajane Smith (2006) to describe how a small group of officials, antiquarians, and scholars employs the public presentation of history as a mechanism of social regulation. The unearthing of this long-lost place has been one step in the process of peeling back physical and cultural layers to reveal an important truth beneath: that this was a real place, inhabited by real people who experienced profound suffering, and redemption. Regardless of whether it is ever re-opened, this site—this history—exists once again in the public imagination in a way that cannot so easily be erased.

East Marshall Street's Nineteenth-Century Well

Richmond filmmaker and psychology professor Shawn Utsey began his documentary portfolio with a film called *Meet Me in the Bottom: The Struggle to Reclaim Richmond's African Burial Ground*. The film captured the zeitgeist of the 2008–2010 period in Richmond, as this struggle was reaching its peak, through a series of interviews with a range of Black Richmonders. Upon learning about the burial ground, activists, scholars, elected officials, cultural workers, and people encountered in the neighborhood gave their opinions and discussed what they thought should be done with the site. Utsey pounded Richmond sidewalks with his film crew recording the comments of folks on the street and in at least one "community center," better known as Harvey's Barbershop on Broad Street in Jackson Ward (Richmond's largest and most famous historically Black neighborhood). Utsey would later describe this film as the first of a trilogy of films depicting attempts by the Black community to assert its collective right to self-determination. By applying humanities as a methodology for community empowerment, *Meet Me in the Bottom* was the first film to record how archaeology, biology, anthropology, sociology, and history were being challenged to face and push through their historically supremacist and Eurocentric demons to better practice.

Utsey's second film, *Until the Well Runs Dry: Medicine and the Exploitation of Black Bodies*, was an exposé on the treatment of the remains found in the early nineteenth-century medical trash pit associated with the Medical College of Virginia. This defunct well was filled with human bones (discarded anatomical material), the aftermath of medical studies conducted on the recently deceased and, most often, stolen bodies of enslaved Black people or free Blacks and whites who were either impoverished, transient, unidentified, or all three (Utsey 2011). Disturbingly, the man most associated with the grave-robbing activities of the Medical College of Virginia at Marshall and 12th Streets was a Black man named Christopher Baker, who had been raised from childhood in the basement of the medical school building. He lived with his mother and stepfather, who, having been purchased to serve the role, had probably trained the younger man in the work. Baker became a well-known figure in Richmond, a ghoul to his own people until his death in 1919.

In 2013, the East Marshall Street Well Planning Committee, an initiative of the Office of the President of Virginia Commonwealth University, implemented a year-long community process that facilitated public learning sessions about the early nineteenth-century human remains rediscovered in 1994. The committee then sought community input in the formation of a Family Representative Council, which would represent the "descendant community" to make recommendations on behalf of those individuals whose remains were discovered. The recommendations of the FRC involved ways to support appropriate study of the remains and associated histories, reburial with dignity, and appropriate memorialization. One of the first steps was the repatriation of the remains from their boxed storage at the Smithsonian Institution in Washington, DC, to Richmond, in the temporary care of the DHR. "A trail of white petals lined East Marshall Street on Monday as drums and bells welcomed home the remains of 53 people, mainly of African descent, whose first resting place had been a 19th-century well on what is now the campus of Virginia Commonwealth University" (Leonor 2019).

Much of the honor bestowed on these remains and the ceremony surrounding their return in 2019 was performed intentionally to counter their initial treatment and the cursory and disrespectful way they were handled upon discovery in 1994. At that time, construction was halted for just three days and the university's archaeological team, led by professor L. Daniel Mouer, was given just two days to recover and record what material they could pull from the pile of debris. "Our university president arrived on the scene and, in no uncertain terms, ordered us to immediately take on this project as a salvage excavation" (Mouer 2015, 3). Within a few weeks, the bones had been boxed up and shipped to the Smithsonian Institute for examination and storage. In spite of Prof. Mouer's best efforts, there they stayed until Shawn Utsey's film *Until the Well Runs Dry* premiered on campus and triggered the Well Project in 2012 (Mouer 2015).

Public imagination was once again sparked by the unearthing and treatment of African American corporeal remains. The president of the university made a decision to "do right" by this project in form and function: the establishment and education of a planning committee to guide the next steps, a commitment of funding for implementation of recommendations, and support for curriculum changes in the medical school's anatomical studies department so that incoming students would learn the history of the institution and evolution of its practices. A website, www.emsw.vcu.edu, was created as an ongoing public archive for purposes of transparency, and the education process undergone by the planning committee was also provided to the Family Representative Council. The archaeologists who had been forced to perform so perfunctorily the exacting work necessary to best practices and preservation still managed to provide scientific data and direction useful to future research. And the very institution that had degraded the remains at the time of their rediscovery was now publicly committed to raising their own bar of behavior.

Figure 3.2. Altar set up at the Lumpkin's Jail site by a local cultural organization, the Elegba Folklore Society, at the start of the excavation in August 2008. A libation ceremony and offerings of food, imagery, and stones served to honor ancestors who were subjected to the slave trade in Richmond and provided to the present-day community a tangible representation of the significance of the site and importance of the investigation in uncovering a critical element of the city's history, 2008. © Ana Edwards

Meanings

Though it would become the most notorious, Robert Lumpkin's slave-trading complex was only one of many such commercial establishments Richmond, Virginia. At the height of his trade over nearly twenty years, Lumpkin sold dozens of men, women, and children every month to traders and private purchasers who would then transport them to destinations throughout the lower South. Perhaps as many as ten thousand humans a month were sold through Richmond alone, adding to the full count of 300,000–350,000 enslaved persons sold from Virginia between 1830 and 1865. These numbers we know as archival facts. But to experience the site through an archaeological excavation—a process designed to produce evidence of long-buried events—was to experience science and scholarship and a bit of reincarnation. Richmonders put their twenty-first-century hands and feet on the bricks and mortar of slavery that year. Robert Lumpkin was a real man who committed the barbarities of the trade on human beings in this place. The foundations of those buildings, the river stone cobble of that courtyard, the remnants of toothbrushes, shoes, and pottery—all were the testaments to his activities and to each of the tens of thousands of Black people forced to count a stay in his jail as one of their lives' commonplace horrors.

The excavation of this one slave-trading site also supported the calls of advocates to recognize and prove the significance for Black Richmonders of the nearby early nineteenth-century municipal cemetery through archaeology. Even if excavations of the cemetery were unlikely given the depth of the historical elevation, the material evidence of the nearby Lumpkin's Jail site showed that Richmond's Black history in Shockoe Bottom was evident and important. The national attention paid to the findings of the Lumpkin's Jail excavation would catapult Richmond onto the world stage of archaeology and heritage tourism and help local scholars and community advocates make the case for the significance of their own city's historical and cultural resources to the country at large. In that moment, Richmonders finally came to experience how the role of a New York City excavation from seventeen years earlier could be a precedent-setting chapter of the growing intersection between the social sciences and social justice in their city.

If not for the public display of human remains tumbling from the bulldozers at the construction site of a federal building project in Lower Manhattan, New York City, in 1991, the scientific community would still have limited understanding of and sensitivity to the missing knowledge embodied by captive and enslaved Africans' experiences in seventeenth- and eighteenth-century British North America. If not for the discovery of a pit of human bones on the campus of the Medical College of Virginia in 1994 (now VCU Health System), Virginia's role in the widespread use of Black bodies for medical study could not have been added to the global roster of medical schools preying upon the poor and vulnerable. The excavation of Robert Lumpkin's slave-trading complex helped make the case for reclamation of the neighboring African Burial Ground. And, without the popularization of this history and the excavation, the scale and depravity of the business of nineteenth-century human trafficking in Richmond, Virginia, would not have become so widely known.

The young people who protested so passionately during the summer of 2020 over George Floyd's death in Minneapolis and, in Richmond, over the killing of Marcus-David Peters—the unarmed African American science teacher experiencing a mental health crisis—were youngsters who grew up with these histories as a visible and audible backdrop of their generation. If pain and grief were the emotions, the motivation was also exasperation and rage over seeing the present connect the historical dots of racial violence and injustice that *remained* embedded in the American society they were expected to inhabit. And they were well prepared to demonstrate that enough was enough. In the face of increasingly unavoidable reckonings with historical injustice, archaeology has evolved, expanding its role from an allegiance to old world hierarchizing of the American narrative to one that levels the narrative out a bit. The term "descendant community," coined by an anthropologist and historical biologist, is now as much a part of the popular lexicon as it is a useful encapsulation of archaeological and anthropological paradigms relating to historically Black sites, especially those with the potential to profoundly impact living communities.

Though beyond the scope of this chapter, it would be hard not to note that the last twelve years of US history is marked by two specific and polar presidencies, those of Barack Obama and Donald Trump. Obama's election represented perhaps the highest symbolic mark of progress for Black people possible in the United States, from noncitizen to head-of-state. Trump's election represented an historical pattern of regression, the negative white response to Black people making progress in American society, draped in populism and nativism. The pushback began as Obama started his term in office and intensified even as the country elected him a second time. This escalated to such an extent that perfectly "decent" white people confided their fears to one another that America did not look like America anymore—a frighteningly blinkered view of the Americans around them.

For some of the public, these "slavery sites" are brimming with the potential to teach us about suffering and oppression before emancipation in 1865 (Chapman et al. 2020). For others, the mere identification of sites as connected to slavery elicits shame, resentment, anger at being stuck in the past, or having one's identity solely associated with enslavement. There is a community preference for sites that tell the stories of achievement, of overcoming, of progress. And for most of the twentieth century, public markers and memorials have focused on the hope-giving and inspirational stories of overcoming and creative progress. But between the two legacy tracks is that space where we continue not only to wonder why these things happen, but *how* they keep happening. What social mechanisms have and continue to "permit" white people to live in active concert with racial hatred and social inequity?

In 1993, the Charlie Rose Show hosted a series of interviews under the theme "The Power of the Question," which resulted in one of author Toni Morrison's most succinct comments on white supremacy: "If you can only be tall because somebody is on their knees, then you have a serious problem." (Morrison 1993). If we—scholars, activists, and community members—truly aspire to achieve justice through historical clarity, it matters that we unearth and examine not only what we find but also the questions we ask about them.

Ana Edwards is a public historian and education programs manager of the American Civil War Museum. Family history, social justice, and the story of Gabriel's Rebellion combined to drive her interest in Virginia African American history and public history landscapes. As a co-founder of the Defenders for Freedom, Justice & Equality, and founding chair of the Sacred Ground Historical Reclamation Project (2004), and in collaboration with other community organizations, she contributed to the reclamation of Richmond's first municipal cemetery for Black burials, known now as the Shockoe Bottom African Burial Ground. Ana holds a BA in visual art from California State Polytechnic University at Pomona (1983) and an MA in history from Virginia Commonwealth University (2020).

Matthew R. Laird, PhD, RPA, is a partner and senior researcher with the James River Institute for Archaeology, Inc. A native of Ottawa, Canada, he has pursued a career in cultural resource management since earning a PhD in American History from the College of William and Mary in 1995. Dr. Laird has directed archaeological investigations at an array of significant sites across Virginia, most notably the Lumpkin's Jail Site in Richmond's Shockoe Bottom district. He lives with his wife and son in Fredericksburg, Virginia.

Notes

1. Established in 1986, JRIA is a private cultural resource management consulting firm based in Williamsburg, Virginia.
2. The site was officially recorded as "44HE1035" with the Virginia Department of Historic Resources.

References

Blakey, Michael L. 2010. "African Burial Ground Project: paradigm for cooperation?" *Museum International* nos. 245–246 (Vol. 62, No. 1–2, UNESCO), 61.
———. 2020a. "Archaeology under the Blinding Light of Race." *Current Anthropology* 61 (S22), S183–S197.
———. 2020b. "On the Biodeterministic Imagination." *Archaeological Dialogues* 27(1), 1–16.
Cep, Casey. 2020. "The Fight to Preserve African-American History." *American Chronicles, The New Yorker*, 3 February 2020. https://www.newyorker.com/magazine/2020/02/03/the-fight-to-preserve-african-american-history.
Chapman, Ellen, Elizabeth Cook, and Ana Edwards. 2020. "Bones in Stasis: The Challenging History and Uncertain Future of the Virginia State Penitentiary Collection." *Journal for the Anthropology of North America*, 22 April 2020. https://doi.org/10.1002/nad.12127.
Chen, Kimberly Merkel, and Hannah W. Collins, 2007. "The Slave Trade as a Commercial Enterprise in Richmond, Virginia," MPS #127–6196. National Register of Historic Places Multiple Property Documentation Form. Richmond: Virginia Department of Historic Resources.
City of Richmond Land Book. 1850. Microfilm copy Richmond, VA: Library of Virginia.
Corey, Charles H. 1876. *Historical Sketch of the Richmond Institute*. Richmond, VA: Clemmit & Jones.
———. 1895. *A History of the Richmond Theological Seminary with Reminiscences of Thirty Years' Work Among the Colored People of the South*. Richmond, VA: J.W. Randolph Co.
Dunlap, David W. 1991. "Dig Unearths Early Black Burial Ground." *New York Times*, 9 October 1991. https://www.nytimes.com/1991/10/09/nyregion/dig-unearths-early-black-burial-ground.html.
Ellis, Nicole. 2019. "How the Discovery of an African Burial Ground in New York City Changed the Field of Genetics." *Washington Post*, 20 December 2019. https://www.washingtonpost.com/nation/2019/12/20/how-discovery-an-african-burial-ground-new-york-city-changed-field-genetics/.
Finder, Alan. 1992. "U.S. Permanently Halts Digging at Cemetery Site," *New York Times*, 31 July 1992. https://www.nytimes.com/1992/07/31/nyregion/us-permanently-halts-digging-at-cemetery-site.html.
Green, Hilary. 2016. *Educational Reconstruction: African American Schools in the Urban South, 1865–1890*. New York: Fordham University Press.
Gudmestad, Robert H. 1993. *A Troublesome Commerce: The Transformation of the Interstate Slave Trade*. Baton Rouge: Louisiana State University Press.
Jackson, Luther Porter. 1942. *Free Negro Labor and Property Holding in Virginia, 1830–1860*. Professor of History, Virginia State College. [The American Historical Association.] New York: D. Appleton-Century Company.
Laird, Matthew R. 2010. *Archaeological Data Recovery Investigation of the Lumpkin's Slave Jail Site (44HE1053), Richmond, Virginia. Volume I: Research Report*. Williamsburg, VA: James River Institute for Archaeology.
LaRoche, Cheryl J., and Michael L. Blakey. 1997. "Seizing Intellectual Power: the Dialogue at the New York African Burial Ground." *Historical Archaeology* 31 (3): 84–106.
Leonor, Mel. 2019. "Remains of African Americans Found in Marshall Street Well Return to Richmond 25 Years Later," *Richmond Times Dispatch*, 25 November 2019. https://richmond.com/news/virginia/remains-of-african-americans-found-in-marshall-street-well-return-to-richmond-25-years-later/article_4d9909bc-b213-5633-803e-efbd5fce10cf.html#tncms-source=login.
Litwack, Leon F. 1979. *Been in the Storm So Long: The Aftermath of Slavery*. New York: Alfred A. Knopf.

Lumpkin, Robert. *Ledger, 1848–1850, #X.60.18.03.* Richmond, VA: Valentine Richmond History Center.
McInnis, Maurie D. 2011. *Slaves Waiting for Sale: Abolitionist Art and the American Slave Trade.* Chicago: The University of Chicago Press.
Morrison, Toni. 1993. "The Power of Questions." Interview by Charlie Rose. *Charlie Rose,* NPR, 7 May 1993. Video, 37:43. https://charlierose.com/videos/18778.
Mouer, Daniel L. 2015. "The Trouble in River City (It's Not Pool!)." Paper presented for RVA Archaeology at the Annual Meeting of the *Society for Historical Archaeology,* Washington, DC, 6–9 January 2016.
Nicholls, Michael L. 2012. *Whispers of Rebellion: Narrating Gabriel's Rebellion.* Charlottesville: University of Virginia Press.
Painter, Nell Irvin. 1976. *Exodusters: Black Migration to Kansas after Reconstruction.* New York: Alfred A. Knopf.
Rosenberger, Jesse L. 1922. *Through Three Centuries: Colver and Rosenberger Lives and Times, 1620–1922.* Chicago: University of Chicago Press.
Rothman, Stephen J. 2004. *Race, Class and Power in the Building of Richmond, 1870–1920.* Jefferson, NC: McFarland & Company.
Schuppe, Jon. 2016. "Rodney King Beating 25 Years Ago Opened Era of Viral Cop Videos." *NBC News,* 3 March 2016. https://www.nbcnews.com/news/us-news/rodney-king-beating-25-years-ago-opened-era-viral-cop-n531091.
Schwarz, Philip J. 2006. "Robert and Mary F. Lumpkin Chronology." Unpublished research notes.
Scott, Mary Wingfield. 1950. *Old Richmond Neighborhoods.* Richmond, VA: Whittet and Sheperson.
Smith, Laurajane. 2006. *Uses of Heritage.* London: Routledge.
Stevens, Charles Emery. 1856. *Anthony Burns: A History.* Boston: J.P. Jewett and Company.
Tucker, Abigail. 2009. "Devil's Half Acre." *Smithsonian* 39 (12), 20–22.
Utsey, Shawn. Director. 2011. *Until the Well Runs Dry: Medicine and the Exploitation of Black Bodies.* Virginia Commonwealth University Department of African American Studies and Burn Baby Burn Productions.
Vlach, John Michael. 1997. "'Without Recourse to Owners': The Architecture of Urban Slavery in the Antebellum South." In *Perspectives in Vernacular Architecture, VI,* edited by Carter C. Hudgins and Elizabeth Collins Cromley, 150–60. Knoxville: University of Tennessee Press.
Wade, Richard C. 1964. *Slavery in the Cities: The South, 1820–1860.* New York: Oxford University Press.
Young, Richard. 1809. *Planning Map of the Town of Richmond.* MS, Library of Virginia.

Chapter 4

Seneca Village Interpretations
Bringing Collaborative Historical Archaeology and Heritage Advocacy to the Forefront and Online

Meredith B. Linn, Nan A. Rothschild, and Diana diZerega Wall

Introduction

Located in what is now Central Park in New York City, Seneca Village was founded by African Americans in 1827. Over the next thirty years, additional African Americans, hailing from eight different US states and from Haiti, joined the community, as did European immigrants, mostly from Ireland. The Village grew to a community of over 220 people, and contained three churches and their corresponding cemeteries, a school, planted fields, orchards, and dozens of homes, some with stables or barns (Figure 4.1). In 1857, the City of New York used the right of eminent domain and an argument about the "greater good" to displace the community and build Central Park. Despite the protests of at least some of the community's landowners, the last of the villagers were forced to depart in the spring of 1857. Within a year, park construction crews removed or buried above-ground traces of the Village's built environment that residents had left behind (Marie Warsh, pers. comm. 2018). The community did not re-form elsewhere, and Seneca Village quickly faded from public memory.[1] It was also neglected in histories of the city or relegated to a footnote at best, until scholars began to unearth the Village's story in the 1990s—first, in a chapter within a ground-breaking history of Central Park (Rosenzweig and Blackmar 1992), then in a highly successful museum exhibition at the New-York Historical Society (N-YHS 1997), and finally in

---

Notes for this chapter begin on page 93.

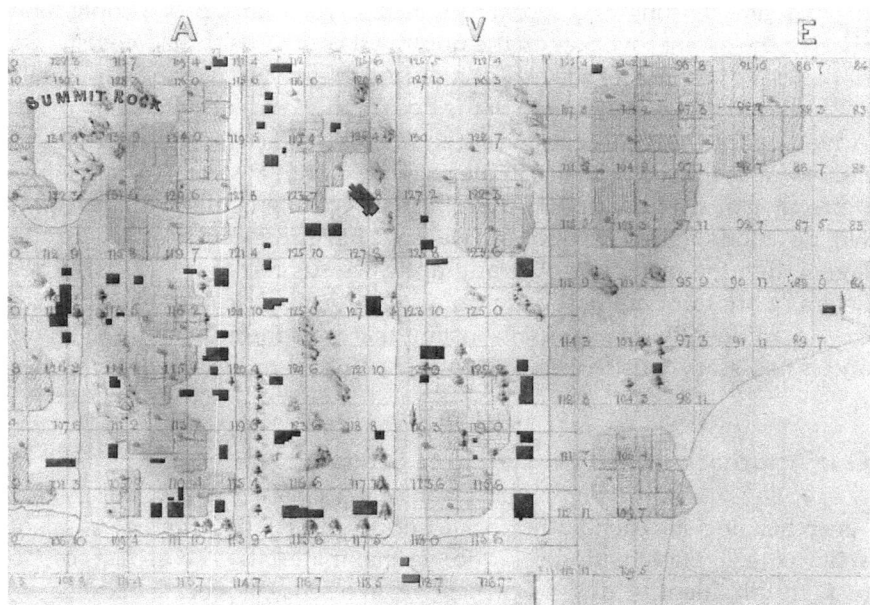

Figure 4.1. A portion of Egbert L. Viele's 1855 "Map of lands included in the Central Park from a topographical survey" showing Seneca Village. Courtesy of Municipal Archives, City of New York.

the ongoing historical archaeology project led by the Institute for the Exploration of Seneca Village History (IESVH) (formerly the Seneca Village Project). After more than a decade of documentary research, planning, networking, and lobbying, the latter was able to perform limited excavations in 2011 followed by analysis and publication of the finds (Wall et al. 2018; Wall et al. 2019).

All of this work received media attention (Foderaro 2011; Rosenbaum 2011) and began to bring the Village and its significance as a once-flourishing nineteenth-century free and predominantly African American community back into public memory. Over the last few years especially, the Village and its residents have captured the imagination of a broader public. This recent surge in interest is at least in part due to both the increased sharing of information enabled by digital media and the growing attention the Black Lives Matter movement has brought to the experiences of Black people in the United States, particularly to anti-Black violence, inequity, and erasure in the past and present. The relevance of Seneca Village for the present has always been something that we, the archaeologists in the IESVH, have attempted to advocate in our approaches to interpreting the site, inviting and working with a diverse group of people, and sharing the group's work with the public. Of course, as archaeologists, we have also advocated for the exploration and preservation of the site and its artifacts and the interpretation of the lives of the residents who used them. Advocacy for these three aspects (the site, its artifacts and residents, and its relevance for social justice in the present) do not always naturally align perfectly, but we have approached them as complementary. This chapter will describe some of the different ways we have advocated for Seneca Village. Using the metaphor of stratigraphy, we suggest that (at least) three layers or strata of advocacy are important for historical archaeology today.[2] Additionally, an essential constant that runs through all these layers and is necessary for successful advocacy is collaboration.

Our Approach to Advocacy: Three Strata

As archaeologists, each author has a special interest in different kinds of artifacts (e.g., glass bottles, ceramics, faunal materials) and aspects of life (e.g., health, identity, diet) for which we, in a sense, advocate because we emphasize them in our own work. We are united, however, in drawing upon feminist, Marxist, and interpretivist approaches, and we are united in our shared excitement about and commitment to bringing to light the experiences of people who are underrepresented and misrepresented in written records and traditional histories, including women, children, minorities, and immigrants. In bringing together fragmentary sources, including documents, oral histories, and artifacts—those "small things forgotten" (Deetz 1977) —we endeavor to rediscover and recognize people whose contributions to our past and present have been underappreciated and, as in the case of Seneca Village, nearly erased entirely.

As a number of Black feminist scholars, in particular, have revealed and described, the history of African Americans in this country is a history of erasure, appropriation, delegitimization, and dehumanization. Seneca Village was born "in the shadow" (Harris 2003) and in the "wake" (Sharpe 2016) of race-based slavery, an institution woven into the economic, political, social, and cultural fabric of the United States. Anti-Blackness, and the binary opposition of the invented (and nonbiologically supported) racial categories of Black and white, structured and continue to structure American society to benefit whites. The Black and white binary is the primary lens through which all other ethnic and racial groups have been viewed in the United States for at least the past three hundred years. We are still caught in the shadow and the wake of slavery, as the scholar of English and comparative literature Saidiya Hartman (2007, 6) describes:

Slavery had established a measure of man and a ranking of life and worth that has yet to be undone. If slavery persists as an issue in the political life of black America, it is not because of an antiquarian obsession with bygone days or the burden of a too-long memory, but because black lives are still imperiled and devalued by a racial calculus and a political arithmetic that were entrenched centuries ago. This is the afterlife of slavery-skewed life chances, limited access to health and education, premature death, incarceration, and impoverishment.

Exposing the contours of the shadow/wake and bringing attention to how African Americans experienced and responded to it is both challenging and necessary. Thus, while uncovering the history of *all* marginalized groups is important, there has long been a special urgency (an urgency made even more apparent by the recent increased attention via the Black Lives Matter movement to the murders of Black men and women by police and to the unfinished project of the civil rights movement) to advocate for and participate in a critical reanalysis of the history of the United States, with an emphasis on the neglected experiences and contributions of Black Americans.

Thus, because archaeological artifacts and features can help to fill silences in the documentary record and counter prejudiced narratives, advocacy for archaeological resources is essential. We will refer to advocacy work related to artifacts and features as Advocacy Stratum III-below ground surface (AS III-bgs). This term is a play on Archaeological Stratum (AS), the term many archaeologists use to describe human-made or natural layers of stratigraphy. Archaeologists number these strata sequentially from the ground surface to the lowest layer in the ground, beginning with the roman numeral I. Bgs is the abbreviation archaeologists often use in recording the depths of stratigraphic layers in centimeters or inches below the ground surface (bgs). We envision advocacy for AS III-bgs as including proper excavation, documentation, conservation, interpretation, and storage of archaeological artifacts, objects that are powerful, tangible evidence of people and their activities.

A critical reanalysis of American history on a broader scale makes clear that the marginalization and erasure of Black Americans is intertwined with displacement and dispersal. The diaspora of peoples of African descent continued on this side of the Atlantic. Black people have been repeatedly forced to move from place to place, by the whims of enslavers and forces of urban development as well as in their own attempts to escape violence and discrimination and seek economic opportunity, community, and safety. We understand these latter desires to have been motivations that contributed to the formation and expansion of Seneca Village. In New York City and other urban areas where real estate is so valuable, development and gentrification continue to displace and disperse Black and brown communities, while simultaneously increasing segregation and concentrated poverty as dislocated families find themselves priced out of all but the most economically challenged neighborhoods. Advocating for greater public recognition of Seneca Village, including commemoration of the physical site, is important because the site is a tangible reminder that African Americans have created stable and successful communities. Eviction from this community and others like it (along with inadequate compensation for seized property), moreover, substantially contributed to the extreme level of residential segregation and the massive gap in wealth between whites and Blacks in the United States today (McIntosh et al. 2020). We will refer to advocacy for the physical site of the Village as Advocacy Stratum II-ground surface (AS II-gs). Advocacy for this layer involves making clear to visitors of the park, to the people who walk on the present-day ground surface, that they are visitors to a special place where Seneca Villagers walked before them.

The approach to studying the Village that Rothschild, Wall, and the original advisory board of the Seneca Village Project/IESVH developed and have implemented throughout the now twenty-plus year history of the project has not just been focused on the recovery of details about villagers' lives, conserving the artifacts, and commemorating the site. Recovery, conservation, and commemoration are all important, but so is interpretation that situates the Village in its broader historical context, unsettles dominant narratives, and incorporates multiple perspectives, especially from Black scholars and community members. Sharing our methods, skills, data, and results with a broader community of scholars, students, artists, and members of the public for them to use for their own purposes has always been a central goal and operating principle. The ultimate aim of our Seneca Village work is to empower individuals and communities toward their own social justice and empowerment goals in the present. This we will refer to as Advocacy Stratum I-above ground surface (AS I-ags). Advocacy for AS I-ags thus includes making our research relevant and accessible in the spaces we live in today, sharing resources and skills, and supporting the mobilization of different interpretations of Seneca Village for social justice.

Like the boundaries between analytical strata in archaeological excavations, the boundaries between Advocacy Strata I, II, and III are often not clear cut; portions sometimes overlap or intermingle. Additionally, just as silt was a component of the soil in all the analytical strata we uncovered at Seneca Village, we see collaboration as an essential element of each advocacy stratum. Collaborative work is not always easy. It is complicated and slow, sometimes seemingly glacial. We do not always agree about how best to proceed or about all aspects of the interpretation of the Village and its residents. But we believe that the project is stronger and its results more significant because it has always been collaborative. It incorporates many different voices and perspectives, and no one person or institution "owns" it. Without our non-archaeologist partners, in particular, it is unlikely that we would have even been able to excavate at the site. One could say that the approach of the IESVH is that it takes a village to investigate one, and, as we will show, it also takes a village to advocate for one. The next sections will explain how we have approached each of these three layers of advocacy in relation to the Seneca Village site.

AS III-bgs: Advocacy for Archaeological Excavation and Cultural Resources Below Ground Surface

The past few decades have seen a major evolution in how most historical archaeologists conduct excavations, especially investigations of sites that continue to be important to living people. In diverse and densely populated urban areas like New York City, many sites are important to one group or another. Urban space is so much in demand, often multiple claimants, developers, and property owners as well as people link the particular location to their history.[3] Today, archaeologists are expected to, at minimum, consult with stakeholders, including direct descendants (kin), the descendant community (people who feel a strong connection to the site or its past occupants, whether they have a direct genealogical connection) (Silliman and Ferguson 2010, 50; Blakey 2020, S186), and others who have stake in the project. Many have gone further and invited stakeholders to join them as collaborative partners (to varying degrees) in the project (McDavid 2004; Colwell-Chanthaphonh and Ferguson 2007; Murray et al. 2009; Cipolla et al. 2019). Full collaboration de-centers the archaeologist(s) and involves stakeholders as partners in each stage of the project, from planning to research to interpretation to publication (Atalay 2006; Flexner and González-Tennant 2018; Sunseri and Gonzalez 2020). This change in how archaeologists work with stakeholders has largely been propelled by Native American and African American communities, who have rightly critiqued archaeologists' assertions of authority over their own material culture and, in some cases, ancestors (Deloria 1988; LaRoche and Blakey 1997; Blakey 2020, S186).

The African Burial Ground project had a major impact on this shift, especially in New York City. This federally funded project, begun in 1991 and administered by the General Services Administration (GSA), unearthed the remains of more than four hundred individuals. The GSA was slow to notify the descendant community of the discovery of the burials and did not allow the community to play an active role in the decision-making process. Descendant community members were only recognized after they repeatedly demanded to be heard. Eventually, through political intervention, the community and its allies were able to halt the project. A panel of archaeologists, historians, politicians, and members of the descendant community then decided that Michael Blakey's team at Howard University should analyze the human remains that had been recovered. Blakey's team was composed of archaeologists and bioarchaeologists who had previous experience and expertise in investigating African American sites. The team listened to the community's concerns and questions and incorporated them into their research and into plans for the subsequent respectful reburial of the remains and for the memorialization of the site (LaRoche and Blakey 1997; Cantwell and Wall 2001, 278–94).

The lessons learned from this project included both the vivid realization of the ethical obligations archaeologists have to stakeholders, and the recognition that involving stakeholders *as partners* (ideally from the beginning) improves the quality of the research project. The close bioarchaeological analysis of the individuals excavated from the African Burial Ground and the invaluable wealth of important information it generated about their origins and life experiences, which is not available in any other sources, was not included in the original research plan. That research was propelled by the demands of descendants and the questions that they posed (LaRoche and Blakey 1997). The descendant community also advocated for the proper care and analysis of their ancestors and related archaeological artifacts and features (AS III-bgs); the creation of a public memorial on the site and a change to the development plan to avoid the disturbance of additional burials (AS II-gs); and educational programming and a visitors' center to share with the public the knowledge gained from the project and the struggle over it in order to change the historical narrative that has been told about African Americans in New York City (AS I-ags).

When Wall, Rothschild, and educator and public historian Cynthia Copeland formed the Seneca Village Project in 1997, the controversy around the African Burial Ground was fresh, and they recognized the importance of collaborating with a diverse group of people. Unlike the African Burial Ground, there were no direct descendants of Seneca Villagers or members of the descendant community who initially came forward, and efforts to find direct descendants failed (until just a couple of years ago, but more about that later). Wall, Rothschild, and Copeland thus decided to form an advisory board. They initially invited scholars who study African American and Irish history in New York, members of the Village's two surviving churches (AME Zion and All Angels'), individuals who had been active during the African Burial Ground Controversy, others identified during previous programming related to the 1997 Seneca Village exhibition co-curated by Copeland and Grady Turner at the New-York Historical Society, and a few of their students, including Herbert Seignoret, who was then a student of Wall (Wall et al. 2004, 104–6). The advisory board (which has grown over time) as well as many other students and non-archaeologists (whom we refer to as the project team), have been involved in all phases of the project. In this section we will discuss how they have contributed to our understanding of and advocacy for Seneca Village's below-ground resources.

The knowledge, political savvy, and outreach work of several members of the board, especially Celedonia (Cal) Jones (Manhattan Borough Historian Emeritus), Sharon Wilkins (Manhattan Deputy Borough Historian), and Cornell Edwards (trustee of AME Mother Zion Church), for example, were essential for securing permission from the NYC Parks Department and the Central Parks Conservancy for the 2011 excavation of the Village. Through their advocacy for the then-potential underground cultural resources, we were able to uncover them in the first place.

Questions asked and archival research conducted by board members and students shaped the excavation project's research design. For example, in her undergraduate thesis, Olivia Ng (1999) not only collected and added to the documentary research conducted by many different project team members, but also interviewed advisory board members about what interested them about Seneca Village.[4] Many of their interests, such as what the relationships between neighbors and the villagers' daily lives were like, informed our research questions for the 2011 excavations. Additionally, the church records that Paul Johnson (a vestry member of All Angels' Episcopal Church, which had been located in the Village) uncovered in the archives of All Angels', for example, greatly increased our knowledge of the family of William Godfrey Wilson, a sexton of the church, and of the relationships among Village families, as reflected in marriages and baptismal sponsorship. It was in part because of Paul's research and his and the All Angels' Church community's interest in discovering material remains associated with the church's Seneca Village original location that Rothschild and Wall chose that location as one of those to examine with ground-penetrating radar (GPR) and then to excavate in that area.[5] There, we uncovered the foundation stones of the Wilson house (Figure 4.2) as well as hundreds of artifacts that they left behind.[6]

Ten undergraduate students and two field supervisors (a PhD student and a recent PhD graduate) were part of the team, co-directed by Wall, Rothschild, and Copeland, that brought to the surface the underground remains of the Village.[7] The physical and intellectual labor of this diverse

Figure 4.2. The foundation wall of the Wilson house uncovered during the 2011 excavation. © Meredith B. Linn and the Institute for the Exploration of Seneca Village History.

group of students was essential in both the field and the lab. Different students gravitated toward different types of material, and their research kept attention on some artifacts that might otherwise have been given less attention. For example, Linn was sometimes jokingly referred to as "the metal advocate," for her interest in rusty, fragile, and fragmentary metal sheets that had been discovered between the demolition layer of the Wilson house and fill that the parks construction crew placed on top of it. Her research, aided by archaeologist Jessica Striebel MacLean, supported the hypothesis that the sheets were remains of tin-coated iron roofing. This metal roofing was less common and more expensive than wood, but was technologically superior for water- and fireproofing homes (Wall et al. 2019, 168). Linn's interest in and identification of this material prevented more of it and some other iron objects from being discarded (after documentation) due to demands for space and limited resources for

Figure 4.3. Curry comb excavated from the Wilson house shown with two of the ribs that hold the teeth next to the body of the comb. A wooden handle would have attached to the arrow-shaped base, secured by the copper alloy cuff. Courtesy of the NYC Archaeological Repository: The Nan A. Rothschild Research Center, public domain.

conserving fragile materials. Her research also suggests that the Wilsons were knowledgeable about the benefits of this material and had made a considerable financial investment in this kind of roofing for their home.

One of the other iron objects (Figure 4.3) that had stumped the crew as well as the subscribers of a large listserv of historical archaeologists that we had queried was, in fact, identified by an undergraduate student who had nothing to do with the project but who happened to be in the lab at Columbia University one day when we were puzzling over it. She leaned over from a neighboring bench and informed us that it was a curry comb, which initially was not so helpful to us, since we were not familiar with such an object, but she then explained that a curry comb is used to groom horses. With a bit more research we were able to find examples of remarkably similar curry combs produced in the 1850s. This identification pushed us to think more about the landscape of the Village and how the Wilson family, in whose home the comb was found, might have interacted with a horse or horses, considering that the historical maps show that they did not possess a stable or barn. Sometimes artifacts raise more questions than they answer.

The curry comb has since become a highlight of many of our outreach presentations to the public and to students. It is also one of the artifacts that Striebel MacLean (2020) included in her digital exhibition of Seneca Village artifacts on the website of the NYC Archaeological Repository (the Repository), which houses city-owned collections. After analysis and cataloging in the archaeology labs at City College and Columbia University and conservation of select objects at NYU (by Linsley Boyer, Brian Castriota, Julia Sybalsky, and Jessica Walthew) and the Metropolitan Museum of Art (by Emilia Cortez and Jennifer Dennis), the artifacts from the 2011 excavation were sent to the Repository for long-term storage.[8] There, Striebel MacLean (urban archaeologist at the NYC Landmarks Preservation Commission [LPC]), Amanda Sutphin (director of archaeology at LPC), Angela Zhinin (urban archaeologist at LPC), and volunteers Carol Weed (retired archaeologist) and John Yarmick (retired banker), have advocated for Seneca Village's artifacts. They rehoused the artifacts in archival-grade storage containers, ensuring that all of this material will be available to future researchers. They also took photographs of the artifacts and uploaded them to the publicly accessible website, along with the corresponding excavation documentation (NYC Archaeological Repository 2020). We see their care for the artifacts as a direct and important form of advocacy for Seneca Village's below-ground resources (AS III) and their publicity of the artifacts as intersecting with all three advocacy strata. Raising public interest in the artifacts draws greater positive attention to the archaeological site itself (AS II), while making available images of the artifacts (the site report and plan and profile drawings) enables visitors to the website to conduct their own research (AS I).

Our advocacy for below-ground resources at Seneca Village did not always include encouraging excavation. In fact, we strongly advocated *against* disturbing any human remains or material culture associated with the burial grounds of the Village's three churches: All Angels' Episcopal Church, African Union Church, and the African Methodist Episcopal Zion (AME Zion) Church. The last two churches had branches downtown and initially purchased land in the Village specifically for burial grounds. Their purchases were likely motivated by a combination of a lack of space and public health–related laws prohibiting additional burials in the crowded downtown at a time when epidemic disease was rife and effective medicines were few. Copeland has long hypothesized that the cemeteries built in the Village, and more specifically, the presence of ancestors, drew at least some people to settle in the Village. As part of our research plan, we approximated the locations of the burial grounds by superimposing a map of the Village made in advance of its destruction (Sage 1856) with a present-day map of Central Park, as there are no above-ground traces of the burials or cemeteries in the park today. We then collaborated with Larry Conyers, geoarchaeologist and specialist in GPR, to pinpoint the boundaries of the burial grounds so that we could make sure to avoid them.[9] We shared this information with the Central Park Conservancy (CPC), the organization that cares for the park today, so that they know where these locations are and will avoid disturbing them in their maintenance work. We see this as an act of advocacy and respect for the deceased who rest below the ground surface. The CPC has shown its respect as well by sponsoring subsequent, more detailed non-invasive GPR surveys of the burial grounds.

AS II-gs: Advocacy for the Site and Its Commemoration on Today's Ground Surface

Sharing the locations of the Village's burial grounds with the CPC was one of several IESVH acts that demonstrated our interest in collaborating with the CPC and to advocate not only for the site's below-ground resources but also for the conservation of the present-day ground surface of Central Park. The site of Seneca Village exists within Central Park, one of the country's most famous and beloved urban landscapes. For many New Yorkers, Central Park is a much-needed greenspace in a city of concrete and steel. It is a place to relax, to exercise, to play, to socialize, to socialize their dogs and children, to think, to breathe deeply, to escape the daily grind, and more. It is also a tourist attraction, drawing people from all over the world, especially for events like the annual NYC Marathon, which ends in the park. Although some park visitors are keenly interested in it as a designed landscape, and how it was created from the plans of Frederick Law Olmsted and Calvert Vaux, many more are unaware of any pre-park history and consider the landscape to be mostly natural, except for obvious modern intrusions, such as lampposts, benches and paths, and playgrounds. With tens of millions of people visiting each year, the CPC's task of caring for the 843-acre park is immense. The CPC was established in 1980 to restore and better care for the park, which had been largely neglected for about two decades prior. As a nonprofit organization, the CPC secures most of its operating funds from private donations. These joint concerns, of managing the park's vast landscape and raising money to pay for that maintenance, might explain some of the hesitancy CPC leaders initially expressed when first approached by members of the IESVH about conducting an excavation to search for Seneca Village. Would our excavation ruin part of the landscape they had worked so hard to restore and to keep beautiful? Would sharing the forgotten story of a successful and predominately African American community forced off their land to build the park tarnish its reputation and deter donors?

Fortunately, the answers to both of these questions turned out to be no, but it took many meetings, a lot of listening, and shows of good faith on both sides to develop a relationship of trust between the two organizations and to secure permission to conduct an archaeological excavation. It was important for IESVH members to show the CPC that we respected and would advocate for the conservation of the present-day park landscape. Thus, we agreed to and followed through with a number of the CPC's requests related to the excavation. In addition to common constraints in terms of the time we were allowed to dig (eight weeks, Monday through Friday only) and the amount of surface area we were allowed to explore (the equivalent of twenty-five one-by-one-meter excavation units), there were a few atypical requests. To protect the park's trees, we agreed not to cut any roots with a diameter larger than a half inch. To protect the park's visitors from potential injury and the site's underground resources from looters, we agreed to secure our excavation site overnight with plywood and snow fencing, to hire a guard to be on site while units were open but we were not present, and to backfill any excavation units that we did not finish on Friday afternoon (thus requiring us to dig them out on Monday morning). The CPC's staff reciprocated by sharing tools, storage space, knowledge (e.g., about different tree species near our excavation units and the locations of underground electrical lines), skills (e.g., how to use a special tool to hammer the snow fencing stakes into the ground), and good humor. Later, when we were completing the excavation report, the CPC (Marie Warsh and Allie Davis) and Hunter Research, Inc. (Richard Hunter, Jim Lee, and Evan Mydlowski) also generously converted our profile and plan view drawings to digital renderings.

Prior to the excavation, we also had agreed to keep a low profile and not to tell any passersby that we were conducting archaeology, which, of course, quickly proved to be impossible. Although we were asked numerous times what kinds of trees or bushes we were planting, most park visitors realized that we did not work for the CPC or a local utility company, and it did not take too long before we were regularly peppered with questions about what artifacts we had found and what had been in that place before the park.[10] Our one-time as well as regular visitors, school groups, and, later (on a date agreed upon with the CPC), reporters, were all fascinated by what we were finding and the story of the Village. Instead of the negative publicity that some CPC leaders might have feared, the reactions of the public and the press were overwhelmingly positive, and garnered further support for the park and for the CPC. The positive outcomes of the 2011 excavation and of the IESVH's and CPC's work to forge a positive relationship have led to ongoing collaborations between the two organizations advocating for the site on all three Advocacy Strata.[11] In this section we will focus on AS II-gs and our collaborative advocacy for commemoration of the site.

The IESVH has always included commemoration as one of its key goals for exploring the Village and has always advocated for the placement of a permanent and prominent marker of some kind at the site itself. As mentioned earlier, because of the racist structure of the United States as well as the racist actions of individuals or groups, Black communities have long faced discrediting, dispersal, and erasure. When the construction of Central Park was first proposed, for example, Seneca Village, as well as other portions of the would-be park, were portrayed negatively by newspapers that supported the park project. These depictions paved the way for the city to seize land from landowners, something that would ordinarily have been extremely unpopular, with little public outcry. Newspapers slandered both the residents and the lands upon which they lived as dangerous, unhealthy, unmanageable, and best to be removed, for the good of the public (*New York Daily Times* 1856, 3).

Our research into the Village, and the evidence that we discovered in other written sources as well as the artifacts we uncovered at the site, shows that these depictions were far from accurate. Although we hesitate to try to sum up the complexity of the Village and what it might have been like in one sentence, we believe that evidence suggests that the Village should be remembered, at minimum, as a successful group of diverse and hard-working people (many of whom were landowners), who worked the land, built and maintained houses, cared for and educated their children, developed communities of faith, and strove to make a better life than they had experienced elsewhere (Wall et al. 2018; Wall et al. 2019). These admirable qualities were not unique to Seneca Village. There were other successful predominately African American communities in New York City and in other parts of the country in the mid-nineteenth century, but they are rarely remembered in mainstream history and even more rarely commemorated. Only 2 percent of the more than ninety-five thousand sites included in the National Register of Historic Places focus on the experiences of Black Americans (Cep 2020). These entries include other free Black communities like New Philadelphia in Illinois and Weeksville in Brooklyn, New York, along with individual house sites such as the W. E. B. Du Bois Boyhood Homesite in Great Barrington, Massachusetts. Furthermore, the African Burial Ground has been recognized as a national monument, with an interpretive center and a large, granite monument. But the more general lack of recognition of *places* of Black American experience, success, and struggle contribute to the erasure in mainstream history of their vital contributions to American society. It is thus of critical importance to prominently mark these places, so that, in their visibility and tangibility in the physical landscape, they become anchored in public memory and impossible to erase or ignore.

Exactly what commemoration should look like and how it should be determined is a difficult puzzle to solve. In 2008, before the excavation, IESVH members successfully partnered with the NYC Parks Department and the CPC to install a sign in an area of the park that had been the heart of the Village commemorating the Seneca Village community. This we considered a small, interim victory in a longer struggle for more significant commemoration. Since the excavation, the IESVH has worked with the CPC and with Community Board 10 (CB 10) of Harlem to continue advocating for more substantial and appropriate commemoration and to brainstorm commemoration ideas. Because of both the importance of the Village site and its location within a New York City park, a number of protocols will have to be followed and many voices will have to be considered before any new commemorative plan can be decided upon.

The three organizations (IESVH, CPC, and CB 10) have stressed the importance of the initial step of educating the broader public, including artists who might propose designs. With this goal (as well as the empowerment goals to be discussed in the next section) in mind, members of the IESVH have given many talks and lectures for various public organizations and schools, some at the site itself, which have included walking tours. Rothschild and her students put together a small exhibition at Barnard College just after the 2011 excavations, and Wall and her students created a more substantial exhibition at City College in 2013. We have also consulted on several CPC projects spearheaded by Marie Warsh, a historian at CPC. These projects include a new temporary outdoor exhibit of interpretive signage, installed in October 2019, that marks sixteen places within the Village and highlights different discoveries about its built and natural environment, residents, and their lives (CPC 2019a), as well as video, text, and photo content for the CPC website. One of the videos features an interview with IESVH member Cal Jones and Ariel Williams, the great-great-great-great-granddaughter of Andrew Williams and the only descendant of a Seneca Village resident we have yet been able to contact (CPC 2019b). Andrew Williams was the first person to purchase land in the Village, and he and his family lived in the Village throughout its thirty-year existence. Jones's extensive research into Andrew Williams and his family has been amplified immensely by the knowledge that Ariel Williams has shared about her own family's history and by the experience of developing a relationship with her.

Figure 4.4. Ariel Williams, descendant of Seneca Village resident, Andrew Williams, with IESVH member and Manhattan Borough Historian Emeritus Cal Jones viewing the new CPC signs interpreting Seneca Village in Central Park. Still from video produced by the Central Park Conservancy. Reproduced with permission.

The short video of the interview shows Williams walking on the present-day park ground surface and vividly illustrates how and why the Seneca Village site and its history are important to her as a descendant. While looking at the CPC sign that provides information about Andrew Williams (Figure 4.4), she explains:

> Being in the Park where Andrew Williams's house was located was really a little bit overwhelming. Overwhelming in a good way, in that so many people would be interested in learning more about my story, and my family, and our involvement with Seneca Village, and where we went after that and what happened after that...Now I feel very connected to not only my father but to my family. I understand the pride behind my name and understand where I came from, and the traits that I took from those people and why my father was the way he was and why I am the way I am today. (CPC 2019b)

Williams's physical encounter with the site, the place where her family had once lived, brought her greater understanding both of the deep history of her family and of herself. The research Jones and other members of the IESVH had conducted into the Village and her family, in particular, along with the CPC's interpretive signage, has encouraged Williams to feel that other people care about her and her family. This positive feeling of belonging and that one's ancestors' lives are valued by a broader public, and, by extension, are to be understood as part of our country's history is, unfortunately, not one that all Black Americans regularly experience.

Advocating for increased investigation into and commemoration of sites where African American communities existed is one essential step in fostering belonging and caring for not only direct descendants of those particular communities but also for Black Americans more broadly, who have repeatedly been excluded from or maligned in mainstream American history. Joan Maynard, an artist and activist, led the effort to have the four remaining houses in Weeksville (an African American community that temporally overlapped with Seneca Village in nearby Brooklyn) added to the National Register of Historic Places because, "we've got to make sure our kids know how they got here, and what those who came before did to try and make a better life" (Cep 2020). Advocacy for African American sites is also important for non–African American audiences both to make them aware of the contributions and experiences of Black Americans and to promote more open dialogue about difficult histories, specifically the roles of white Americans in creating and perpetuating structural racism.

The Seneca Village site encourages both kinds of necessary conversations. On the one hand, its existence as a successful village of African Americans (many of them landowners) and Euro-American immigrants testifies that there were places of co-existence and significant African American freedom-, place-, and community-making. It is a place that inspires us to imagine what could have been had the community not been dispersed. As Seignoret pointed out in a recent public talk sponsored by City College (Copeland et al. 2021), these other stories of the African American past that focus on freedom and success as opposed to the dominant narratives of enslavement are very important to tell. Citing the Nigerian writer Chimamanda Ngozi Adichie (2009), Seignoret underscored "the danger of a single story" in creating stereotypes about African Americans or any other groups of people.

On the other hand, the reasons the Seneca Village community formed away from the city center, the community's displacement and erasure, and the residents' dispersal all encourage a deeper examination of anti-Black racism in American history as well as in our present. Today, Black communities continue to suffer disproportionately from many of the same problems that encouraged Black residents to settle in Seneca Village—anti-Black violence, lack of good job and educational opportunities, lesser investment in infrastructure and buildings that creates increased health risks, and so forth. Black communities continue to be displaced by application of the right of eminent domain and the forces of development and gentrification, while the rights of Black communities and individuals to privacy, voting, and even life itself, continue to be threatened. A statement made by Ana Edwards, an artist and historian and contributor to this volume, in support of archaeological investigation and commemoration of an African American burial ground known as Shockoe Bottom in Richmond, Virginia, aligns with how we have long thought about the site of Seneca Village and why we continue to advocate for its commemoration. She said, "I don't know if this space can do all the work our society needs it to, but we need this place" (Cep 2020). For us, making the presence of the Seneca Village site known to the public and commemorating its physical space in the landscape pushes necessary conversations that both complicate our understanding of the past and compel us to contend with how that past still affects our present, in which white Americans unjustly benefit from a social system at the expense of all other people, especially Black Americans.

AS I-ags: Advocacy for Social Justice in the Present through Seneca Village, in Real and Virtual Spaces above the Ground Surface

The ultimate aim of the historical archaeological project to investigate Seneca Village has always been to use the project to advocate for social justice and to foster more of it in the world. The primary ways we have attempted to do this have been through the commemoration initiatives previously discussed and through a variety of endeavors that we categorize under the broad tent of education. Many of our efforts have focused on our own students, but we have also worked with younger students and teachers and other members of the public. This section will describe how we have approached this above-the-ground-surface stratum of advocacy, and our efforts to create new digital projects that aim to empower a broader group of collaborators and the members of the public.

As archaeologists who teach in institutions of higher learning, much of our work has focused on sharing our knowledge and skills with undergraduate and graduate students. Wall and Rothschild were inspired to create the Seneca Village Project in part because they knew it would be an excellent endeavor in which to involve students. Like many academic fields, archaeology lacks diversity and has a "whiteness problem," both in terms of the racial identity of the vast majority of practitioners in the field and orientation of its interests, approaches, and interpretations (Franklin 1997; Blakey 2020; White and Draycott 2020). This problem is a complex one caused by many factors, but a significant one is that most archaeologists have not adequately demonstrated to Black and other minority students that archaeology is a field that can benefit them or their communities or that it will welcome their contributions. Prior to the mid-1990s, historical archaeology in the United States had largely focused on sites associated with famous white men or Euro-American immigrants. When archaeologists did investigate sites associated with the experiences of African Americans, they focused on sites of enslavement, which are absolutely important, but their investigations tended to reinforce a "single story." Most of those plantation studies were led by white archaeologists who rarely involved descendant communities or Black students (Franklin 1997).

Wall and Rothschild felt that in investigating Seneca Village, a free African American community, they could also encourage Black and minority students to consider historical archaeology, because of the project's potential to shed light on *different* historical African American experiences. They hoped that inviting students into the project as collaborators and giving them agency would also show care for them and their communities and, in turn, those students' contributions could change the field itself. Thus, not only was the site and its history significant but also *how* the project leaders welcomed all students, and particularly minority students, into the project and supported and respected them was critical. Wall and Rothschild placed diversity as a top priority when selecting students for involvement in the project. They have also included monetary compensation, either in the form of work-study funds or grant-funded stipends. We recognize that the costs associated with attending field schools or doing work outside of required courses, which, in the past had been considered part of the "price of admission" to the field, is deeply unjust. It devalues the work of students, privileges those who can afford to work for free and/or pay field school fees, and creates insurmountable barriers for students from economically disadvantaged backgrounds, who, because of structural racism are more likely to be members of minority communities. Thus, we see offering fair compensation to students as a form of social justice work that also has benefits for our project and the field of historical archaeology as a whole, because it welcomes and supports collaborators who bring different perspectives and strengths.

Even if our students do not go on to become historical archaeologists, we hope that involvement in the Seneca Village Project can provide them with positive experiences and useful skills that can help them to achieve their own goals. Historical archaeology, in common with other forms of archaeology, is unique in the academic world in the level of teamwork it requires. So many different kinds of skills are needed to investigate a site. No one person can do it all. It is a field that, in theory, should invite and have plenty of room for people with many different interests. Over the years, the Seneca Village Project has engaged students in a number of activities, many of which involve learning skills that are transferable to other kinds of work. These activities include: archival research, oral history interviewing, mapping, soil analysis, developing research questions and plans, excavation, drawing, team management, database creation, multiple types of artifact analysis, quantitative analysis, artifact cataloging, artifact conservation, oral presentations, poster presentations, writing scholarly articles, writing for the public, and creating real and virtual exhibitions. Whenever possible, Wall and Rothschild, and more recently, Linn, have invited students and former students to coauthor publications (Wall et al. 2004; Wall et al. 2018; Wall et al. 2019) or to publish their work independently (Birkett 2019) or have nominated them for writing awards (Ng 1999; Mazzone 2019; Althoff 2020; Aubey 2020). Advocacy for the recognition of our students' contributions to the project both is fair and advances social justice because they benefit from that recognition when applying to MA or PhD programs or jobs.

Some of our most recent efforts to involve and empower students have included digital projects, which we have found to have a number of benefits. Digital projects encourage students to become adept with transferable digital skills, they can foster more collaboration than most traditional class projects, they can be "published" easily online and thus garner broader recognition for the students' work, and they have the potential to reach a much larger audience to share knowledge of Seneca Village. Linn, for example, co-developed and co-directed the 2020 program for Bard Graduate Center's (BGC) Lab for Teen Thinkers Program, with BGC Senior Manager of Education, Carla Repice, and PhD student Tova Kadish. We selected twenty-three students from racially, ethnically, and economically diverse backgrounds from all five boroughs to participate in the program and funding from BGC enabled us to provide them with stipends. The program was initially planned for in-person learning with multiple field trips but had to be shifted to an all-online experience because of the COVID-19 pandemic. During the five-week program, we introduced students to the broader history of New York City and especially the history of African Americans in the city; contemporary issues affecting African American and minority communities; archaeological excavation methods and the importance of context; methods of studying objects and written documents together to access marginalized histories; the history of the IESVH's efforts to explore the village from political negotiation to the 2011 excavation to the creation of the excavation report (Wall et al. 2018); writing for the public; oral presentation techniques; creative writing and drawing; and web page design and construction.

The Teen Thinkers Program, like the larger Seneca Village Project, was also collaborative. We emphasized the value of diverse voices by modeling it throughout the program. For example, we invited a number of guests (including IESVH members and BGC staff) to share their expertise, often in pairs. Whenever possible, we invited the students themselves to share their own knowledge, and many expressed first-hand experience of the issues affecting Black and brown communities in New York City today. The students' final project was also collaborative. Groups of four students brought together the individual research they had conducted about one object excavated from the Village. They created digital exhibitions, with support from BGC digital humanities specialist Jesse Merandy and BGC graphic designer Jocelyn Lau. Their exhibitions centered on one of the following preselected themes that they were tasked with interpreting and exploring together: work, recreation, kitchen and table, tea, care of the body, presentation of the self. The students shared their websites in a celebratory online oral presentation, and the websites are publicly accessible (Lab for Teen Thinkers 2020). Student feedback about the project was very positive and highlighted their appreciation for skill-building, working collaboratively, and learning about a history that helps them to understand the present differently. In a postprogram survey, one student noted, for example, "I learned so much and had the honor of spreading the history of Seneca Village and its people . . . it gave me a sense of different career paths and future research I would like to do . . . [I left] the program with a new perspective and improvements in [my] research, writing, presentation skills, and more." Another wrote, "It made me want to learn more and changed my perspective on many topics," and a third stated they came to understand "the way history is framed. How our biases influence how we analyze objects. How different perspectives give different understandings to things." Many also commented upon how they wished Seneca Village was taught in all New York City schools, unknowingly hitting on a long-term goal of the IESVH and of the Teen Program organizers.

The authors and the other members of the IESVH have long advocated for introducing the study of Seneca Village into New York City public schools, and many of us have given talks in schools and libraries and tours to school groups, but not on a regular or systematic basis. Making Seneca Village part of the New York City public lower, middle, and high school curriculum could have tremendous positive social justice impact, in teaching transferable skills that prepare students for college and careers; building confidence in and finding recognition for the value of their own knowledge and experience; learning a more balanced version of American history that exposes both systemic racism and the contributions of Black Americans, and one that enables them to better understand and engage with social justice issues in the present. BGC's Teen Program was designed to be one step in a longer-term project to create a social-justice-centered

Seneca Village curriculum for public schools. We repeated the Teen Thinkers Program in 2021 and refined it in response to student feedback. Repice, Linn, BGC education coordinator Nadia Rivers, and poet and social justice educator Ama Codjoe have also organized professional development workshops for teachers about Seneca Village. Alice Baldwin-Jones, a longtime IESVH member and cultural anthropologist, in consultation with Wall and Linn, created and led one of the lessons, which has been shared with the teachers who participated to adjust for their own classrooms and with the public on BGC's website. Our aim is to invite different people to create different lessons each year and use the feedback we receive from teachers and our BGC Teens to develop a flexible Seneca Village curriculum that can be shared freely online.[12]

The expansion of Seneca Village–related projects (operating within and across the three different advocacy strata), combined with the increased public interest in Seneca Village, has also made clear that our advocacy goals could be advanced by creating a central "place" to share our knowledge and resources. A website is the best solution, at the present, because it can make most of these resources available to anyone anywhere and can provide a platform and a framework for increased collaboration. Linn is currently leading the "Seneca Village Digital Project" to create a new and expanded website that includes or links to pre-existing resources and provides space and incentive for the development of new ones, created both by long-term IESVH members and others who are new to researching the village. A group of archaeology professors and staff from the following institutions and organizations as well as independent scholars have been involved in planning meetings thus far: BGC, Brooklyn College, CCNY, Columbia, Barnard, the NYC Landmarks Preservation Commission, CPC, and All Angels' Church.

This website also helps us to address something we have encountered, especially in the last few years, that some archaeologists might see as a conflict between our social justice advocacy goals (AS I-ags) and the two other advocacy strata, advocacy for the site (AS II-gs) and for its residents and archaeological resources (ASIII-bgs). Among the people who have become interested in Seneca Village are a number of talented artists and writers, who have incorporated their ideas about the village into their own work. As three white female archaeologists who have been researching and advocating for Seneca Village for decades and incorporating social justice methods in our endeavors, we are elated that the village is finally receiving recognition and that it is inspiring others in their own efforts of self-empowerment and building a more just society. We, in turn, are inspired by the artists' interpretations that are different from our own. Our interpretations are limited by our own knowledge and experience as well as our training within the social scientific discipline of archaeology.

From the traditional perspective of that discipline, some of the artists' interpretations diverge from available "evidence" and/or "facts." For example, John Dowell's beautiful and enthralling series of photographic works show cotton, a crop that does not grow in the Northeast, flourishing in Seneca Village (Voeller 2019). Sara Bunn's 2019 exhibition "We Wore More Than Shackles ~ A Day in the Life of Seneca Village" presented mannequins named after real Seneca Villagers, some Bunn provided with imaginative personal histories, wearing clothing inspired by 1830s fashion and containing twenty-first-century details (afinelyne 2019). Marilyn Nelson's (2015) book of poems *My Seneca Village* contains many thought-provoking and creative scenes, including how a named female Seneca Villager might have responded, if she had been there, to a white riot at a Black theater (an event noted in historical sources) by punching a man in self-defense. Tourmaline's lush film highlights the ingenuity and power of a historically known transgender woman, and places her in the filmmaker's vision of Seneca Village as a place of refuge, although it is unknown if the woman had ever been there (Tourmaline and Lax 2020). Last, Brent Staples (2019, 2022), a writer for the *New York Times*, presents the Village as a Black utopia.

Perhaps the most dramatic expression of an increasing awareness of Seneca Village emerged in late 2021 at the Metropolitan Museum. There, a group of curators created an exhibit "Before Yesterday We Could Fly," centered on an Afrofuturistic Period room, based on ideas of what Seneca Village might look like today, had its residents not been evicted by eminent domain. The authors of this article met with the curators, and two members of the IESVH Board were on the advisory board of the exhibit and contributed material for it (Cynthia Copeland and Cal Jones). One of the exhibit's goals is a vision of a more socially just future than that existing today or in the past. It displays a few objects inspired by similar artifacts recovered from the Village in our excavations, but the exhibit is more artistic than historical; it incorporates a number of works of art created for the room that reference African origins, the creative blending of traditions in the African diaspora, and complex futures (Sarah Lawrence, pers. comm. 2022). The product is a beautiful and kaleidoscopic home space.

Some archaeologists, who, as they have been trained to do, feel tied to evidence and yet also weave interpretive stories from it, might worry when artists take imaginative license, especially if they do so without explaining their choices to their audience. Do such leaps do an injustice to the people of Seneca Village themselves, people whom we feel we have come to know in our embodied engagement with their former possessions and traces of their daily lives, from the plates the Wilson family set their table with to a shoe that cradled one of the children's feet, to the soil they walked upon? In our own work, we too have taken imaginative leaps, though we try to point out to our audiences when we are on solid ground and when our toes have left the floor.

It is precisely this letting go, however, or, more precisely, supporting others in their own endeavors to leave the ground surface, that is perhaps the most challenging and yet most important aspect of archaeological advocacy, especially for this advocacy stratum (AS I-ags). We archaeologists do not have exclusive rights to interpreting the past. There are many aspects of Seneca Villagers' lives that are not represented in the fragmentary evidence that remains, and there are things that Seneca Villagers experienced that we, as white, female archaeologists today, might not ever be able to access or imagine. Artists and writers, who specialize in imagination, and especially those who themselves come from Black communities, can reveal aspects of and questions about the experiences of Seneca Villagers—deeper layers of truth—that can't be found by digging in either the ground or the archives. Their work can also connect powerfully to the truths in our present and provoke meaningful feelings and discussion about injustice and how to overcome it (Whitney Museum 2019).[13] We thus see the work of artists who engage with Seneca Village as providing invaluable insight. Supporting that work is a crucial part of our advocacy. That support means sharing our research resources with them, citing their work, and respecting their artistic interpretations.

Conclusion

The potential dilemmas posed by the differences between our ways of knowing as archaeologists and those of writers and artists encouraged us to reflect more deeply upon the history of the Seneca Village Project, upon our interpretations and our goals. It inspired us to participate in the "Advocacy in Archaeology" session organized by Kelly M. Britt at the 2020 annual meeting of the Society for Historical Archaeology in Boston and to rewrite that paper for this collection. So much has changed in the years since that conference. The urgency to advocate for sites of African American heritage and for the roles they can play in social justice endeavors has only grown, as has our reliance on digital media, and simultaneously, our need for real places and tangible things. We are responding to these challenges by investing further, in both real and digital spaces, in our multilayered approach to advocacy, that focuses on the below-ground archaeological resources (AS III-bgs), the site itself (AS II-gs), and how the project can promote social justice (AS I-ags). Central to all three advocacy strata are the collaborative principles that have guided the project from the beginning.

Acknowledgments

We are grateful to the many people who have collaborated with us and contributed in many different ways to the ongoing historical archaeological investigation of Seneca Village. In addition to those we have already mentioned, we acknowledge and thank John Krawchuk, then of the New York City Department of Parks and Recreation, and Douglas Blonsky, Christopher Nolan, Maria Hernandez, and Matt D'Amico of the CPC, who helped make the 2011 excavation possible. We are grateful for our continued collaboration with the CPC, especially with Marie Warsh, historian, and John Reddick, director of community engagement projects. We greatly appreciate the assistance and counsel of the many other scholars who have been part of the Seneca Village Project Advisory Board: Elizabeth Blackmar, George Brandon, C. Virginia Fields, Joan Geismar, Venus Greene, Leslie Harris, Jean Howson, Cheryl LaRoche, Edward O'Donnell, Warren Perry, Rodger Taylor, David Hurst Thomas, Eric K. Washington, Craig Wilder, Sherill Wilson, and the late Cornell Edwards and Roy Rosenzweig. We extend great thanks also to new academic collaborators who have joined the new Seneca Village Digital initiative: Kelly Britt, Zoe Crossland, Jesse Merandy, Caspar Meyer, Matt Reilly, and Mia-Michelle Russell. Funding for the excavation and/or other research was generously provided by the National Science Foundation, National Geographic, Friends of Cornell Edwards, the Richard Gilder Foundation, the Durst Foundation, the Columbia Institute for Social and Economic Research and Policy, the Professional Staff Congress of the City University of New York, City College Division of Social Science, and Barnard College. We are very appreciative of the support of all of these organizations. We thank Kelly M. Britt and Diane F. George for the opportunity to write this article, their helpful feedback, and the space to explain our approach and to highlight the contributions of our many collaborators. To those we have neglected to mention by name, we are also indebted and most appreciative.

Meredith B. Linn is assistant professor of historical archaeology at the Bard Graduate Center. She holds a PhD from Columbia University, an MA from the University of Chicago, and a BA from Swarthmore College. Her research projects have focused upon the health-related experiences of Irish immigrants in nineteenth-century New York City and upon Seneca Village. Linn coauthored, with Nan Rothschild and Diana diZerega

Wall, the Seneca Village archaeological site report. She has also published articles about her Irish immigrant research and is currently working on books about both projects.

Nan A. Rothschild is a social and historical archaeologist whose fieldwork has been in New York City and the American Southwest. She taught at Barnard College from 1981-2006 and at Columbia University until 2019. She has published several books, among them "New York City Neighborhoods, the 18th Century," "Colonial Encounters in a Native American Landscape," and with Diana Wall, "The Archaeology of American Cities."

Diana diZerega Wall is an archaeologist who specializes in New York City. Her interests include colonialism and the intersection of class, race, ethnicity, and gender. Professor emerita at City College and the CUNY Graduate Center, her books include *The Archaeology of American Cities* (with Nan Rothschild, 2014) and the award-winning *Unearthing Gotham* (with Anne-Marie Cantwell, 2001). She is currently working on two books, one on New Netherland with Anne-Marie Cantwell and one on Seneca Village, with Nan Rothschild.

Notes

1. A *New York Herald* article from 1871 illustrates that the village was largely forgotten by the public within the span of a generation of its destruction. Laborers removing trees near 85th and 8th Avenue unearthed formally buried human remains in two caskets, and in 1959 a park gardener unearthed a human skull and then multiple burials (*New York Herald* 1871, 4; *The New Yorker* 1959, 24; Rosenzweig and Blackmar 1992, 89). Anyone who remembered the village should have known that it had included multiple cemeteries; at the very least, the Parks Department should have been aware.
2. We are grateful to Kelly Britt for her suggestion to develop this stratigraphic metaphor.
3. In the not too distant past, some sites did not elicit attention from possible kin and descendant communities. In the authors' experience, sites with heterogeneous past occupants are less likely to attract the attention of stakeholders, unless one or more of those individuals was a historically significant figure (as was the case with the 7 Hanover Square site when a descendant of Robert Livingston, an occupant of a structure on that site made himself known to Rothschild and Wall). Since the discovery of and controversy surrounding the African Burial Ground, African Americans have been the most active and proactive descendants involved with archaeological sites in New York City.
4. Several other students from Barnard College, Columbia University, and City College also conducted important research early in the project. They include Kristi-Lynn Cassaro, Siobhan Cooke, Jessica Davis, Nina Finch, Ericka Haskin, Cornelia Jarvis, Yvette Kelley, Iciar Lucena, Nyla Manning, Marina Massey, Tyrah McGregor, Oscar Oliva, Kueita Saint Louis, Christina Spain, Christine Seeholzer, and Alicia Senia.

5. There were other reasons why this area was chosen for excavation. Minimally invasive soil testing conducted by Suanna Selby in 2004 suggested the area was less disturbed by the construction and operation of the park than other areas of the former village, while non-invasive GPR testing conducted by Larry Conyers in 2005 and 2011 detected the presence of underground anomalies. Both of these projects involved students from City College, Columbia University, and Barnard College. They included Linn and Seignoret as well as Heather Atherton, Debra Karstadt, Robert Kristek, Mary Kuhns, Shahirah Majumdar, Lizzie Martin, Amanda Murphy, Zinnia Rahman, Jenny Ruvulo, Hatem Samhan, David Silver, and Sarah Zimmet.
6. All Angels' Church was the one building that we know of that escaped destruction when villagers were evicted. The wooden frame church was picked up off of its foundations and moved a few blocks to the west. A photograph showing this structure in its new location is the only photo of a building from Seneca Village that has yet been discovered (All Angels' Church 2020). Unfortunately, the building was destroyed in 1889.
7. The undergraduate students were Ashley Anderson, John Anderton, Ariane Dandeneau, Ashton Dorminvil, Randy Henry, Madeline Landry, Victor Luna, Julianne Maeda, Nelson Sinchi, and Andrea Lee Torres. Jenna Coplin and Meredith Linn were the field supervisors. Seignoret provided additional assistance. Matt Sanger mapped the site.
8. The team of students from the excavations performed the cleaning, labeling, and initial cataloging of the artifacts. Additional artifact analysis was conducted by the authors, Seignoret, and other City College students. The faunal remains were analyzed by Adam Watson and students Sydney Pickens, Sarah Reetz, and Amanda Rossillo. Specialist consultants Heather Trigg, Susan Jacobucci, and Justine McKnight analyzed pollen and macrobotanical remains in our soil samples. Students Denisse Fernandez, Frances Jin, Debra Karstadt, and Iciar Lucena entered this cataloging and other primary source data.
9. Bruce Bevan and Roelof Versteeg also conducted geophysical testing early in the project.
10. Anderson and Linn kept a database of the questions posed to the crew by passersby.
11. With regard to protection of the site's archaeological resources (ASIII- bgs), CPC has committed to leaving burials undisturbed and archaeological monitoring and testing prior to playground renovation projects in the former residential zones of the Village. CPC has contracted Hunter Research, Inc. to do that testing work and has included IESVH members as consultants.
12. Lizzie Martin, a contributor to this volume, who assisted with GPR testing in the village many years ago, is helping us to refine this lesson plan in her classroom.
13. Tomashi Jackson's work is among the most directly political so far. Her brilliantly colored multimedia artworks draw clear parallels between the eviction of Seneca Villagers and the City's recent unjust seizure of property in Black and brown communities via New York City's Third-Party Transfer Program (Whitney Museum 2019).

References

afinelyne. 2019. "A Day in the Life of Seneca Village on View at Port Authority Terminal." *GothamToGo* (blog), 21 March. https://gothamtogo.com/a-day-in-the-life-of-seneca-village-on-view-at-port-authority-terminal/.

All Angels' Church. 2020. "Our History, All Angels' Church." https://allangelschurch.com/our-history/.

Adichie, Chimamanda Ngozi. 2009. "The Danger of a Single Story Presented at the TED Conferences." https://www.youtube.com/watch?v=D9Ihs241zeg.

Althoff, Amanda. 2020. "Archaeollage: Fragments of Seneca Village." Unpublished manuscript and research paper for "Writing Archaeology," Zoe Crossland (instructor). Columbia University, New York, NY. Awarded the Bert Salwen Prize by Professional Archaeologists of New York City.

Atalay, Sonya. 2006. "Indigenous Archaeology as Decolonizing Practice." *American Indian Quarterly* 30 (3/4): 280–310.

Aubey, Madison. 2020. "Seneca Village: Some artifacts and their Poems." Unpublished manuscript and research paper for "Writing Archaeology," Zoe Crossland (instructor). Columbia University, New York, NY. Awarded the Bert Salwen Prize by Professional Archaeologists of New York City.

Birkett, Jordane. 2019. "The Kettle of Community." *BGC Commons*. https://senecavillageteapot.commons.bgc.bard.edu/.

Blakey, Michael L. 2020. "Archaeology under the Blinding Light of Race." *Current Anthropology* 61 (S22): S183–97.

Cantwell, Anne-Marie, and Diana diZerega Wall. 2001. *Unearthing Gotham: The Archaeology of New York City*. New Haven, CT: Yale University Press.

Central Park Conservancy (CPC). 2019a. "Discover Seneca Village." https://www.centralparknyc.org/activities/guides/discover-seneca-village.

Central Park Conservancy (CPC). 2019b. "Seneca Village: The Williams Family Legacy." Video. https://www.centralparknyc.org/locations/seneca-village-site.

Cep, Casey. 2020. "The Fight to Preserve African-American History." *The New Yorker*, 27 January 2020. https://www.newyorker.com/magazine/2020/02/03/the-fight-to-preserve-african-american-history.

Cipolla, Craig N., James Quinn, and Jay Levy. 2019. "Theory in Collaborative Indigenous Archaeology: Insights from Mohegan." *American Antiquity* 84 (1): 127–42.

Colwell-Chanthaphonh, Chip, and T. J. Ferguson. 2007. *Collaboration in Archaeological Practice: Engaging Descendant Communities*. Lanham, MD: AltaMira Press.

Copeland, Cynthia R., Alexandra Jones, and Herbert Seignoret. 2021. "Archaeology and the Making of the American Past: Race, Community, and the Struggle for Social Justice." City College of New York, 11 March.

Deetz, James. 1977. *In Small Things Forgotten*. Garden City, NJ: Anchor Press/ Doubleday.

Deloria, Vine Jr. 1988. *Custer Died for Your Sins: An Indian Manifesto*. Norman: University of Oklahoma Press.

Flexner, James L., and Edward González-Tennant. 2018. "Anarchy and Archaeology." *Journal of Contemporary Archaeology* 5 (2): 213–19.

Foderaro, Lisa W. 2011. "Unearthing Traces of African-American Village Displaced by Central Park." *New York Times*, 27 July 2011. https://www.nytimes.com/2011/07/28/nyregion/unearthing-an-african-american-village-displaced-by-central-park.html.

Franklin, Maria. 1997. "'Power to the People': Sociopolitics and the Archaeology of Black Americans." *Historical Archaeology* 31 (3): 36–50.

Harris, Leslie M. 2003. *In the Shadow of Slavery: African Americans in New York City 1626-1863*. Chicago, IL: University of Chicago Press.

Hartman, Saidiya V. 2008. *Lose Your Mother: A Journey Along the Atlantic Slave Route*. New York: Farrar, Straus and Giroux.

Lab for Teen Thinkers "Seneca Village." 2020. Bard Graduate Center, New York, NY.

LaRoche, Cheryl, and Michael L. Blakey. 1997. "Seizing Intellectual Power: The Dialogue at the New York African Burial Ground." *Historical Archaeology* 31 (3): 84–106.

Mazzone, Jacqueline. 2019. "The Story of a Button: Understanding Life in Seneca Village." Research paper for 964. Excavating the Empire City. Bard Graduate Center, New York, NY. Awarded the Bert Salwen Prize by Professional Archaeologists of New York City.

McDavid, Carol. 2004. "From 'Traditional' Archaeology to Public Archaeology to Community Action: The Levi Jordan Plantation Project.'" In *Places in Mind: Public Archaeology as Applied Anthropology*, edited by Paul A. Shackel and Erve J. Chambers, 35–56. New York: Routledge.

McIntosh, Kriston, Emily Moss, Ryan Nunn, and Jay Shambaugh. 2020. "Examining the Black-White Wealth Gap." *Brookings* (blog), 27 February 2020. https://www.brookings.edu/blog/up-front/2020/02/27/examining-the-black-white-wealth-gap/.

Murray, Wendi Field, Nicholas C. Laluk, Barbara J. Mills, and T. J. Ferguson. 2009. "Archaeological Collaboration with American Indians: Case Studies from the Western United States." *Collaborative Anthropologies* 2 (1): 65–86.

Nelson, Marilyn. 2015. *My Seneca Village*. South Hampton, NH: namelos.

New York Daily Times. 1856. "The Present Look at Our Great Central Park," 9 July 1856, 3.

The New-York Historical Society (N-YHS). 1997. "Before Central Park: The Life and Death of Seneca Village." New York, NY. Website accompanying the exhibition co-curated by Cynthia Copeland and Grady Turner and designed by Carol May and Tim Watkins of May & Watkins Exhibition Inc. https://www.nyhistory.org/seneca/.

The New Yorker. 1959. "Paddy's Walk," 10 January 1959, 24.

New York Herald. 1871. "New York City," 11 August 1871, 4.

Ng, Olivia. 1999. "Seneca Village Perspectives." Senior thesis, Department of Anthropology, Columbia University. Manuscript on file with the Institute for the Exploration of Seneca Village History, New York, NY.

The NYC Archaeological Repository: The Nan A. Rothschild Research Center. 2020. Seneca Village Project (2018). http://archaeology.cityofnewyork.us/collection/map/seneca-village/project/seneca-village-project-2018.

The NYC Archaeological Repository: The Nan A. Rothschild Research Center. 2020. Iron Curry Comb. Qi#: 210725, Cat #: 9531.129. Seneca Village Project (2018). https://archaeology.cityofnewyork.us/collection/search/seneca-village-210725-iron-curry-comb/.

Rosenbaum, Phil. 2011. "History Unearthed in New York's Central Park." CNN International. http://www.cnn.com/video/#/video/world/2011/07/29/bs.seneca.dig.nyc.cnn?iref=allsearch.

Rosenzweig, Roy, and Elizabeth Blackmar. 1992. *The Park and the People: A History of Central Park*. Ithaca, NY: Cornell University Press.

Sage, Egbert. 1856. Central Park Condemnation Map. Municipal Archives, New York, NY.

Sharpe, Christina. 2016. *In the Wake: On Blackness and Being*. Durham, NC: Duke University Press Books.

Silliman, Stephen, and T. J. Ferguson. 2011. "Consultation and Collaboration with Descendant Communities." In *Voices in American Archaeology*, edited by Wendy Ashmore, Barbara Mills, and Dorothy Lippert, 48–72. Washington DC: The SAA Press.

Staples, Brent. 2019. "Opinion: The Death of the Black Utopia." *The New York Times*, 28 November 2019. https://www.nytimes.com/2019/11/28/opinion/seneca-central-park-nyc.html.

———. 2022. "In Search of the Black Utopia." *The New York Times*, 8 January 2022. https://www.nytimes.com/2022/01/08/opinion/seneca-village-central-park-new-york.html.

Streibel MacLean, Jessica. 2020. "Seneca Village Unearthed." NYC Archaeological Repository: The Nan A. Rothschild Research Center. 2020. http://archaeology.cityofnewyork.us/collection/digital-exhibitions/seneca-village-unearthed/page/1/view_as/grid.

Sunseri, Jun, and Albert Gonzalez. 2020. "Honoring and Embodying the Mandate of Community-Accountable Archaeology: Perspectives from the Indo-Hispano/a Southwest." *Historical Archaeology* 54 (4): 738–55.

Tourmaline and Thomas J. Lax. 2020. "Anything We Want to Be: Tourmaline's Salacia | Magazine | MoMA." *The Museum of Modern Art Magazine*, 25 January. https://www.moma.org/magazine/articles/360.

Viele, Egbert L. 1855. "Map of lands included in the Central Park from a topographical survey," 17 June 1855. Parks and parkways drawings and plans collection, dpr_d_3172. Municipal Archives, City of New York. https://nycma.lunaimaging.com/luna/servlet/detail/NYCMA~15~15~6495~1226534?qvq=q percent3Aviele&mi=36&trs=37.

Voeller, Meghan. 2019. "Cotton: The Soft, Dangerous Beauty of the Past" Review of an exhibition of John Dowell's work at the African American Museum in Philadelphia, PA. *Hyperallergic*, 20 February. https://hyperallergic.com/485798/cotton-the-soft-dangerous-beauty-of-the-past/.

Wall, Diana diZerega, Nan A. Rothschild, Cynthia Copeland, and Herbert Seignoret. 2004. "The Seneca Village Project: Working with Modern Communities in Creating the Past." In *Places in Mind: Public Archaeology as Applied Anthropology*, edited by Paul Shackel and Erve Chambers, 101–17. New York: Routledge.

Wall, Diana diZerega, Nan A. Rothschild, and Meredith B. Linn. 2019. "Constructing Identity in Seneca Village." In *Archaeology of Identity and Dissonance: Contexts for a Brave New World*, edited by Diane F. George and Bernice Kurchin, 157–80. Gainesville: University Press of Florida.

Wall, Diana diZerega, Nan A. Rothschild, Meredith B. Linn, and Cynthia R. Copeland. 2018. "Seneca Village, A Forgotten Community: Report on the 2011 Excavations." New York, NY: Institute for the Exploration of Seneca Village History, Inc. A report submitted to NYC Landmarks Preservation Commission, the Central Park Conservancy, and the NYC Department of Parks and Recreation.

White, William, and Catherine Draycott Draycott. 2020. "Why the Whiteness of Archaeology Is a Problem." *Sapiens*, 7 July 2020. https://www.sapiens.org/archaeology/archaeology-diversity/.

Whitney Museum of American Art. 2019. "From Seneca Village to Brooklyn: A Conversation with Tomashi Jackson." https://whitney.org/events/tomashi-jackson. Event recording available here: https://whitney.org/media/43518.

Chapter 5

Right to the City
Community-Based Urban Archaeology as Abolitionist Heritage

Kelly M. Britt

> How two theories of the future of America clashed and blended just after the Civil War: the one was abolition-democracy based on freedom, intelligence and power for all men; the other was industry for private profit directed by an autocracy determined at any price to amass wealth and power. The uncomprehending resistance of the South, and the pressure of black folk, made these two thoughts uneasy and temporary allies.
>
> —W. E. B. Du Bois, *Black Reconstruction in America 1860–1880*

> Without community, there is no liberation.
>
> —Audre Lorde, *The Master's Tools Will Never Dismantle the Master's House*, 1984

Prologue

87 MacDonough Street: Home to The United Order of Tents

26 December 2020. A post on the Bedford-Stuyvesant Brooklyn community Facebook page asks: "Question . . . Does anyone know the status of 87 MacDonough Street?" The post stated that many fond memo-

---

Notes for this chapter begin on page 123.

Figure 5.1. The United Order of the Tents Eastern District #3 Headquarters, 87 MacDonough Street, Brooklyn, NY. 2019. © Kelly M. Britt.

ries were experienced there as a child, and the writer was even able to bring their organization there for a summer camp from 2005 to 2007. This posting was paired with an image of a house (a mansion by New York City standards), known locally by its street address 87 MacDonough Street (Figure 5.1). While mansion in form and size, its weathered look with peeling paint, broken windows, and tattered curtains alludes to a haunted house, with the only glimpse of its owner and use situated in a sign above its front door that states "1888–1988 EASTERN DISTRICT GRAND TENT #3 GRAND UNITED ORDER OF THE TENTS OF BKLYN. JRG JU" (Figure 5.2). Few know that the United Order of Tents Eastern District #3 (Tents) is the oldest Black women's benevolent society in the United States. Secret in nature, the historic mutual aid organization was founded prior to the Civil War by Annetta M. Lane and Harriett R. Taylor, two formerly enslaved women. They were supported by two abolitionists, J. R. Giddings and John Joliffe, and together they formed a union—hence the JRG (J. R. Giddings) JU (Joliffe Union) in their official name, with Union referring to the Tents united as one.

At the time of writing this chapter, 189 comments follow the 26 December Facebook posting. Through a cursory subjective categorization of comments, I found over seventy of them directly related to inquiries about

Figure 5.2. The United Order of the Tents Eastern District #3 Sign. 2019. © Kelly M. Britt.

Tents' history, memories of community members with a relationship to the physical house and space, or comments regarding its preservation for the "community." While the notion of community was not expressly defined in these comments, many referred to it as "our community," "the culture," even "US" in opposition to "European interventions." In addition to the comments reflecting on the history and legacy of 87 MacDonough Street, approximately fifty comments focused on the property as real estate (comments regarding if it was for sale, etc.) including a comment that listed the property currently for sale for $9.75 million on the Zillow real estate app. This ad, after further inquiry, turned out to be fake, created as part of the Great Gotham Challenge,[1] which is essentially an online scavenger hunt focused on team building through learning about history and culture. This posting of the property's seemingly "for sale" status prompted much response, from desires to purchase to outright opposition to any sale. It was here that the comments included stories and memories of the organization or property or both. While no one was aware then, this posting of a fake ad put into motion a set of actions guiding the Tents to emerge from secrecy and share its organizational and site history, invoking a real community dialogue about heritage.

Those comments about the history and memories associated with the site and organization, the real estate value of this historic house, and issues of displacement that plague this historical Black community lie at the heart of this chapter, which initiates an investigation of how heritage and heritage management can create what Ruth Wilson Gilmore calls abolitionist geography or what I suggest may be called abolitionist heritage. Alternative land-use patterns and geographies have always existed and are embedded in individual and collective memories. Can these alternative patterns and memories provide a counter heritage discourse that could influence historic preservation policies evidenced in the tangible built environment while also supporting and sustaining the intangible social fabric of a place? How can archaeology more generally be used as a tool of advocacy to empower communities fighting erasure?

Introduction

This chapter explores archaeology's role in advocacy and activism, in particular through historic preservation initiatives, and grounds the work methodologically in a community-based archaeology through emancipatory participatory action research (PAR). For purposes of this chapter, I consider archaeology as historic preservation or heritage management due to the interwoven connection between the two in historic preservation law within the United States. To connect placemaking to urban planning, particularly in historic preservation contexts, I explore David Harvey (2008) and Henri Lefebvre's (1968) concept of the "Right to the City"—what it means, and how people have, can, and do claim this right particularly within the urbanization and planning process of New York City. This exploration is set in the history of displacement in New York City and the neighborhood of Bedford-Stuyvesant (Bed-Stuy) in particular and focuses on mid-twentieth-century policies and projects by Robert Moses to more recent planning ventures by former mayor Michael Bloomberg. Discussion surrounds how these projects have tried to justify the purposeful erasure and displacement of many New York City residents for the greater good. Economic and housing policies that have fueled gentrification and have led to what Samuel Stein has coined the "Real Estate State" (2019) will be teased out as well. Finally, local preservation processes and their role in urban planning will be examined to call attention to the transactional realities of heritage and how these processes work in capitalist urbanization efforts. I briefly highlight examples, all situated in New York City, where residents' voices were heard through the local preservation process. Interwoven throughout is a case study focused on The United Order of Tents Eastern District #3 headquarters described above, which needs preservation both materially (structure) and socially (membership).

This case study, which is in the beginning stages of research, will serve as both prologue and epilogue to this examination of erasure and endurance, focusing on potential future endeavors that may provide ways for historic preservation to be used as a tool of resistance and resilience.

What or Who Is the United Order of Tents, You Ask?

This was a question I asked myself every time I walked by the house and read its sign. Also known as the "Tents," it is a Black women's fraternal order dating back to the mid-nineteenth century (The United Order of Tents handout n.d). The fraternal lodge began as a stop on the Underground Railroad, with tents set up to assist enslaved persons escaping north. Originally formed in New York State in 1847, the Tents moved to Pennsylvania to work with the Quakers and the first Tent, Rebecca Tent #1, was formally organized in Philadelphia that same year (The United Order of Tents handout n.d.). Known informally as "tents of salvation," the organization is rooted in Christian charity work providing food, places to bathe, nursing care to those in need, and proper Christian burial to all.

The United Order of Tents is a secret society, out of necessity to protect its members and mission through Reconstruction and Jim Crow, therefore not much is known about the history of the organization, especially about Eastern District #3. The building at 87 MacDonough Street has been part of a national historic district since 1996 (USN 04701.004141) and is located in the listed Stuyvesant Heights Historic District. While the property is in disrepair and looks abandoned, it is used regularly, yet its lifeforce is almost invisible to those that walk by (Britt and Gregory 2019).

There are few remaining members left in Eastern District #3, and of those that attend meetings, many are elders and require assistance. The once-coveted aspect of secrecy, which protected them and provided insulation, now could be a force of demise and erasure. They realize they need to recreate themselves to entice new members to carry on their legacy. While this project is in the infancy stage, I have joined with other scholars and community members to propose the creation of the "Friends of the Tents," an auxiliary support group to assist as needed by recording oral histories, conducting archaeology, helping raise funds for the restoration of the building, and supporting the organization in whatever way is needed to ensure that the materiality and the memory of the Tents are not erased. Historic preservation efforts are currently in the planning phases as the Tents await nonprofit status.[2] These efforts, which will focus on restoration of their headquarters and home, are directly built upon the foundation of historic preservation laws and regulations—local ones such as

New York City Landmarks Preservation Commission (LPC) guidelines as well as the National Register—and will provide the impetus and potential funds for restoration.

Many racist urbanization methods such as redlining through the National Housing Act of 1934, restrictive covenants, and local urban planning policies have included displacement of working- and middle-class communities of color, specifically Black communities, throughout the United States. These intentionally discriminatory housing policies, even when deemed illegal, were underwritten in the structured process driving communities to the periphery of the urban landscape, many to industrial zones or fringe housing stock. Largely forgotten, these communities now find themselves on what has become hallowed capitalistic ground: waterfronts with views or historic districts with "character" that are coveted by developers. Climate change resiliency projects on waterfronts and private investment in historic districts complicate the current cycle of urban re-creation, at times erasing entire Black communities or places important to these communities through neoliberal policies of urban renewal. While waiting for the Tents to acquire nonprofit status and the ability to apply for grants and funds, I continue to consider the question of what role this project can play in the larger look at historic preservation in urban planning.

Advocacy and Archaeology: Participatory Action Research (PAR) and Community-based Archaeology as Method

This volume highlights the changing nature of archaeology in the twenty-first century and seeks to expand the concept of what public archaeology is and the role it has in the larger public domain, in particular in advocacy and activist efforts in urban settings. As Margaret Purser discusses eloquently in the foreword, advocacy efforts by archaeologists have primarily focused on *the resource*. This includes efforts to study the resource through archaeological inquiry, protect it from destruction, or in some cases complete excavation of it when destruction is imminent. As stated above, for purposes of this piece, I consider archaeology as a form of historic preservation or heritage management due to its connection with historic preservation laws and ordinances. Much of archaeology done globally is associated with urban development, and historic preservation laws generally dictate and govern archaeology in these spaces, thereby advocacy for the preservation of the resource has been paramount.

What has shifted, or perhaps taken center stage, from the latter portion of the twentieth century onward due to the influence of community-based archaeological endeavors is advocacy *for the people* associated with the resource. In this instance, archaeology becomes translational, using advocacy for the resource to advocate for the community associated with the resource. These communities can vary in definition. Many definitions pertain to descendant communities, but as seen in this volume with Elizabeth D. Meade and Douglas Mooney's work with historic cemeteries, as well as that of Ana Edwards and Matthew R. Laird, the notion of community can be more expansive. This can include present-day communities that reside in the same location as the heritage site or communities that are not directly connected to the site through genealogy but through a larger diaspora for whom the site represents a history lost, forgotten, or erased. However, for most heritage sites, multiple communities with multiple voices are in dialogue. This is true in my work with the Tents, where dialogue is occurring among current and former Tents' members, former juvenile members, those related to members, others with memories connected to events at the physical space, neighbors, and many individuals directly connected to the history of the African diaspora.

Community-based archaeology emerged in the late twentieth century as a way to create a more democratic process of conducting archaeology with descendant groups, particularly Indigenous groups, who are directly connected to the research being conducted (Atalay 2012; Marshall 2002). These projects incorporate non-archaeological voices into the entire research project, making for a more democratic process of knowledge production of the past. Urban archaeology by necessity incorporates this broader notion of community, for archaeology within urban spaces takes place within communities living with these sites. Some members may have a direct link to the history these sites held through family, stories, or ownership of property, but others may have a more indirect link to a site with memories, events, and other actions tied to the sense of place. Some may not have any relationship at all, but the research in and of itself may impact them directly. We can see this especially with projects tied to historic preservation, heritage, placemaking, and maintenance—all of which directly tie people to place.

Emancipatory PAR methodology provides the framework for this translation from resource to people and is at the heart of the United Order of Tents project. PAR is a nontraditional research methodology designed for researchers and participants to work together in a collaborative research design to challenge inequities and strive for social change. Rather than telling, PAR seeks collaborative knowledge production. An emancipatory PAR method uses a critical theory paradigm (Jacobs 2018, 42) grounded in action and based on critiques of social inequities and structures of power in order to promote change (Jacobs 2018, 42).

Methodologically, much of what I bring to this discussion and the Tents project is based on historical research, early stages of ethnographic and oral history work, and historic preservation documentation. As a resident of Brooklyn and community member of Bed-Stuy, I also bring personal experience from living in the area and being witness to, as well as part of, the changing physical, social, and economic landscape. This includes my personal impact as a white woman on the gentrification process within the community, one complicated and exacerbated due to the recent COVID-19 pandemic. This personal connection to the area brings with it a responsibility to try and understand these processes and to address the dislocation associated with this changing landscape, including my own actions in this process. Lending my services and knowledge in historic preservation as a Friend to the Tents is part of the process of reflecting on my role within the gentrification process. What is this role? How can I contribute to the larger understanding of dislocation in urban settings and potential ways it can be mitigated or resisted? On a more personal note, I am a mother to a child with a multiracial ancestry, one tied directly to the African diaspora and Underground Railroad history, thereby in many ways connected to the larger legacy of the Tents. Thus, I feel a personal responsibility to understand and protect this history for her, to not only comprehend the intangible, but also actively preserve the tangible and its effect in the urbanization process. I strive to carry out my work with the Tents to preserve the tangible (their home at 87 MacDonough Street) and the intangible (their legacy) in light of these considerations, being continuously reflexive and mindful of my positionality within Bed-Stuy and racialized socioeconomic structures more broadly.

The Right to *Their* City

My approach in this chapter draws on David Harvey's notion of the right to the city, which is rooted in an anti-capitalist collective struggle pushing back against the forces of capitalist urbanization. It is this collective struggle I hope to build upon in this chapter using historic preservation and urban archaeology as a means for the collective to resist the racist urban planning initiatives that stem from capitalist urbanization. Bed-Stuy today faces a rapidly changing landscape due to the powers of gentrification. In addition to the longtime Black residents at risk of losing their homes, at stake are the places that hold history through memories and events embedded in the landscape. Much like New York City's African Burial Ground, the Tents' home serves as a symbol to the African American community, one whose history is steeped in mutual aid, community empowerment, and advocacy. With membership at an all-time low, and the building in need of repair, however, the Tents home and their organization is not immune to the risk of dislocation. In 2011/2012 the Tents sold the northern portion of its lot to a developer, and by 2014 a five story, twenty-eight-unit apartment building was erected in that spot, with studios starting at $2,000/month (Brownstoner 2014). The Tents sold this portion to raise funds to pay for the stabilization of the western wall of the house. While this kept one wall standing, the contractors did damage to the interior, and the sale erased any potential below-ground history from this portion of the lot, which once held the carriage house. This disastrous and heartbreaking episode shows the precarity of many community sites of memory. Can the right to preserve the Tents' legacy through preservation of place serve as a unifying symbol of empowerment for the community to claim its right to placemaking here as well?

What Is the Right to the City?

The right to the city is "the power of an idea of a new kind of urban politics that asserts that everyone, particularly the disenfranchised, not only has a right to the city, but as inhabitants, have a right to shape it, design it, and operationalize an urban human rights agenda" (Right to the City). As Robert Park (1967) and David Harvey (2003) have discussed, this right goes beyond citizens having access to the material attributes of urban space. "The right to the city is not merely a right of access to what already exists, but a right to change it after our heart's desire" (Harvey 2003, 939). Harvey (2003, 939) notes that this desire promotes creativity and destruction of urban spaces; essentially "the city is the historical site of creative destruction." This is the art of the process of urbanization at its core. It exceeds the material process of creating structures that shape urban space and into the actual lives of the people who live there.

Harvey (2003, 1–2) draws on the urban sociologist Robert Park (1967) in shaping this idea of the right to the city:

> "Man's most consistent and on the whole, his most successful attempt [is] to remake the world he lives in more after his heart's desire. But, if the city is the world which man created, it is the world in which he is henceforth condemned to live. Thus, indirectly, and without any clear sense of the nature of his task, in making the city man has remade himself." If Park is correct, then the question of what kind of city we want cannot be divorced from the question of what kind of people we want to be, what kinds of social relations we seek, what relations to nature we cherish, what style of daily life we desire, what kinds of technologies we deem appropriate, what aesthetic values we hold. The right to the city is, therefore, far more than a right of individual access to the resources that the city embodies: it is a right to change ourselves by changing the city more after our heart's desire.

The right to the city, therefore, is not just about creating, changing, destroying, and producing the physical aspects of the city but also the right to create oneself in the process and embody a space that reflects who we are. The created physical place of home, neighborhoods, and amenities exemplifies this embodiment as the built environment can reflect important collective cultural ideals through design and social use of space. Harvey ties the right to the city directly to the labor that produces urban spaces such as developers and contractors, but also the organizations and groups that provide the services that give life to the spaces produced.

Harvey's main arguments focus on the violence perpetrated to this right by capitalist urbanization of physical and relational space. Sotirios Frantzanas' (2014, 1074–75) review of Harvey's work explains Harvey's definition of capitalist urbanization as a "class phenomenon where the capitalist class uses predatory practices of exploitation and dispossession against vulnerable populations, reducing their capacity to sustain the necessary conditions for social reproduction." Frantzanas (2014, 1075) continues clarifying Harvey's notion of capitalist urbanization as "the better the common qualities a social group creates, the more likely it is to be raided and appropriated by private profit-maximizing interests. So those who had created interesting and vibrant neighbourhoods lose them, through the use of predatory practices, to upper class consumers and capitalists." Harvey calls for collective action to resist this dispossession. This type of dispossession by urbanization requires planning—planning the creation/destruction of the physical built environment as well as creation/destruction of the social networks—such as community-based organizations, local businesses, or community activities—that inhabit that environment. Urban planning can be designed and enforced by a few for maximum profit return. An alternative to this capitalist dispossession can be a collaborative means to a collective product. By listening to the needs of the community, and observing the social networks already in place, planners could build upon them to create a built environment that reflects not only the physical space needed and wanted but existing social networks as well.

Harvey (2008, 23) is explicit in stating that this right to the city is not an individual right but a collective one, building from Park's point that the kind of city we desire and want to interact with cannot be separated from the people we are and want to be: "The right to the city is . . . moreover, a collective rather than an individual right since changing the city inevitably depends upon the exercise of a collective power over the processes of urbanization. The freedom to make and remake ourselves and our cities is, I want to argue, one of the most precious yet most neglected of our human rights." This human right to the city has been claimed in a variety of ways, some more successful than others. In the late 1960s, Henri Lefebvre wrote about the use of this right by the physically marginalized and socioeconomically disenfranchised residents of a city to reclaim the services and resources of urban living that had been taken away or denied through means such as displacement to the periphery of the city. Others have taken and used the words "right to the city" as a rallying cry to not only reclaim physical space, as Lefebvre intended, but also demand changes to the process of urbanization through the social space, such as better education, transportation, and employment opportunities, within the urban sphere (Insensee 2013).

Two examples of claiming rights to cities bear discussion here, one from Brazil and one from New York City. An example of an initially successful collective claim that went awry can be seen in Brazil, where in 2001 the Right to the City was written into the federal law. While on paper it guaranteed the social over the commercial value of the land and democratic access for all to this urban space, in practice this pledge was not enforced. Contrary to the law, many socioeconomically poor communities were evicted for the planned development of structures for the 2014 World Cup (Insensee 2013). As with most policies, this one was only as strong as its enforcement. This is a cautionary tale or lesson learned: advocacy should not stop just because one's rights to claim the city are words written into law—they require vigilance.

Claims to one's right to the city have also been executed via heritage preservation efforts, where communities not only claim the physical space but also the historical, symbolic, and cultural components (see DeCesari and Herzfeld 2015). Perhaps one of the more well-known New York City examples is the African Burial Ground, excavated in 1991 and detailed in several contributions to this volume. Due to the persistence of community leaders, community descendants, and select archaeologists, this site was not only preserved and memorialized through the creation of a National Historic Landmark and interpretation center, but also fundamentally changed the way public archaeology was conducted and reshaped bioarchaeological methods surrounding the concept of race.

Moses to Bloomberg—Building a City on a History of Erasures

> When you operate in an overbuilt metropolis, you have to hack your way with a meat ax.
> —Robert Moses, 1954 (quoted in Caro 1974, 849)

New York City was founded on displacement and erasure. As Dutch and English colonial settlers embarked on a new beginning to expand their material and monetary horizons by creating New Amsterdam and then

New York, they did so by displacing the original inhabitants of the area, the Lenni Lenape. Just as the Dutch and the English prioritized New York City's landscape as a commodity to be used, modified, and consumed through various modes of extraction, the urban landscape continues to be commodified, with the added aspect of commodifying everything that lies on top of this landscape, including the built environment (Stein 2019). Removing people from their homes, the places with memories and meaning, seems to be another step in the capitalist pyramid upon which the city was built.

From Ruth Glass's (1964) coining of the term "gentrification" in the 1960s to explain the increase in middle-class residents displacing lower-class ones in urban neighborhoods, to Sharon Zukin's definition in the late 1980s as a process "of private-market investment capital into downtown districts of major urban centers" (Zukin 1987, 129), the term has migrated into public discourse including comedic sketches and has been the focus of many grassroots community movements. Most recently the term has been coupled with defining signifiers from various subareas, such as "green," "resiliency," and "preservation" (Denton 2019; Gould and Lewis 2018), describing the various causes of and effects on the wide variety of displacement processes. While the potentiality of green, resilient, or preservation-rooted projects leading to gentrification is tied to context, the unifying factor of them all is the planning policy that preceded them.

Many leaders in New York City have presided over urban planning through the years; however, no one personified the desire for prestige and wealth at the expense of others better than the twentieth-century public official Robert Moses. Moses worked in the New York City area from the 1920s to the 1970s, when New York City entered a severe economic crisis. While Moses never held an elected office, he was known as the "Master Builder" and later the "Power Broker" (see Caro 1974). Moses, like the Dutch and English colonial settlers before him, was a man yearning to extract material wealth and social prestige from the city. These projects were marketed "for the greater good" of society yet were conducted through racial capitalist mechanisms with little to no empathy for the lives of the displaced. This disregard is exemplified by Moses's order to build the Southern State Parkway bridges extra low to exclude those who commuted via bus—in other words, members of lower socioeconomic communities—from easy access to Jones Beach (Campanella 2017). A more notorious act of displacement, the creation of the Cross Bronx Expressway in the mid-twentieth century, intentionally displaced Black, Brown and working-class families and lowered property values, structurally sealing some in poverty. In response to Robert Caro's critique of him in *The Power Broker* (1974), Moses famously stated, "I raise my stein to the builder who can remove ghettos without moving people as I hail the chef who can make omelets without breaking eggs" (Boeing 2017, 1).

Jane Jacobs, the journalist and community activist who, in many ways, embodied the right to the city philosophy, mobilized communities to fight back against Moses's programs and claim a say in the development of their neighborhoods through protest and publicity in public space. Due to these collective pushbacks, several of his plans toward the end of his career were never realized. While he left a legacy of large public projects, that work also erased countless communities and city residents, displacing over 250,000 people from low-income tenements alone (Caro 1974,19).

The Real Estate State

While cities have always been in a cyclical creation/destruction process, urbanization in the twenty-first century seems to be accelerating, with the development of private property being the prime method to the madness. This push has given rise to what Samuel Stein terms the "Real Estate State," in which real estate is the "primary commodity, revenue stream, and political priority" within urban spaces (Stein 2019, 38). This commodification of land produces capital that feeds directly back into urbanization.

The role that the commodification of residential trends plays in displacement is a prominent discussion in gentrification debates (see Zukin 1987). This commodification has been recently witnessed in urban spaces like Williamsburg, Brooklyn, and the Lower East Side in Manhattan, two neighborhoods that became popular in the late-twentieth and early-twenty-first centuries with the influx of artists who moved there due to an availability of excess space at affordable or even free (squatters') prices. These artists were then displaced as real estate in these neighborhoods skyrocketed from the popularity the art scene brought to the area. That popularity did not form organically but rather was planned. Urban planners, developers, and others forecast a trend and marketed it, catering to the development of the physical space and not to the social networks that produce the life within the space, and (or while) promoting this development for the "betterment of society." With this *Field of Dreams* notion of development, "build it and they will come," supply exceeds demand, and we begin to see surplus real estate—particularly private as opposed to public residential space—and therefore more forced displacement of disenfranchised groups, erasing physical and social traces of once-collective communities.

This private property focus is evidenced in many of the historic preservation and environmental laws that developed in the middle of the twentieth century, which generally pertain to projects on public lands or using public funds, protecting the right of private property commodification. While they protect the private sphere from collective action, they also provide a space for public engagement, allowing communities to voice agreement or disagreement with the structural aspect of the urbanization process. The question remains whether historic preservation efforts are used as a means for communities to access the right to their portion of the city *or* if the process is too mired in discriminatory planning policy for this right to truly be claimed, leading only to gentrification and displacement.

Gentrification: Societal Myth and Economic Reality

> The mythology has it that gentrification is a process led by individual pioneers whose sweat equity, daring and vision are paving the way for those among us who are more timid. But . . . it is apparent that where urban pioneers venture, the banks, real estate companies, the state, or other collective economic actors have generally gone before.
> —Neil Smith, "Gentrification, the Frontier, and the Restructuring of Urban Space"

An increase in gentrification urged on by the late twentieth- and early twenty-first-century shifts in housing policy encouraged more private development with fewer funds supporting or creating public housing. This trend fostered not only a lack of affordable housing but also an increase in Airbnb rentals, displacing formerly affordable or middle-class apartment rentals.[3] This is an example of the market-based competition cycle at work. As housing policy shifted, outside investors purchased cheap property to flip and rent out at higher rates, increasing property taxes, which led residents to Airbnb their apartments to make more money to pay the higher property taxes. This cycle forced many longtime community members to relocate. While these neoliberal policies have been occurring for some time, no other political leadership embraced and marketed these changes to the public like billionaire philanthropist and former New York City Mayor Michael Bloomberg.

Mayor Bloomberg came into office months after 9/11 and his twelve-year term ended the year following Hurricane Sandy's landfall. These massive disasters provided the justification for Bloomberg's neoliberal planning policies that focused on remaking the city into a luxury destination, as can be seen in the rebuilding or creation of new buildings on the waterfront, despite climate crises issues like sea level rise and storm surge.

For example, the "$20 billion post–Sandy flood-prevention plan illogically calls for a 'Seaport City' to be built right into the East River" (Katch 2013).

Despite current Mayor Bill de Blasio's stance on spreading the wealth, his building and rebuilding of affordable housing are directly tied to Bloomberg's policies. Many current projects, while touting the terms "green," "resilient," and "sustainable" to the world community, are undertaken at the expense of erasing many who live in areas the projects are intended to help. These liminal spaces lie on the periphery—public housing on the waterfronts where the risk is higher and the need greater for climate change adaptive solutions—or in historic districts that may not be at a higher risk due to climate change but have been home for decades to disenfranchised communities living in the formerly unwanted historic housing stock. New or redeveloped privately funded luxury residential spaces are being built in these areas, creating new communities existing in all-encompassing residential silos, many demarcated not only by the model of car one drives but by the color of one's skin. Here, as seen historically, race intersects with the economic force behind the displacement and extraction processes at play both directly and indirectly.

Race, Class and Power: Redlining, White Flight, Urban Planning, and Historic Preservation

> White people do not have to expressly target black people in order to exploit them. They only have to locate their interests in private and public policies that have disparate impact. Freed from involvement in color-specific political decisions and specific acts of racial oppression, white Americans can more easily imagine the injustices of their society to be natural or irrational.
>
> —Craig Steven Wilder,
> *A Covenant With Color: Race and Social Power in Brooklyn*

As seen in New York City's planning policies—from the efforts of Moses in the twentieth century to the luxury developments spearheaded by Mayor Bloomberg in the twenty-first century—race and class are at the heart of the planning power dynamic at play on the urban landscape. These dynamics were evident in Bloomberg's "affordable" housing program, which actually decreased housing for low-income residents. The promise of affordability relied on building the real estate state, essentially by creating tax incentives for developers to make a percentage of units in new housing "affordable." The question is, affordable for whom? The guidelines for affordable housing in New York City allow it to be priced at a rate that is unaffordable for those in most need of housing. These spaces become investments, primarily for private profit, making the planning process for public space a mechanism of commodification and gentrification (Stein 2019, 39). Additionally, despite these so-called affordable housing developments, many of these areas become the most desirable places to live (gentrification), and rents and purchasing prices increase, while residents with lower incomes, particularly those on minimum wage struggle to make ends meet (Rodriguez 2013; Stein 2019).

These housing disparities can be seen throughout the city, but particularly in the highly desired borough of Brooklyn and the historically Black neighborhood of Bed-Stuy. This is illustrated in the rise in the median market-rate rent in Brooklyn, which increased by over 50 percent in less than ten years (Rodriguez 2013).[4] Bed-Stuy has ebbed and flowed throughout time with demographic and economic shifts. Some of these shifts included revitalization projects, such as those in the 1960s that produced new amenities for the neighborhood's constituents but did not address the issues of education, high unemployment, and high infant mortality rate. Redlining encouraged people to own homes in other neighborhoods or the suburbs, but only for those of a particular hue. By the late 1960s and into the 1970s, white flight driven by racist housing policies and urban renewal programs created a primarily Black community in Bed-Stuy, living in turn-of-the-century brownstones with little civic oversight—leading to the nickname "Do or Die Bed-Stuy."

Recently, there has been a shift in community makeup as gentrification and Airbnb usage increase; however, new ways for people to resist and counter these forced erasures have also emerged. Social media serves as a platform for resistance for many individuals to voice thoughts, opinions, and concerns. Facebook groups that may or may not require membership approval, like Bed-Stuy Friends or Bed-Stuy Parents group, have had many posts initiated by community members that have focused on gentrification, particularly around the neighborhood. These discussions have been instrumental in getting people to discuss displacement on a personal level as well as to post articles that highlight some of the predatory practices many developers and the city have used on older generations in the neighborhood (e.g., Culliton 2019). Many conversations focus on the racial disparities gentrification produces and less on the economic and planned forces behind much of the development. While individual developers may target specific homeowners, generally older longtime residents of color, they are working off sanctioned city planning efforts to redevelop areas of the city (e.g., Anderson 2013). These social media sites provide a collective space to voice, but not always a collective means of action to resist.

Some countermeasures can be seen in the arts and historic preservation efforts through citywide nonprofit groups that advocate for the preservation of historic properties, like the Historic Districts Council (HDC) or the Professional Archaeologists of New York City (PANYC) (Geismar, this volume). Additionally, historic sites and organizations that host events such as webinars on particular social justice topics or offer spaces to conduct more citizen science preservation efforts conduct advocacy through various modes of heritage management. Some occur through required national, state, and local historic preservation review processes enacted in new development. Others are promoted through public programs and engagement.

This is where an urban anthropological lens, particularly through historic preservation and archaeology, may be able to work to sustain the right to the city. Weeksville Heritage Center's June 2019 event on reparations and housing is a case in point. Free and open to the community, this event had a panel of local activists from organizations such as Equality for Flatbush and JACK, a performance venue dedicated to art and activism with a particular focus on reparations, as well as a Weeksville oral historian, to discuss the history of disempowerment and the case for reparations seen through a housing lens. As reparations is seen as restorative justice, the question posed by the oral historian was, what period are we trying to reclaim? And with the reclaiming of a neighborhood in a particular time by a particular group, are we stating that space is a commodity—one that can be claimed, lost, and reclaimed? Comments emerged on collective land purchasing, which poetically is exactly how Weeksville was first established and supplies a model of how heritage and historic preservation could provide a means for communities to claim their right to the city.

Urban Heritage, Archaeology, and Advocacy

Evidenced by the saving of Washington Square Park in Manhattan in the mid-1950s is a notion that heritage and preservation are alternative forms of urban planning that can (though do not always) demand a pause to consider history, the meaning of place, and the embodied presence of social networks in the way urban spaces are made. Preservation bolsters abstract claims to the right to the city with the specific stories, places, and people that matter, yoking the sociological aspects of place with the geographical and one's right to both. This builds on what David Harvey (2009, 23–24) has called the "spatial consciousness" or "geographical imagination." As Harvey (2009, 24) unfolds this idea, this consciousness or imagination "enables the individual to recognize the role of space and place in his biography, to relate to the spaces he sees around him, and to recognize how transactions between individuals and between organizations are affected by the space that separates them." It links individuals to surrounding geography, building their biography and creation of self, which in turn links groups of individuals to place through social networks and the built environment—placemaking. It is this connection to place that enables people to use preservation as a means to claim their right to the city. As Gilmore (2008) has illustrated through her work in fighting the prison industrial complex in California, the environmental review process, in which many historic preservation projects lie, can be a space for community voices to be heard and actions taken.

What Is Abolitionist Geography?

In the Black radical tradition, W. E. B DuBois's notion of abolition democracy influenced Ruth Wilson Gilmore (2018), noted urban geographer, professor, activist, and co-founder of many grassroots organizations that focus on social justice. She uses the modern prison system to explore the institution of carceral geographies through a racial capitalist lens but makes clear that this is not the only way to use the concept and encourages conceptual reimaginings (Gilmore 2018). Abolitionist geography starts with the premise that freedom is place—geography that "understands freedom as a provisional place or as one built by people with their resources at hand" (Gilmore 2018, 57). Rather than erase and forget the divisive past, one "build[s] the future from the present, in all the ways that we can" (Gilmore 2018, 14). In essence, it advocates dismantling oppressive institutions through the action of placemaking. The Tents' heritage is built on processes focused on access to their historic narratives, particularly ones that have been lost, forgotten, or erased. Building on Gilmore's notion of abolitionist geography, the Tents' heritage is placemaking in the present built on the acrimonious past of confinement and forced mobility through urban policies such redlining, racial covenants, and gentrification. It is abolitionist heritage.

Within New York City, there are several historical archaeological examples associated with communities that collectively mobilized to fight against destruction of the site. Most notably is the African Burial Ground located in Lower Manhattan, whose archaeological excavation ignited a response from various communities situated within the African diaspora, resulting not only in re-writing an aspect of Black history that had been erased from the landscape through decades of building directly on top of ancestral resting grounds, but also in forcing archaeology as a discipline to rewrite how it works with communities. For purposes of this chapter, I will highlight two other examples in New York City: 227 Duffield Street and the Weeksville Heritage Center, both located in the borough of Brooklyn.

#BlackLandmarksMatter: 227 Duffield Street

A recent site that has captured the public eye and sparked outrage is a three-story Greek-revival row house located at 227 Duffield Street in Brooklyn, New York. Located on a block that was designated in 2007 as "Abolitionist Row" due to the amount of abolitionist activity that took place here in the nineteenth century, 227 Duffield is the last surviving structure with links to this history and was threatened by demolition as part of the ongoing renewal of downtown Brooklyn initiated by the Bloomberg administration. The physical links are tentative in that the "significance" of the site cannot be "corroborated" by direct physical material evidence. Additionally, the building has been renovated so much that it is not considered to have "integrity." Yet the emotive links to the past have integrity and have sparked public outcry and protests with the slogan "Black History Matters." This outcry proved fruitful, for the Landmarks Preservation Commission voted to landmark the property in February 2021. It was purchased by the city one month later. In the words from DeBlasio's briefing on the purchase, to be "protected and celebrated for a very long time" (Gannon 2021b) (Figure 5.3).

As Jeremy Wells (2011, 13) has articulated, the evaluation of a site's "significance" for the National Register of Historic Places is based only on sensorial observations, ignoring other aspects such as experiential and cultural significance associated with the property. Preservation standards need to move beyond a primarily visual evaluation based on empiricist criteria and employ more of a holistic view of what is considered "significant." Michael Allen (2016, 47) similarly challenges historic preservation initiatives by stating "we need to abandon the historicizing motivations that seek easy emblems for eras, styles, and building types; and we need to listen to and support communities that ask open questions about the future of sites, not walk away when communities choose preservation plans that do not fit our models."

Christopher Matthews (2020) recently discussed the necessity of centering people within these communities and their needs in the historic designation process. Matthews uses George Lipsitz's (1998) notion of the "possessive investment in whiteness" to illustrate how white racial privi-

Figure 5.3. 227 Duffield Street, Brooklyn, NY, protest. *Left:* 227 Duffield Street front facade. *Right:* Author's daughter at protest to save the building. 2019. © Kelly M. Britt.

lege has permeated all aspects of American culture, both material and social. "The point here is that historic preservation not only reinforces racist practices that have barred people of color from fair access to the material benefits of whiteness, it also celebrates property ownership and thus very much embodies the post–World War II racism that defines the urban-suburban landscape of the United States" (Matthews 2020, 59). Matthews (2020, 59) counters the National Trust for Historic Preservation's *Preservation for the People,* which still adheres to many of these "reinforced racial practices," and provides a hypothetical counter preservation framework—a People's Preservation. This framework does not see the quality or integrity of a building as the only aspects worthy of preservation, but rather considers the ways that many of the buildings and places within the community continue to serve it despite challenges and the erasure of historic narratives (Matthews 2020, 59).

In the 227 Duffield Street example, communities did choose preservation and made their voices heard. While this site was denied landmark status several times through New York City's LPC process, it was finally granted status in February 2021. This victory came after a long advocacy campaign supported by various local groups such as Brooklyn Anti-gentrification Network and by individual residents. The public hearing for landmarking this property took place in July 2020, at the height of the COVID-19 pandemic and after the recent brutal murders of George Floyd, Ahmaud Arbery, and Breonna Taylor, when #BLM protests were taking place throughout New York City. Despite or maybe because the hearing was held on Zoom, "more than 40 people spoke in favor of landmarking 227 Duffield, including Attorney General Letitia James, Council Member Stephen Levin, and several preservation and racial justice advocacy groups, and over 80 letters in support of designation were submitted" (Gannon 2021a). Of these forty people who spoke, several were archaeologists, including myself, Cheryl LaRoche, and Joan Geismar (from this volume). Since designation, the city purchased the property for $3.2 million (Gannon 2021b) to ensure protection. Possible interpretation of local Underground Railroad history may be forthcoming. In its long quest for preservation landmark status, 227 Duffield Street illustrates not only how important historic Black sites of resistance are to a community, but also how historic preservation can be a form of reparations of sorts within the urbanization process by claiming the right of heritage placemaking. However, I do question whether this site would have been granted landmark status without the public outcry against police brutality and systematic racism. Time will tell if LPC's decision was just a response to friction or indeed a shift in local preservation philosophy.

Weeksville Heritage Center, Brooklyn, NY

Weeksville Heritage Center, located on the border of the Bed-Stuy and Crown Heights neighborhoods, provides a model of how heritage can shape the community, how the community can shape heritage, and how individuals can work collectively to claim their right to the city. Weeksville was a nineteenth-century free Black community that managed to withstand the phases of urban transformation to the landscape that other communities did not. It was started by James Weeks, an African American from Virginia who purchased the land in 1838 from another free African American land investor. The act of owning land was a form of resistance and activism, for in New York, men of color could only vote if they owned and paid taxes on $250 worth of land. Weeksville, as it became known, developed into a thriving community of free Black investors and activists (Figure 5.4).

As Brooklyn was incorporated into New York City in 1898 and the neighborhood grew, Weeksville's legacy continued locally but drifted from the larger public consciousness. In 1968, historian James Hurley along with

Figure 5.4. Historic Hunterfly Road Houses, Weeksville Heritage Center, Brooklyn, NY. 2017. © Kelly M. Britt.

several other preservation-minded citizens mobilized and created the Society for the Preservation of Weeksville and Bedford-Stuyvesant History, now known as Weeksville Heritage Center. With Hurley's rediscovery of the Historic Hunterfly Row Houses of Weeksville, the organization focused on documenting the history of the community through archaeology and archival research on the Weeksville Gardens site, which was threatened by urban renewal. (Weeksville Heritage Center). The public archaeology project, which involved the neighborhood residents, provided the material evidence that served as the impetus for LPC to work to preserve Weeksville.

Due to the preservation efforts of the community and local leaders, the Historic Hunterfly Row Houses were placed in a National Register Historic District and were listed as a New York City landmark in the 1970s. Since then, several archaeological investigations have been conducted by academics and cultural resource management firms. The archaeological and historic research provided a space for community engagement with their past. It bridged the individual and collective past and present while looking toward the future, both socially (how this historical information shapes people's identities) as well as geographically (how this manifest through space and the making of place). Through the work of preservationists, historians, archaeologists, community members, and activists, the Historic Hunterfly Row Houses were saved, restored, and interpreted as part of Weeksville Heritage Center. This center is now a multidisciplinary museum whose mission is not only to preserve and interpret the history of Weeksville but also to encourage current uses of Black history in education, the arts, and civic engagement (Weeksville 2019).

While Weeksville Heritage Center has been successful in its mission, in early 2019 it faced a financial crisis and almost shut its doors due to budgetary constraints. As it did in the 1970s, the community once again came together to support this center of heritage. Within nineteen days of crowdsourcing requests, it surpassed its goal of $200,000 in donations and city support. Additionally, City Council Member Robert Cornegy Jr. rallied with other city officials to nominate Weeksville Heritage Center for the Cultural Institutions Group (CIG), a group of thirty-three organizations on city-owned property that receive consistent municipal funding (Spivack 2019). This nomination was accepted, making Weeksville the first historically Black CIG in Brooklyn. These actions speak to the place heritage plays in a community's identity. The interwoven fabric of past and present plays an active role in the community's civic engagement with resisting unwanted urbanization. While this neighborhood is rapidly gentrifying, using historic preservation as a tool of resistance, community members were able to claim their right to the city and design an urban space that holds meaning to the members who live in and use that space.

While not all historic preservation efforts have outcomes that have resisted displacement (see Brown-Saracino 2010; De Cesari and Dimova 2019; Listokin et al. 1998; McCabe and Ellen 2016; Smith 1998), there is a growing awareness of the role preservationists can have in the process, and the need for preservationists to become activists, particularly anti-gentrification ones (Sanchez 2016). This call for advocacy is rooted in the need to preserve the tangible structures that history has created *and* the intangible networks people have in these spaces. With that call to action, Weeksville provides a beacon of hope and a model for the Tents to look to for guidance as they move forward with their preservation efforts just blocks away.

Epilogue: Claiming One's Right:
An Abolitionist Heritage—The United Order of Tents

This chapter highlights race, gentrification, and resistance, focusing on how an understanding of the intersection of historic and current housing policies and race illustrates the power dynamics at hand. This can be seen as a form of slow violence, which environmental scholar Rob Nixon (2013, 2) defines as "violence that occurs gradually and out of sight; a delayed destruction often dispersed across time and space." It also sheds light on the resistance movement to gentrification that is growing in Brooklyn, and Bed-Stuy more specifically, and the role archaeology and historic preservation can play in this movement through community-led placemaking. Additionally, this chapter initiates an investigation of community-supported placemaking in the historically Black neighborhood of Bed-Stuy as a response to these latest waves of displacement. The questions that thread throughout this chapter include: As the community grows a larger historic district, and historic structures become a material outgrowth of community identity, can community-led heritage and heritage management play a role in the social sustainability of this community? Or will it contribute to the gentrification process? Can archaeology and historic preservation processes and policies provide the space between an idea (urban planning) and action (physical construction) for communities to claim what Lefebvre and Harvey have called their "right to the city"? Or can they serve as a means to achieve Ruth Wilson Gilmore's notion of abolitionist geography (or abolitionist heritage)? And if so, what do these processes look like today in New York City?

An Equitable Future? Or a Displaced Dystopia?

Jane Jacobs's (1961, 238) idea that "cities have the capability of providing something for everybody, only because, and only when, they are created by everybody" is theoretically possible, but it requires that people regain or retain their "right to the city." If we become completely obedient communities not looking for those spaces to question authority and not taking advantage of the places of freedom—essentially those places between plan and action—we could be led like zombies down the neoliberal path to urbanization (Monbiot 2016). This same prospect holds true within the discipline of archaeology. As our world outside the discipline shifts, so too should we and the nature of archaeology. Archaeology does not need to be a discipline that only looks to the past for better understanding of that past, but can also be used as a tool to situate the present and to shape the future.

After the Facebook postings and the fake Zillow ad were removed, the Tents and Friends of the Tents (of which I am a member) put together a public event to bring some of the histories of this organization to the larger public. The event took place in March 2021 in celebration of Women's History Month and was hosted by the Brooklyn Public Library's Macon Street

Branch African American Heritage Center, a local library within the neighborhood of Bed-Stuy. While we expected many community members to join, the unexpected Tweet before the event by Erica Buddington from the Langston League,[5] highlighting the Tents organization, its history, and the upcoming event, went viral. Registration for the event went from forty to 450 almost overnight. By the weekend of the event, over 650 people were registered and on the day of, close to two hundred connected through Zoom and stayed with the panel of speakers from the Tents, Friends of Tents, and community representatives for over an hour and a half. Thanks to the work of undergraduate student Julia Leedy, an intern with the Tents through Brooklyn College, the Tents have a website where people could follow up, and membership requests and additional inquiries on how to help started to come in.

It is too early to determine whether the *structural* preservation will provide the needed *social* preservation of the Black community to fight back the waves of gentrification that at times feel like tsunamis. Racial and economic inequities that have historically divided continue to divide. However, in keeping with Gilmore's idea of freedom as a provisional space actively built by people with resources they have and Harvey's notion of the right to the city, and with the New York African Burial Ground, 227 Duffield Street, and Weeksville Heritage Center serving as role models, historic preservation and urban community-based archaeology may provide a space for the community to claim its right to the city, offering a space of freedom and purposeful placemaking long-denied. For Bed-Stuy and Brooklyn, only time will tell if this rings true.

Acknowledgments

I am deeply grateful to all the people that have helped assist this project along its journey, particularly Dr. Robyn Spencer for her generous words of wisdom and support. Dr. Spencer along with Dr. Safiya Bandele were instrumental in initiating the Friends of the Tents. Several undergraduate and graduate students from CUNY and Columbia University (now at UCLA) have worked with me and the United Order of Tents in myriad ways and have been instrumental in helping me gather data, particularly Scott Ferrara, Madison Aubey, and Julia Leedy, and students from my 2019, 2020, and 2021 ANTH 3420 Urban Archaeology course, whose research projects always brought new insights to the understanding of the history of the Tents home. I am also forever grateful to the Brooklyn Public Library, especially Nicole Bryan, the Macon Branch Supervisor, and Sheena Miller, formerly with the African American Heritage Center for being so supportive and hosting the 2021 talk connecting the Tents with the community. Additionally, I would like to thank CUNY's Professional Staff Congress, the Tow Faculty Research Grant, and the LaundroMat Project Create and Connect fund for funding to help support this project. My deepest gratitude though goes to the amazing women of the United Order of Tents Eastern District #3, particularly, Mrs. Essie Gregory, president of the executive board, for coming to my classes for oral history interviews, working directly with students to help create a Tent's website, co-writing an article, and welcoming me as a Friend of the Tents. I truly value the friendship that has blossomed and treasure it deeply.

Kelly M. Britt, PhD, RPA is an Associate Professor of Anthropology at Brooklyn College whose research focuses on community-based historical archaeology of urban spaces. She completed her PhD in Anthropology from Columbia University in 2009 and spent seven years at FEMA as their Regional II Archaeologist before joining Brooklyn College.

Notes

1. See website for The Great Gotham Challenge: https://info.ggc.nyc/.
2. Since the initial writing of this piece, the Tents obtained 501(c)(3) status in 2022.
3. According to New York City's 2018 Housing Supply Report, half of the Airbnb listings in 2016 were concentrated in seven neighborhoods in Manhattan and Brooklyn. In these seven neighborhoods, rents rose between 21.4 percent and 62.6 percent between 2009 and 2016, with 10.7 percent to 21.6 percent of the increase attributed to Airbnb (New York City Rent Guidelines Board 2018, 10).
4. Rents went from $925 to $1,400 from 2002 to 2011.
5. The Langston League is a "multi-consultant curriculum firm that specializes in teaching educators how to create culturally responsive and sustaining instructional material, for all students" (http://www.langstonleague.com/).

References

Allen, Michael. 2016. "What Historic Preservation Can Learn from Ferguson." In *Bending the Future*, edited by Max Page and Marla Miller, 44–48. Amherst: University of Massachusetts Press.
Anderson, Kelly, dir. 2012. *My Brooklyn*. New Day Films. Film/https://www.newday.com/films/my-brooklyn.

Atalay, Sonya. 2012. *Community-Based Archaeology: Research with, by, and for Indigenous and Local Communities*. Berkeley: University of California Press.

Boeing, Geoff. 2017. *We Live in a Motorized Civilization: Robert Moses Replies to Robert Caro*. Berkeley: Department of City and Regional Planning, University of California Berkeley.

Britt, Kelly M., and Essie Gregory. 2019. "Clubhouse Excavation: The United Order of Tents." *Dilettante Army*. http://www.dilettantearmy.com/articles/united-order-of-tents.

Brooklyn Anti-Gentrification Network website. https://bangentrification.org/.

Brown-Saracino, Japonica, ed. 2010. *The Gentrification Debates: A Reader*. New York: Routledge.

Brownstoner. 2014. "Rental Building on Former Order of Tents Property Just About Done." 26 June 2014. https://www.brownstoner.com/brooklyn-life/rental-building-on-former-order-of-tents-property-just-about-done/.

Campanella, Thomas J. 2017. "How Low Did He Go?" *CityLab*. https://www.citylab.com/transportation/2017/07/how-low-did-he-go/533019/.

Caro, Robert. 1974. *The Power Broker: Robert Moses and the Fall of New York*. New York: Alfred A. Knopf.

Culliton, Kathleen. 2019. "Bed-Stuy Man Tricked into Selling Home at Block Party." *Patch*, 25 June 2019. https://patch.com/new-york/bed-stuy/bed-stuy-man-tricked-selling-home-block-party-bp?utm_source=facebook.com&utm_medium=social&utm_term=real+estate&utm_campaign=autopost&utm_content=bed-stuy&fbclid=IwAR2hpESKZgAXuRCgFvZHCQh8WTppdG6OwWHCdQsRs0bO0IN7KqvgERoYF7o.

De Cesari, Chiara, and Michael Herzfeld. 2015. "Urban Heritage and Social Movements." In *Global Heritage, A Reader*, edited by Lynn Meskell, 171–95. New York: Wiley-Blackwell.

De Cesari, Chiara and Rozita Dimova. 2019. "Heritage, Gentrification, Participation: Remaking Urban Landscapes in the Name of Culture and Historic Preservation." *International Journal of Heritage Studies* 25 (9): 863–69. DOI: 10.1080/13527258.2018.1512515.

Denton, Jack. 2019. "Is Landmarking a Tool of Gentrification or a Bulwark Against It?" *Pacific Standard*, 3 July 2019. https://psmag.com/economics/is-landmarking-a-tool-of-gentrification-or-a-bulwark-against-it.

Frantzanas, Sotirios. 2014. "The Right to the City as an Anti-Capitalist Struggle: Review of Rebel Cities: From the Right to the City to the Urban Revolution." *Ephemera Journal*. http://www.ephemerajournal.org/sites/default/files/pdfs/contribution/14-4frantzanas.pdf.

Gannon, Devon. 2021a. "19th-Century Abolitionist Home in Downtown Brooklyn Is Now a City Landmark." *6sqft*, 2 February 2021. https://www.6sqft.com/historic-abolitionist-home-in-downtown-brooklyn-may-become-city-landmark/.

———. 2021b. "New York City Buys Downtown Brooklyn's Abolitionist Rowhouse for $3.2M." *6sqft*, 15 March 2021. https://www.6sqft.com/new-york-city-buys-abolitionist-rowhouse-in-downtown-brooklyn/.

Gilmore, Ruth Wilson. 2008. "Forgotten Places and Seeds of Grassroots Planning." *Engaging Contradictions Theory, Politics, and Methods of Activist Scholarship*, edited by Charles R Hale, 31–61. Berkeley: University of California Press.

———. 2018. "Making Abolition Geography in Southern California: Interview with Ruth Wilson Gilmore, interview with Léopold Lambert." *The Funambulist: Politics of Space and Bodies* 21, 14–19.

Glass Ruth Lazarus. 1964. *London: Aspects of Change*. Vol. 3. London: Centre for Urban Studies and MacGibbon and Kee.

Gould, Kenneth A., and Tammy L. Lewis. 2018. "From Green Gentrification to Resilience Gentrification: An Example from Brooklyn." *City and Community* 17 (1): 12–15. https://doi.org/10.1111/cico.12283.

Great Gotham Challenge. https://info.ggc.nyc/.

Harvey, David. 2003. "The Right to the City." *International Journal of Urban and Regional Research* 27 (4): 939–41

———. 2008. "The Right to the City." *New Left Review* 53 (September–October), 23–40.

———. 2009. *Social Justice and the City.* Athens: University of Georgia Press.
Insensee, Patrick. 2013. "What is the Right to the City?" *RioOnWatch.* https://www.rioonwatch.org/?p=11668.
Jacobs, Jane. 1961. *The Death and Life of Great American Cities.* New York: Random House.
Jacobs, Steven Darryl. 2018. "A History and Analysis of the Evolution of Action and Participatory Action Research." *Canadian Journal of Action Research* 19 (3), 34–52.
Katch, Danny. 2014. "Mayor Michael Bloomberg: A depreciation." In *Internationalist Socialist Review* 90. https://isreview.org/issue/90/mayor-michael-bloomberg-depreciation.
Lefebvre, Henri. 1968. *Le Droit à la ville.* Paris: Anthropos.
Listokin, David, Barbara Listokin, and Michael Lehr. 1998. "Contributions of Historic Preservation to Housing and Economic Development." *Housing Policy Debate* 9 (3), 431–78.
Lipsitz, George. 1998. *The Possessive Investment in Whiteness: How White People Profit from Identity Politics.* Philadelphia: Temple University Press.
Marshall, Yvonne. 2002. "What is Community Archaeology?" *World Archaeology* 34 (2), 211–19.
Matthews, Christopher. 2020. "A People's Preservation: Urban Erasures in Essex County, NJ." *Journal for the Anthropology of North America* 23 (1), 47–66.
McCabe, Brian J., and Ingrid Gould Ellen. 2016. "Does Preservation Accelerate Neighborhood Change? Examining the Impact of Historic Preservation in New York City." *Journal of American Planning Association* 82 (2): 134–46.
Monbiot, George. 2016. "Neoliberalism—the Ideology at the Root of All Our Problems." *The Guardian.* https://www.theguardian.com/books/2016/apr/15/neoliberalism-ideology-problem-george-monbiot.
New York City Rent Guidelines Board. 2018. "Housing Supply Report." *New York City Government Website.* https://www1.nyc.gov/assets/rentguidelinesboard/pdf/18HSR.pdf.
Nixon, Rob. 2013. *Slow Violence and the Environmentalism of the Poor.* Cambridge, MA: Harvard University Press.
Park, Robert. 1967. *On Social Control and Collective Behavior.* Chicago: Chicago University Press.
Right to the City. https://righttothecity.org/about/mission-history/.
Rodriguez, Cindy. 2013. "As Bloomberg Built Affordable Housing, City Became Less Affordable." *WNYC News.* https://www.wnyc.org/story/304422-new-york-remade-city-more-desirable-ever-also-too-expensive-many/.
Sanchez, Graciela Isabel. 2016. "Preservationists Must be Anti-Gentrification Activists." In *Bending the Future: 50 Ideas for the Next 50 Years of Historic Preservation in the United States,* edited by Max Page and Marla R. Miller, 214–218. Amherst: University of Massachusetts Press.
Smith, Neil. 1998. "Comment on David Listokin, Barbara Listokin and Michael Lahr's 'The Contributions of Historic Preservation to Housing and Economic Development' Historic Preservation in a Neoliberal Age." *Housing Policy Debate* 9 (3): 479–85.
———. 2013. "Gentrification, the Frontier, and the Restructuring of Urban Space." In *Gentrification of the City,* edited by N. Smith and P. Williams, 15–34. London: Allen and Unwin.
Spivack, Caroline. 2019. "Brooklyn's Cash-Strapped Weeksville Heritage Center Surpassing Fundraising Goal." *Curbed New York.* https://ny.curbed.com/2019/5/20/18632349/brooklyn-crown-heights-weeksville-heritage-center-fundraising.
Stein, Samuel. 2019. *Capital City: Gentrification and the Real Estate State.* New York: Verso.
United Order of Tents. *History of the United Order of Tents J.R. Giddings and Jolliffe Union.*
Weeksville Heritage Center. https://www.weeksvillesociety.org/
———. 2019. "What We Do: Document. Preserve. Interpret." https://www.weeksvillesociety.org/our-vision-what-we-do.
Wells, Jeremy. 2011. Historic Preservation, Significance and Phenomenology." *Environmental & Architectural Phenomenology* 22 (1), 13–15.

Wilder, Craig Steve. 2001. *A Covenant With Color: Race and Social Power in Brooklyn*. New York: Columbia University Press.
Zukin, Sharon. 1987. "Gentrification: Culture and Capital in the Urban Core." *Annual Review of Sociology* 13, 129–47.

Chapter 6

"Think Like a Historical Archaeologist"
Moving Beyond the Primary Source Document in K–12 Education

Elizabeth Martin

Introduction

As historical archaeologists, we understand the situated and partial nature of archives, and their power to marginalize and erase populations. After years of working in education across all grade levels in New York City, I had started to come to terms with the primacy of the documentary record in public-school classrooms to the exclusion of nontextual material culture while gently promoting my own beliefs in the strengths and importance of material culture studies and landscape and historical archaeology. However, upon learning about the various curricula offered to social studies teachers, such as "Thinking like an Historian" from the Stanford History Education Group (SHEG), I began to envision a way that I could more effectively advocate for the richness of the material past while also aiding student engagement in their own learning. This chapter will present that approach, describing the current state of the social studies curriculum in New York State, advocating for change, and presenting a different data set for educators throughout the country to use. The value of introducing this new approach lies both in helping kindergarten (K) through grade twelve learners in the present by better preparing them

---

Notes for this chapter begin on page 143.

with the knowledge and skills they will need for college or whatever postsecondary-school future they envision, and in helping postsecondary educators gather knowledge about their students before they meet them in a college or university setting. Ultimately, the value of this new approach is in educating with equity and in producing graduates who can think critically and constructively about the past and the future.

While this chapter utilizes my experiences specifically in New York, the country as a whole has largely adopted the Common Core Learning Standards (CCLS),[1] standardizing learning goals for all students in K through twelve. While testing is not mandated by the CCLS, it is mandated by the federal government, and the CCLS have become connected to high-stakes testing in all states (with the exception of Nebraska). Because this educational model is so widely used across the country, the ideas proposed in this chapter are relevant to many state curricula beyond New York, even if they vary somewhat from those described here. While there are exceptions, the vast majority of public K through twelve education only provides the historians' perspective in a social studies class even though *social studies* is supposed to be a diverse package of varied humanities-based perspectives.

Unfortunately, these tools have not closed the achievement gap, which requires addressing the inequities students face outside of the classroom as well as inside. In 2019, WBEZ in Chicago reported that "school districts that are well-resourced—and that have typically been high-achieving—continue to score well under the Common Core exams. But many districts that have majority low-income students, and that have typically performed below the state average, continue to be low-performing" (An and Cardona-Maguidad 2019). Until COVID-19 upended education, New York City's Department of Education (NYCDOE) used a student's test scores for admissions to gifted and talented programs, which in turn created a culture of private tutoring and test prep centers for those who could afford it. While the president of the United States has decided to reinstate state testing, New York City has recently changed the admissions process for all public schools, removing the state test score requirement due to the inequities in opportunities offered to low-income and immigrant students laid bare by COVID-19. I offer this analysis while experiencing the reality of teaching right now, during the two years of COVID-19, but students who speak English as a second language or have been disenfranchised from their education by economic and racial biases in our society have always struggled with social studies classes. These changes to the city's admissions process have long been sought by advocates for the desegregation of the New York City public-school system.

Additionally, a New York educator's individual rating is still partially dependent upon the number of students who pass the Regents or other state tests.[2] This does not encourage an "out-of-the-box" curriculum. Instead, teachers must focus most of their time on subjects that appear on these tests. Although many argue that the tests are truly a measure of what a person should know to succeed in life, in reality they do not allow for all students to gain this success. The standardized tests work for some of the students inculcated into white middle class American culture at a young age, with no interruptions in their education and a home that is not food-insecure, yet the majority of our students do not fit that bill.

If we want to bring equity to our society, there are three related things we must do: broaden the official umbrella of the social studies curriculum; allow for more flexibility in testing; and move beyond the primacy of document-based research. MA programs for social studies education teach that "social studies" includes all humanities (history, geography, political science, anthropology, sociology, psychology, and economics) but most K through twelve curricula do not teach more than history. Geographical skills are side-lined and, often, government and economics are brought into classrooms only in twelfth grade, after the tests are taken. Sociology, psychology, anthropology? Never. Students have to pass tests, and the tests only ask history-based questions, labeled "DBQs" (document-based questions), that focus mainly on document-based archival material. Curriculum packages such as Thinking Like a Historian tailor curricula to this test, which in turn limits the scope of topics taught in the classroom. Bringing the technical skills and subject matter of historical archaeology into our public-school classrooms could aid in making education more diverse and more equitable for all students in the system.

I advocate here for bringing historical archaeology into the social studies classroom as it will offer students the twenty-first century skills that our country's learning standards require. By sticking solely to the documentary record, we reiterate the narrative constructed by those (white men) traditionally in power. By using the historical archaeological resources from within the multitudes of our local built environments, we can offer students a critical view of such a historical narrative. The work of the historical archaeologist is to uncover such a narrative, critique its purpose, and offer an alternative to the past lived experience that is not rooted in the dominant narrative that particular documents often construct. These critical-thinking skills are some of the most important ones we can offer to students in the social studies classroom in order to help them succeed in the twenty-first-century world.

Mixed Messages for Educators:
Constructivism in the Classroom vs. Common Core Learning Standards (CCLS) and College-Ready Skills

The New York State Education Department (NYSED) has two mandates for educators: use of student-centered project-based learning (PBLs) and assessment of that learning through standardized testing that matches the CCLS. The first mandate has many positives while the second is more problematic. Important early-twentieth-century research on childhood psychological development by Jean Piaget and Lev Vygotsky, along with educator John Dewey (McLeod 2019; Stuckart 2018), has been introduced into classroom experiences. As theorized in education, constructivism is meant to treat the student as more than a passive learner; rather students are regarded as playing a constructive role in their own lives.[3] The more they are given the opportunity to build their own knowledge, the more they learn. "Constructivism's central idea is that human learning is constructed, that learners build new knowledge upon the foundation of previous learning. Learning is an active and social process" (McLeod 2019). As John Dewey explains, the act of doing (practice) teaches students more than rote memorization. For him, doing is learning. This type of educational practice may be familiar from Waldorf and Montessori schools but it is fairly new to public schools. The process is key—making meaning does not happen if students are passive learners. Inquiry-driven, student-centered lessons are the new norm for the classroom experience. And classroom instruction mostly matches this theory-driven structure now. Students are learning through practice and imagination, and many classrooms are joyful places throughout the full day of school. While the CCLS have changed as result of this theoretical approach, the state's standardized Regents tests in no way reflect the constructivism for which developmental psychologists have advocated.

Unfortunately, educators are being given a conflicting mandate. As described in the Common Core State Standards, CCLS are designed to prepare students for life "outside the classroom." The standards teach "critical reading, . . . cogent reasoning and use of evidence that is essential to both private deliberation and responsible citizenship in a democratic republic." (CCSSI 2010, 3). The standards lay out a vision of what it means to be a literate person prepared for success in the twenty-first century (Table 1). The CCLS goals conflict, however, with the mandate for problem-based learning (PBL). Education departments teach future educators that there are four types of learners: visual, auditory, reading/writing, and kinesthetic, and that teaching real-world PBLs in classrooms helps all of these types (see Malvik 2020). Regardless of the fact that the anthropologist in me believes that all humans are, in fact, kinesthetic or tactile learners in addition to whatever else they may be, with teachers primarily focusing on what is covered by the standardized test, they rarely have time to branch out into real problem-based learning based in constructivist theory. Thus, the PBL projects often become something like "Write an op-ed endorsing a presidential candidate from the 1860 election." The assignments fit in with the document-based questions (DBQs) that students must learn in order to pass, but teachers are forced to manipulate tasks to look "real world." The teacher is placed between a rock and a hard place—making learning accessible to all students and ensuring that they pass a test that is not actually accessible to all students.

Teachers must support both of these often-contradictory mandates: engage students with PBL, which has lessons that can connect to the world outside the classroom, while also teaching to a test that is supposed to prove both student literacy and teacher effectiveness at once. When one examines the student body throughout the state, there is a clear segregation for success here. *All* students can learn to write op-eds, grow hydroponic vegetables, or create renewable energy, but they cannot all translate this knowledge into scores on the Regents exams. These exams prioritize students who have had a stable educational history and family life, as well as English as a first language, while the problem-based work discussed above helps more students with college-readiness and twenty-first century skills in general.

There is a constant push and pull between the needs of the student and the test results. For example, a New School study for New York City public schools told educators that to focus "most heavily on the demands of standardized testing is of only limited use in a world where deeper academic preparation and critical thinking are prized by colleges and employers" (Nauer et al. 2013). There are mixed messages for teachers here. First, teachers need to help students pass tests based on memorization of test-taking strategies while also becoming analytical, critical, and evaluative of the world around so they can take these skills beyond the classroom and succeed by becoming a helpful and beneficial member of society. Second, teachers must follow the prescribed content matter from state curricula while also creating an environment in which students feel empowered in their own education. Teachers cannot do both perfectly, so they often have to choose to focus on one over the other. If you are a teacher whose rating, and potentially job stability, is based on your students' pass-rate, there is no question about which obligation gets a short shrift.

An Overview of the High School Learning Experience

All criticism of the curriculum or mixed messaging aside, the student experience has advanced from rote memorization of the textbook. Group work and collaboration are the new norm. Students sit at tables not desks and open books, tablets, computers, or newspapers, not textbooks. Teachers introduce material in mini-lessons, not lectures. In the twenty-first century classroom, teachers are facilitators of the learning experience but their instruction is not the only way students learn. Students are encouraged to talk constantly on purpose. They often share information with each other and it is not called copying but a "jigsaw"; thus, they teach one another. Teaching twenty-first century skills gives opportunities for equitable, collaborative experiences for young people to promote mediation and dialogue in adulthood. However, while the delivery method (the lesson plan) for K through twelve education may have changed, the material (sources for instruction) has not because these are, by necessity, still connected to the tests. Practically speaking, the curriculum map is as follows: elementary-aged students learn some about Native American cultures as well as their local town and state histories. Middle school–aged students delve into Mesopotamia, Greece/Rome, and then circle back to American history in eighth grade. And finally, most high schoolers begin the cycle again, although spending more time on concepts of colonial encounter and imperialism in the world's political history, before United States government and economics in the twelfth grade. (Figure 6.1).

To help with the discord of tests versus real-world learning skills, various curricula have been developed to bridge the divide. The Stanford curriculum "Thinking Like a Historian," which is used across the country, has developed a language for teachers to use. Students learn skills referred to as sourcing, contextualization, corroboration, and close reading using the same primary source documents educators have always used. (Figure 6.2).

- *Sourcing* is a basic understanding of the who, what, when, where, why of the written document.
- *Contextualization* is asking students to "understand how context/background information influences the content of the document. Recogniz[ing] that documents are products of particular points in time."
- *Corroboration* asks students to "establish what is probable by comparing documents to each other. Recogniz[ing] disparities between accounts."
- *Close reading* helps students "identify the author's claims about an event. Evaluat[ing] the evidence and reasoning the author uses to support claims."

Although teachers are not encouraged to use textbooks anymore, this curriculum, when taken as a whole, has many similarities to traditional

"Think Like a Historical Archaeologist" 133

Unit 1: Colonial
Examining Passenger Lists   Mapping the New World
Pocahontas   The Puritans
The First Thanksgiving Mini Lessons   King Philip's War
Salem Witch Trials   Portola Expedition
California Missions

Unit 2: Revolutionary and Early America
Great Awakening   Stamp Act
American Revolution SAC   Boston Massacre
Loyalists   Battle of Lexington
Declaration of Independence   Shays' Rebellion OUT
Federalists and Anti-Federalists Slavery in the Constitution
Hamilton v. Jefferson

Unit 3: Expansion/Slavery
Manifest Destiny   Second Middle Passage
Slavery Narratives   Louisiana Purchase
Lewis and Clark SAC   *Freedom's Journal*
Texas Revolution   Irish in 19th-Century America
Gold Rush and San Francisco   Evaluating Sources on Juana Briones

Unit 4: Civil War and Reconstruction
John Brown's Motivation   Radical Reconstruction
Reconstruction SAC   Sharecropping
Thomas Nast's Political Cartoons Fort Sumter
Civil War Photographs   Biddy Mason

Unit 5: The Gilded Age
Battle of Little Bighorn   Carlisle Indian Industrial School
Great Plains Homesteaders   Chinese Immigration and Exclusion

Figure 6.1. Examples of history lessons using primary sources, geared to the Regents test. Stanford History Education Group. Screenshot by Elizabeth Martin.

bound textbooks.[4] And, while no scholar would deny the importance of these skills, prioritizing them alone does not encourage the practice-based learning that the Department of Education maintains is so important for student success in the twenty-first century. The experience in the classroom is altered but the primacy of history as the only way to learn social studies is not. Why even call it social studies? Students learn about and form an opinion on a historical event by reading between two and four primary sources, potentially analyzing a political cartoon or photograph, and then either answering multiple choice questions or writing short answers to DBQs in a graphic organizer.[5]

In the lessons shown in Figure 6.1, students read document after document, both primary and secondary, from different perspectives on the

Historical Reading Skills	Questions	Students should be able to . . .	Prompts
Sourcing	• Who wrote this? • What is the author's perspective? • When was it written? • Where was it written? • Why was it written? • Is it reliable? Why? Why not?	• Identify the author's position on the historical event • Identify and evaluate the author's purpose in producing the document • Hypothesize what the author will say before reading the document • Evaluate the source's trustworthiness by considering genre, audience, and purpose	• The author probably believes . . . • I think the audience is . . . • Based on the source information, I think the author might . . . • I do/don't trust this document because . . .
Contextualization	• When and where was the document created? • What was different then? What was the same? • How might the circumstances in which the document was created affect its content?	• Understand how context/background information influences the content of the document • Recognize that documents are products of particular points in time	• Based on the background information, I understand this document differently because . . . • The author might have been influenced by _____ (historical context) . . . • This document might not give me the whole picture because . . .
Corroboration	• What do other documents say? • Do the documents agree? If not, why? • What are other possible documents? • What documents are most reliable?	• Establish what is probably by comparing documents to each other • Recognize disparities between accounts	• The author agrees/disagrees with . . . • These documents all agree/disagree about . . . • Another document to consider might be . . .
Close Reading	• What claims does the author make? • What evidence does the author use? • What language (words, phrases, images, symbols) does the author use to persuade the document's audience?	• Identify the author's claims about an event • Evaluate the evidence and reasoning the author uses to support claims • Evaluate the author's word choice; understand that language is used deliberately	• I think the author chose these words in order to . . . • The author is trying to convince me . . . • The author claims . . . • The evidence used to support the author's claims is . . .

Figure 6.2. Historical Thinking Chart, recreated from original chart by the Stanford History Education Group.

same event and then answer questions about them. For example, they may analyze a map of the Triangular Trade or read speeches for and against the Chinese Exclusion Act. They might be asked to question whether Columbus was a great explorer or the harbinger of mass genocide by reading excerpts of his diary and excerpts of history books. Manifest Destiny and slavery are packaged together. The curriculum's scope and sequence lead the teacher and student along the same path as before. History is presented not as actions made by people but as inevitabilities on a continuum leading to the present. Further, primacy is given to the written record, placing power directly back into the hands of those individuals who had access to it in the past. Although the traditional textbook is absent, and students do employ the historical thinking skills described above, they are funneled toward a conclusion about the inevitability of historical events by using the same documentary record that has been used for generations—with all research done for them prior to their involvement, and hence all student-inquiry removed.

A brief analysis of a recent United States History and Government exam illustrates the above point further.[6] The exam itself is three parts, split into multiple choice questions, DBQs, and two essays. The exam analyzed here has two multiple choice questions about the Civil War and enslaved African Americans. One asks the student to look at a primary source document (a poster) calling for African American men to join the Union army. Students are expected to choose which recent legislative proclamation is behind the creation of the poster. The other question requires the student to know why Abraham Lincoln said he had to fight the war. There are methods that would show a student's understanding of this time period in more complex ways, however. For example, one could ask the high school student to research and evaluate whether Lincoln's words were history or narrative, and what the difference might be. Next, the DBQs are excerpted primary source documents that the student is asked to use for short responses as well as "evidence"[7] in the final essays. No prior knowledge is necessary for these responses, as the student is only expected to use the excerpted sources, meaning that all research has been done for the student by the test-makers. The particular DBQs in the exam in question focus on the work of Thomas Paine, Harriet Beecher Stowe, and Upton Sinclair, which also connect to one of the essays asking the student to discuss how important pieces of writing have helped change societal problems. The other essay asks students to do a cost/benefit analysis of the United States' nineteenth century expansionist policies. What is the product of teaching students the correct answers to this exam if it is not to make true our country's approved narrative? The test emphasizes that government and elite upper-class responses to injustice are what helped enslaved African Americans and the impoverished working classes in American cities and justifies United States territorial expansion into Native American lands. Are there two sides represented here? Is there agency found for those people marginalized in the past? How might they have resisted or responded to their own unjust treatment? Is our student body learning that the only way to change the world is to wait for someone with more power to do it for them?

Additionally, student success on this type of exam depends completely on the child being literate in test-taking as well as in the curriculum map sequence utilized by the state from kindergarten through twelfth grade, which allows them to fit each lesson into the historical narrative and then translate those lessons to their proper order on the test. Yet America is not, and never has been, one size fits all. The student body is very diverse in my home state as in many states and students do not all have the same educational background. This is particularly true of the many immigrant children who do not arrive conveniently at kindergarten age, are not in stable housing, and are experiencing food insecurity, now exacerbated by COVID-19. "The population of first- and second-generation immigrant children in the United States grew by 51 percent from 1995 to 2014, to 18.7

million, or one-quarter of all U.S. children. Those totals are only expected to increase, especially in light of students streaming across the border . . . from South America and an influx of Syrian refugees fleeing the crisis in their country" (Camera 2016). These students are people we must prioritize in American society right now. They also need to practice and learn skills to become college-ready or to make their postsecondary education plan, yet they are automatically held back by the standards that prioritize a white, American middle- to upper-class child.

Another Style of Classroom and Curriculum: The Consortium Revolution

Although passing the Regents exams is the most common path to graduation in New York State, there is a growing movement against it. In reaction to the challenges presented by teaching to the Regents test, the New York Performance Standards Consortium and Center for Inquiry was formed in 1998. Today's consortium is a group of thirty-one schools that have a contract with the New York State Board of Regents promising to uphold the same state standards, but testing students in a very different manner. Students from a consortium school pass performance-based assessment tasks (PBATs) in all four core courses rather than the Regents exams in order to graduate from high school. Teachers at these schools choose their own curriculum, which has allowed social studies educators to jettison the concept of the inevitable timeline of history, and US history classes are more often taught thematically (imperialism, power and war, immigration, etc.)

The PBAT is generally a seven-to-fifteen-page paper written and then defended to a panel of teachers about a topic of the student's own choosing.[8] The thesis defense is the "performance" aspect of the requirement. Students have built wind-powered cars for physics; done analytical math to show the difference in inaugural-day crowd sizes for President Obama and President Trump; read *Lolita* and *Reading Lolita in Tehran*; and have written argumentative essays about the inequality in policing between white and Black and brown communities. These schools serve both traditional and nontraditional American students and are succeeding on most fronts because they are finding ways to help nontraditional American students flourish next to their traditional counterparts. They offer more ways into education for students of all abilities. Some gain high honors and some just pass. Either way, they do not suffer taking and failing the Regents test multiple times.[9]

Proponents say the alternative system is worth the effort because it engages students and encourages them to think creatively. They also point to data. According to the consortium, 77 percent of its students who started high school in the fall of 2010 graduated in four years, versus 68 percent for all New York City students. . . . The schools have done particularly well getting English language learners and special needs students to graduation. Last year, 71 percent of students learning English at consortium schools graduated on time, versus 37 percent of English learners citywide. (Robinson 2015)

Think Like a Historical Archaeologist: Historical Archaeology for the Social Studies Classroom

The archaeological record is not simply history, but tangible history as well. Using material records in classrooms does not simply check boxes on a rubric, it brings out the qualities of the past that documents lack. The things that people touched in the past can still be of use to people today. The need for more tactile-based learning has been widely accepted and brought into the mainstream through the concept of makerspaces. These are tinkering workshops where students of all ages (even adults) are given access to tools such as a hammer and screwdrivers and other materials that teach them creative but logical thinking and offer lessons that help with dexterity. Robotics and computers can be involved, but the basic makerspace is a workshop with real tools and open-ended problems for people to solve for themselves. Most makerspaces are in libraries and museums although some have received funding to be built into public schools, reversing the loss to education of home economics and woodshop. This movement is connected to a fear that humans are forgetting how to make things. What happens if we lose our fine motor skills due to underdevelopment? According to Martinez and Stager (2013), constructivism means that "although the learning happens inside the learner's head, this happens most reliably when the learner is engaged in a personally meaningful activity outside of their head that makes the learning real and sharable. This sharable construction may take the form of a robot, musical composition, papier-mâché volcano, poem, conversation, or new hypothesis" (32). A document-based learning experience is not constructivism, yet historical archaeology and the inclusion of material culture studies are. The popularity of makerspaces in education today demonstrates the utility of teaching the skills of archaeological analysis. Material culture studies will make historical events accessible and meaningful for students because it is personal as well. While the student may not be "making a project," the skills of the archaeologist involve the active and physical manipulation of objects in space; they could be constructing meaning quite literally. This skill appears even more important for students at this moment in time. Consider the 2020–2021 school year, a year of remote learning and deep isolation. Children touching objects and making things will be both academically and emotionally supportive for children.

Additionally, material culture studies will not be hard for teens to understand. Work from material culturalists such as Gosden and Marshall (1999) and Appadurai (1986) show us that there is value in the context of the Thing. "A watch bought in a shop as a commodity can be given as a gift with the social force of an item made and intended from the first to be a gift. For Appadurai, context is all and, rather than making blanket distinctions between objects, we need to look at the political and social circumstances surrounding exchanges" (Gosden and Marshall 1999, 174). Objects are both political and social because of the relationships inherent in exchange. Further, Daniel Miller's (2001) theory that the act of shopping can be a physical manifestation of love will connect immediately. Gifts are not for the person gifted the object as much as they are about the person giving the thing. High schoolers probably already know this. Things really do matter. An exploration of the object histories of artifacts from local collections will connect to students through explorations of gender, class, race and power, exposing the similarities between past and present landscapes and material records, and potentially help them address their own need for an $800 Canada Goose coat.

Teachers may get overwhelmed at the suggestion of yet more curriculum, but introductory sessions could be offered through the already-existing structure of professional development (PD) fairly easily. Using the archaeological resources already available but under-utilized in their local communities would also make this effort less complicated. There is an archaeological site for almost every topic in the state's scope and sequence, and these sites might make the subjects come to life more than a Regent's prep class. Historical archaeologists have published material about many events that students are already expected to learn.[10] Historical archaeology as a discipline works to give voice precisely to those people removed from the power structure of the past. Their names may appear in census records but in few personal documents. Locally, we have many urban archaeological sites that would help students see the lived experience of the past from the outsider's perspective. Utilizing local urban archaeological resources can help a teacher engage with the urban built environment with which students interact on a daily basis: for example, Seneca Village and The African Burial Ground in Manhattan, Weeksville in Brooklyn, and The Lighthouse in Connecticut.[11] Acknowledging that the past is still present then becomes a simple yet powerful teaching tool. None of the above archaeological sites appear in the current high school curricula but are occasionally introduced in archaeology courses in colleges and universities. When you halt the primacy of the documentary record you see more of the people who lived those historical events. Young people also learn to look at multiple perspectives by using more than one skill. They learn to read maps, look at statistical data, and connect objects from the past to their present. I do not argue for removing documents from the classroom but to ask educators to understand that documents are not always fact but are constructed narrative and should be treated as one of many resources for student engagement in a social studies unit.

While the Department of Education says that students should learn more than that historical events happen, the curriculum offered follows the same rote series of events on a timeline, making history seem inevitable and solidifying the current power structure. For students with backgrounds of violence, environmental racism, and poverty these lessons might lead them to question the current power structure; this is not learning but indoctrination into a system our other students have already bought into. Alternative themes about power and hegemony are hard to explore unless the teacher builds their own curriculum map. Teachers who teach to standardized tests do not have time to do this, given all of their other responsibilities.

However, although the consortium schools have changed the city education system for the better, there is still room for improvement. In the social studies department, the task that has been assigned to replace the Regent's exam in US history is an argumentative essay, a research project centered on individualized student interest that also has a rubric to which the State of New York has agreed. As of the time of this writing, this essay is a must for a student who graduates from a consortium school, basically making teachers teach to a different kind of test. I believe that this essay could easily be structured to allow for evidence from the material record and the built environment, offering other topics of inquiry to students. Historical archaeology works to discard the bias of the documentary record, hoping to help question past and current power structures. By looking past, the documentary record, historical archaeology brings us the lived experience of more people. Students could learn to argue for agency in the experiences of people marginalized from the documentary record but visible in the material one. This arrangement would re-focus education onto those left out of the power structures of the past, bringing poignant meaning and agency to today's students left out of our modern power structures.

Conclusion

To revolutionize social science education, we need to think in revolutionary ways. Historical archaeology is not an arcane practice but one that is important and relevant for the present day. We research objects and landscapes, and the everyday lived experiences of people in the past by using documentary and archaeological/material research backed up by a strong scientific method. We constantly collaborate with many other academic disciplines as well, calling on geology, philosophy, geography, anthropology, statistics, biology, and even history in order to better understand our own research. We try to destabilize today's cultural norms by giving voice to those who had it taken away in the past. The very nature of our discipline can become powerful for a child left out of America's contemporary power structure. We should teach students to think like historical archaeologists instead of like students trying to pass an exam, thus empowering them to question the very society they have been thrust into. As of now, students are not being taught to think critically at all but to follow guiding questions given to them after readings about historical events. Although a critique of the past is now built into the lesson, it is spoon fed to students, eliminating their research skills. Teaching the skills and content of historical archaeology will help our pre-college students practice those "college-ready," twenty-first-century skills that our society has decided will help them succeed. In the end, such a curriculum could give more students power over their own voice and desegregate educational structures by opening up access to success for learners of diverse backgrounds. This would change the current hierarchy, which keeps the same people in power generation after generation because they have been given all of the tools they need before they were even born.

Dr. Elizabeth Martin is a historical archaeologist from New York City. She has worked in higher ed, professional archaeology, museum education, and the public schools for close to twenty years. Dr. Martin's early work on marginalized outsider communities in the Northeast taught her to construct classrooms that help students explore and critique the historical narrative because it is through this type of experience that young adults find agency in their present and future lives.

Appendix

> Who Built the United States of America?
> Case Studies of American Historical Archaeology

Explanation of Unit:
This unit encourages students to think beyond the typical timeline of events discussed in the chapter. It introduces students to the methodology of Historical Archaeology and Material Culture, reframing the types of evidence utilized by the student and bringing out diverse voices from the past. Through historical archaeology, "case studies" will connect American cultural experiences of today to the spaces and places that took place in the past, offering students the chance to meet people often left out of history books because they did not have the social status or literacy to leave behind a documentary record.

Meaning of the unit: This unit is about helping students construct an understanding of the United States as we all experience it now, through the multivalent interactions, meetings, encounters, and middle grounds that all people across have constructed for themselves since they arrived. The framers of the constitution wrote some documents, but millions of people have made meaning for themselves in this country and their voices matter just as much as those of the framers.

Teaching implementation: "Case studies" could be offered to the students on bands that designate different styles of lessons.

- All would have to be modified for the specific classroom culture of each teacher.
- The particular topics/sites/histories covered in each version for students would be the same.
- They all promote heterogeneous student dialogue and a cohesive classroom environment through student collaboration and exploration of the subjects planned.
- All Voices Matter in the past and the present

*This is not a complete list.

Table 6.1. Unit with suggestions.

Theme and Thematic Essential Questions	Case Studies/Lessons/ State Framework Alignment
UNIT 1: EQ1: Who built America? EQ2: How do archaeological techniques help me think about historical events? EQ3: How can I find human agency in the objects and environments of the past?	General Ideas for Case Studies: **Indigenous and Colonial Encounter** • L.T. Ulrich's Molly Ocket's Pocket • St. Augustine Indigenous and Spanish • Jamestown/Roanoke • Custer's Last Stand GIS map of arrows • Middle grounds: La Florida, Puerto Real, American Southwest; Canadian Meti; The Lighthouse **Race and Enslavement** • African Burial Ground • Seneca Village • Weeksville • Jim Crow Museum • The Tents, Brooklyn • Mapping the Freedom Rides • The Great Dismal Swamp • Modern Movements: BLM sites of protest or demarcation • Monuments and memorials **Immigration** • Down by the station (Chinatown in LA) • Five Points • Museum of the Chinese in America (MOCA) • Ellis Island/Tenement Museum **Material Culture Studies** • Shopping/Consumerism • Why some things matter • Landscapes of Power/Capitalism

Notes

1. http://www.corestandards.org/ELA-Literacy/RH/6-8/; http://www.nysed.gov/common/nysed/files/programs/curriculum-instruction/ss-framework-k-8a2.pdf.
2. The rating is the grade a public-school teacher receives every year (highly effective, effective, ineffective). It is based on classroom observations by the administrators of the school and the pass rate of their students, called the Measure of Student Learning (MOSL). Most teachers who teach a class that ends in a Regents exam have to use the pass rate from the students who take that test as well as the pass rate of their students in general.
3. Constructivism from theory in development and education is similar to practice theory in archaeology (Ortner 1984).
4. Engage NY is the state curriculum, but many teachers prefer others. Two others in circulation are a CUNY-written curriculum called Debating United States History (DUSH) and one from the New Visions schools. Both teach historical thinking skills along with the same subjects framed as a timeline of historical events. Howard Zinn's *Peoples' History of the United States* and the accompanying curriculum that he helped create, along with CUNY's American Social History Project (2022), are both notable and often overlooked exceptions here, although they are both still taught from an historian's perspective. Sociological and anthropological could add richness to their lessons.
5. "Graphic organizer" from CUNY's High School Education Framework: "Use graphic organizers and templates. When asked to use other texts as springboards for their writing, students often struggle to manage both their own "voice" and the "voice" of the author, which leads to copying large portions of the source text verbatim. Taking notes in a graphic organizer can provide students with an intermediate step between the source text and the text they are writing" (Brandt 2015, 11).
6. Due to copyright restrictions, I am unable to reprint any image of the Regents exam itself but anyone interested can easily look up old exams at https://www.nysedregents.org/USHistoryGov/home.html.
7. "Evidence" is quotations from a primary or secondary source. Students are taught to "gather evidence" that support their main ideas for essay writing.
8. Some schools say PBA, some PBAT.
9. Students in New York State have a lower pass rate on the US History Regents than any other test. I have witnessed English language learners (ELLs) attempt to pass this exam more than five times before barely passing with a sixty-five.
10. The GIS study of the Battle of Little Big Horn from the Indigenous perspective gives more nuance to the lived experience. Roberta Greenwood's *Down by the Station* study of Chinatown in Los Angeles does the same.
11. Table 1 at the end of this chapter has a model of a unit organized around archaeological sites rarely included in K–12 education.

References

An, Susie, and Adriana Cardona-Maguidad. 2019. "Common Core: Higher Expectations, Flat Results." *WBEZ Chicago Public Radio*, 3 December 2019. https://www.npr.org/local/309/2019/12/03/784224482/common-core-higher-expectations-flat-results.

Appadurai, Arjun. 1986. *The Social Life of Things: Commodities in Cultural Perspective*. Cambridge: Cambridge University Press.

Brandt, Kate. 2015. *THE CUNY HSE Curriculum Framework: Social Studies: Integrating Reading & Writing*. www.cuny.edu/wp-content/uploads/sites/4/page-assets/academics/academic-programs/model-programs/cuny-college-transition-programs/adult-literacy/cuny-hse-curriculum-framework/Section2CUNYHSEFrameworkSocialStudies.pdf.

Camera, Lauren. 2016. "The Increase of Immigrant Students Tests Tolerance." *US News and World Report*, 5 January 2016. https://www.usnews.com/news/blogs/data-mine/articles/2016-01-05/number-of-immigrant-students-is-growing.

Common Core State Standards Initiative (CCSSI). 2010. Common Core State Standards for English Language Arts and Literacy in History/Social Studies, Science, and Technical Subjects. https://learning.ccsso.org/common-core-state-standards-initiative.

Greenwood, Roberta S. 1996. *Down by the Station: 1880–1933*. UCLA: The Cotsen Institute of Archaeology Press.

Gosden, Chris, and Yvonne Marshall. 1999. "The Cultural Life of Objects." *World Archaeology* 31 (2): 169–78.

Malvik, Callie. 2020. "4 Types of Learning Styles: How to Accommodate a Diverse Group of Students." *Rasmussen University Education*, 17 August 2020. https://www.rasmussen.edu/degrees/education/blog/types-of-learning-styles/.

Martinez, Sylvia Libow, and Gary Stager. 2013. *Invent To Learn: Making, Tinkering, and Engineering in the Classroom*. Torrance, CA: Constructing Modern Knowledge Press.

McLeod, Saul. 2019. "Constructivism as a Theory for Teaching and Learning." *SimplyPsychology.org*. https://www.simplypsychology.org/constructivism.html.

Miller, Daniel. 2001. *The Dialectics of Shopping*. Chicago: University of Chicago Press.

Nauer, Kim, et al. 2013. "Creating College Ready Communities: Preparing NYC's Precarious New Generation of College Students." *Center for New York City Affairs Milano School of International Affairs, Management, and Urban Policy. The New School*, September 2013. https://static1.squarespace.com/static/53ee4f0be4b015b9c3690d84/t/540f681ee4b00d55a4d3ddbb/1410295838929/CollegeReady.pdf.

Robinson, Gail. 2015. "NYC Schools That Skip Standardized Tests Have Higher Graduation Rates." *Hechinger Report*, 30 October 2015. https://hechingerreport.org/nyc-schools-that-skip-standardized-tests-have-higher-graduation-rates.

"Social History in Every Classroom." 2022. American Social History Project/Center for Media and Learning at CUNY. https://shec.ashp.cuny.edu/.

Stanford History Education Group. 2019. sheg.stanford.edu.

Stuckart, Daniel W. 2018. *Turning Pragmatism into Practice: A Vision for Social Studies Teachers*. Lanham, MD: Rowman & Littlefield.

Zinn Education Project: Teaching Peoples' History. 2021. https://www.zinnedproject.org/materials/peoples-history-for-the-classroom.

Chapter 7

"DIVERS[]S" and the Political Legacies of an "Experience-Exhibition"

María Fernanda Ugalde and O. Hugo Benavides

> An experience is something you come out of changed. If I had to write a book to communicate what I have already thought I'd never have the courage to begin it. I write precisely because I don't know yet what to think about a subject that attracts my interest. In so doing, the book transforms me, changes what I think.
> —Michel Foucault, "How an Experience-Book is Born"

Introduction

The exhibition "DIVERS[]S" at the National Museum (MuNa) in Quito, with its focus on gender relations and gender-sexual diversity in Ecuador's pre-Hispanic past, was the most visited museum exhibition in the country in 2019. It far exceeded the popularity of MuNa's permanent exhibits and registered return visitors in record numbers (Museum guides, personal communication). DIVERS[]S provided a transgressive understanding of gender/sexuality and gender relations not only in terms of the past but also in contemporary terms. The exhibition hit a powerful chord for a traditionally homophobic, transphobic, misogynistic, and heteronormative country like Ecuador. For example, it was less than three decades ago, in late 1997, that the state decriminalized homosexuality—although quite surprisingly, the state recently (in 2019) legalized homosexual marriages.

Notes for this chapter begin on page 166.

In this vein, the exhibition is a prime example of the manner in which archaeology in urban spaces can have a profound impact upon the national and transnational landscape. In the following chapter, we will explore the development and curating of the exhibition in the urban space of Quito, placing particular emphasis on how the exhibition contributed in multiple ways to broadening people's understanding of gender and sexual diversity in the national and larger Andean landscape. The particular urban location of the MuNa in the country's capital afforded two unique elements to the exhibition: first, the urban landscape of Quito and its prominence as the capital of the country, which make it a focal point for the nonurban population, provided a sense of prestige that allowed the exhibition to be taken in beyond Quito itself. Second, it allowed a particular dialogue between the urban landscape/highland visitors and the archaeological material being exhibited, which was mostly of rural coastal provenience. This urban-rural dialogue established by MuNa's locality in relation to the pieces themselves contributed very positively to the primal dialogic nature of the exhibition we were looking to establish.

In this article, we seek to analyze how the exhibition was imagined less as an authoritative voice on the sexual/gender truths of the pre-Hispanic past than as a manner of asking questions and considering how little we actually might know about gender/sexual relations and concepts in the past. Or perhaps worse yet, how much of what we think we know might be less a result of empirical evidence than of projections of contemporary patriarchal, sexist, and heteronormative biases and assumptions. The exhibition incorporated an active sense of inquiry and was not compelled by the logic of normative museums to tell the visitors what they should think or even provide them with an authoritative lesson on archaeological knowledge. Rather, our purpose was to have the public consider what they knew about the gender/sexual diversity of the past, and perhaps even more importantly, ask themselves how they came to know of that past. It was our hope to contrast these queries of their knowledge with the many examples of figurines from over five millennia of ceramic production in the region and see what incongruities would be brought to light.

For this enterprise, we took into account the particular archaeological discourse on gender/sexuality as it has evolved over the last forty years, since the initial archaeological research contributions on gender and women in the 1970s (Conkey and Spector 1984; Gero and Conkey 1991; Slocum 1975). It also was important to acknowledge the colonial legacies that are an integral part of Ecuadorian culture. It was not only imperative to assess the particular national and local discourses on gender/sexual difference in Ecuador, but also to appraise how those discourses could be addressed, confronted, and transformed through a more alternative and interactive archaeological exhibition.

In the following pages, we explore this disciplinary context of the manner in which archaeology (however slow or tardy) has sought to develop a more progressive understanding of sexual/gender diversity as well as the national and localized (and even contradictory) manner in which gender/sexual diversity is articulated in Ecuador. After this brief contextualization, we will describe the exhibition DIVERS[]S and analyze its impact. We very much believe that the exhibition allowed us to learn and listen while also inquiring and proposing new ideas about gender relations in general—and sexual/gender diversity in particular—in the Ecuadorian pre-Hispanic past.

The experience of the exhibition itself allowed us to see alternative forms of multiple sexual/gender discourses embedded in the archaeological material—something that was made more powerful by the public's bold reactions to the exhibition's inquiry. It also allowed us to reflect upon the defensive stances of many that seemed too terrified to let go of assumptions that solidified their contemporary identity. In this sense, the exhibition-experience as a form of knowledge and methodological proposal for artistic creation (Villalobos and Cabanzo 2020), like that of Foucault's book-experience, profoundly changed all those involved: not only the public, as expressed in the comments that they and guides shared, but also us as archaeologists and Ecuadorians.

Gender/Sexuality Archaeological Discourse as Praxis: Archaeological Advocacy

> If you are gay and Irish, your parents must be English.
> —David Beriss, *Identities*, Introduction to Queer Studies, 2001

Since the 1980s, archaeology has benefited from many contributions that highlighted not only the discipline's profound avoidance of studying gender and sexual variation in the archaeological record, but also provided a series of theoretical and methodological contributions about how one could address this lacuna in the discipline. During the last four decades these contributions have matured in range geographically, theoretically, and methodologically. Nonetheless, sexual and gender diversity as a viable and legitimate area of archaeological research continues to be questioned and challenged by the traditional patriarchal circles in the discipline.

In many ways, however, the research in archaeology on gender/sexual variation has allowed the field to further its own interdisciplinary vocation, incorporating the work carried by myriad scholars from different subject areas. Particularly important in this regard have been the works of Judith Butler (1993), Monique Wittig (1981), Paul Beatriz Preciado (2002) and Rita Segato (2016).

These archaeological contributions also heightened another long-term tension present in the discipline since the postprocessual critique of the 1980s, highlighting (to paraphrase Britney Spears) that archaeology may not be so innocent. Rather, far from being the objective and neutral scientific tool that it often feigns to be, archaeology has actively been an element of not only gender and sexual domination but also the maintenance of class and political hierarchies (particularly from the Global North vis á vis the Global South). This new transgressive research on gender/sexual diversity in the past provides concrete examples of how contemporary biases and colonized thinking are projected into the past and continuously read into the archaeological record.

The different theoretical approaches expressed in this research also allowed a political praxis that has aligned archaeology with other academic pursuits like queer studies, disability studies, postcolonial studies, and decolonized thinking, again to name a few. This interdisciplinarity has enabled a wealth of knowledge production and epistemological questioning that has been valuable in illuminating the close relationship between past and present as well as the ways in which our notions of the past continue to determine many of our contemporary legacies. Archaeological research on gender and sexual diversity has contributed to breaking down disciplinary boundaries, taxonomic constraints, and fictional chronological divides.

Precisely because of the rich transgressive contributions of gender/sexual archaeological research, however, its impact has not been always readily accepted or deemed benign. On the contrary, the recent gender/sexual archaeological contributions show what archaeology can do in terms of bold social contributions and advocacy. Gender/sexuality archaeological research is the theoretical companion of blocking the construction of dams, fighting against the destruction of heritage, and not allowing the patriarchal and heteronormative bias of our societies to continue to be legitimized and go unchecked.

Particularly relevant, and an essential motivation for our exhibition-experience, was the importance of the notion of belonging, of being included, and of the production of safe spaces (Ahmed 2012). For both authors, the ongoing commitment to the research that led to DIVERS[]S was less an exclusive academic concern than one that came from both of our personal and lived experiences, where research and feminist/queer activism are an indissociable whole. It was precisely these political ramifications of gender/sexual research that allowed us to see in the work an anchor that could translate our experiences into a worthwhile endeavor, not only in terms of making sense of our anti-patriarchal advocacy, but also of providing support to the future and upcoming younger queer feminist brethren.

Perhaps the work of two African American scholars, bell hooks (1994) and James Baldwin (1963), provide insights into the political implications of the work. For bell hooks, her approach to theory and writing (and, in our case, the museum exhibition), was not an academic enterprise but rather a sincere attempt to understand the basis of her social pain. Or, as Foucault (1991) has expressed, delving into theory was very much about his desire to learn and come to terms with why it was so painful to be who he was. For these authors, the queer element is an important element, if not almost the pivotal source, of that painful existence. All of them, in one way or another, and in different national, racial, and religious experiences, were confronted with the lasting legacies of being told that their sexual desires and gender identities were perverse and wrong. These discriminatory legacies inflict long-lasting scars and internal forms of psychological damage. As Baldwin (1963, 9) explains in his famous letter to his nephew, "to be committed is to be in danger," and for most of us, that commitment is too much to handle. Therefore, the majority choose to avoid danger only to find that they continue to reproduce those exacting social conditions that perniciously affect their and their loved ones' existence.

In this manner, DIVERS[]S combined years of research in different fronts with the authors' lived experiences. It also expressed our political desire to use our gained academic knowledge to answer why it is often so painful to be who we are, including having to seek self-exile to escape the sexist and homophobic repression of the nation. We also looked to provide through this archaeological exhibition into the country's ancient gender/sexual past a kind of buffer, or at the very least a more humane understanding of the Ecuadorian queer subject—what the Ecuadorian author Jorge Dávila Vazquez (1985) lovingly refers to as "Las criaturas de la noche/ The creatures of the night." The hope always was that the exhibition could contribute, however slightly, to lives lived in less harsh national terms than ours.

At least in this regard, it seemed that the exhibition achieved its goal. As two of the museum guides discussed with us, the museum itself was turned into a safe queer space of sorts. Not only did out members of the LGBTQ+ community come to see the exhibition, but they also returned with their friends, families, partners, and spouses, many time holding hands in the museum (something infrequent in the MuNa or country itself). In some instances, however, this outward expression of their queer and transgendered experience was negatively received by the museum's heteronormative administration, including the security guards who had to be told not to admonish or disrupt this homosexual or homosocial behavior.

Both guides also described how there was a sense of pride in the visitors to the exhibition. It was as if they were visiting and learning about their ancestors, their own past, as if the exhibition was finally providing them a kind of access to their history—one that had been erased and razed from the historical record. The exhibition made intimate sense to them. It was a missing link (of sorts) to a collective past that intuitively they knew to be true.

The National Ecuadorian Context of Gender/Sexuality

> I was haunted everywhere by the hilarious phrase: A man kicked to death! And all the letters danced before my eyes so merrily that I finally resolved to reconstruct the street scene or to penetrate, at the very least, the mystery of why a citizen was killed in such a ridiculous way.
> —Pablo Palacio, *Un Hombre Muerto a Puntapiés* (our translation), 2013 (1927)

Pablo Palacio's paradigmatic short story "A Man Kicked to Death" was originally published in 1927. During the century since the story's publication, Ecuador has seen enormous transformation, including several recent milestones for LGBTQ+ communities, despite the fact that the first of these, the decriminalization of homosexuality, was not achieved until 1997. This struggle was led by the brave and tireless effort of many people, primarily of the transgender community, and particularly of groups like Coccinelle and one of its fiercest members, Purita Pelayo (Cabral 2017; Viteri et al. 2021). Since 1997, there have been more significant milestones, including the ability to change one's gender in one's *cédula* (national identification document) in 2018 and the legalization of homosexual marriages in 2019, both protected by the nation-state's constitution.

However, as you can see from the above dates, these social transformations in the LGBTQ+ communities were a long time coming, despite the strong advocacy of many local, regional, and national groups fighting for decades with the support of international legal aids groups for equality and sexual rights. In many ways, such slow social transformation rightly captures the conservative milieu of Ecuadorian society, and particularly the manner in which colonial legacies, especially notions of *buenas costumbres* (good customs), permeate the social, moral, and normative order. This conservative structure and the permanency of strong traditional Catholic beliefs have made it hard for women and sexual minorities to claim equality under the law and be accepted in their full worth as equally valid human beings in mainstream society.

It is this particular repressive environment that Palacio captures so well in his succinct short story of a man being lynched (literally kicked to death) in the streets of Quito because he had made some subtle homoerotic overture to the murderer's son. It is to Palacio's credit that he develops the story with very little moral or judgmental overtones, neither in terms of condemning the gay man or the homophobic murderer. Rather, the story is told from a more noir perspective that highlights the darkness of the context but also its banality, as something that happens every day and, as such, something that otherwise would not even be worthy of reporting in detail. It is perhaps in this choice of the scene as a worthy element of focus and further investigation that we garner Palacio's powerful progressive contribution. Perhaps it is in this description of the homophobic murder as banal that we can actually capture the powerful imaginary that the narrative has held among the LGBTQ+ Ecuadorian communities over the last century.

It is also this violent transphobic and homophobic context, so explicitly detailed in the narrative, that expresses what most of the country's queer experience has been like over the last century. In many ways, the most recent progressive LGBTQ+ milestones, such a long time coming, can be registered as evidence of how repressive and homophobic the nation's history has been. The particular conservative reality of the country is hard to understand because it is not simply a response to the long-standing history of colonial, religious, and social legacies. These colonial legacies are shared throughout the continent, but they seem to have had a stronger foothold in the small nation of Ecuador. It is also interesting to see that often the Catholic church (particularly its regional highland representatives) has been more liberal than many other social forces. For example, in 1997, one of their bishops spoke out not necessarily in defense of homosexuality but definitely against its criminalization. As it was stated at that time, many things are seen as a sin, but just because they are a sin does not mean they are a crime.

Precisely this desolate sexual context might have contributed (perhaps, albeit unconsciously) to the large immigrant exodus of Ecuadorians to other countries, first to Venezuela in the 1970s, then to the United States from the late 1960s until now, and later to Europe—particularly, Spain,

Italy, and England—since the 1990s. All of these social mobilizations were predominantly expressed as an economic necessity and the desire to better one's livelihood. But one must wonder how much of that socioeconomic necessity was also driven by a desire to better one's social conditions, including one's gender identifications—that is, to be considered in one's full right as a gendered being, particularly as both a woman and/or queer subject, something not readily possible in Ecuador in the latter half of the twentieth century.

Although more research will need to be done to support this "sexile" hypothesis (Mogrovejo 2020) as an unconscious motor for Ecuadorian migration, what is factual is that around 20 percent of Ecuadorians have lived or continue to live outside of the country. This includes both of the authors of this article, who spent their formative years living abroad and carried out their education outside of the national fold (see Ugalde and Benavides 2018). Like us, tens of thousands have interacted with other less conservative sexual and gender mores and returned to the country, impacting the national debate on gender and sexuality and on what constitutes an independent and liberated sexual subject. Therefore, it is not surprising that the last decade has seen a backlash against this progressive turn in the struggle for sexual rights in the country.

Since the early 2000s, the conservative battle cry has consolidated along two different axes. The first one is the attack against the "gender ideology" (*Ideología de Género*), while the second has been part of the continental movement of "Leave my Children Alone" (*Con mis hijos no te metas*). What is striking about both is how they readily stress the notion that they are the defenders and protectors of authentic gender (read: heteronormative) traditions and good customs (*buenas costumbres*).

It is against this backdrop, and to some degree against this conservative ideological gender agenda, that we thought of and put together the DIVERS[]S exhibition-experience. The challenges were manifold. First, and foremost, we saw this exhibition as coming from our lived-in struggle as queer subjects as well as from our research, and ultimately as an effort to fight against the repressive colonial ideologies that had decimated us and so many LGBTQ+ subjects over the centuries. It was our hope to strike back against the homophobic and sexist structure of the Ecuadorian State and society in the national space of its largest state museum, the MuNa in Quito.

Second, and equally important, was how to undertake this academic/political work without being lynched in the process ("*sin morir en el intento/* without dying in the process," in Ecuadorian parlance). The exhibition was a life dream for both of us and something we had discussed as the most optimistic of opportunities, but we also were quite aware of the impossible odds of carrying it out, and even the physical danger that arranging such an exhibition could entail. Precisely as a strategy against this hegemonic stronghold of neocolonial thinking, we thought the approach of presenting questions, rather than truths, would be most conducive. In the process, we would also be questioning the colonial order of things, which presents facts as known truths as opposed to ideas in the process of construction.

Finally, we were aware that gender and sexuality are always intimately tied to notions of race and the nation. It was clear that the exhibition would bring up questions and assumptions about what it means to be Ecuadorian, and above all of the role and place of the Indigenous subject in the national imaginary. The racial element is particularly relevant because it problematizes both of the conservative movement's assumptions that they are the stalwart of tradition by proposing alternative understandings. The exhibition would present possible evidence of Indigenous sexual and gender diversity destroyed by European colonialism and most recently by Western homophobic scholarship.

In many respects, what the exhibition would put forward was the question of a more accurate portrayal of Indigenous communities expressing greater non-Westerns forms of gender and sexual diversity. We were readily aware that because the Ecuadorian nations claims itself as a multicultural and multinational state (i.e., a mestizo miscegenated state in which the Indigenous community is central), our asking of questions about that original ancestral subject would easily bring shudders to the hegemonic ideology and Ecuadorian national identity. We also understood that these questions might expose the two conservative movements for what they are: not the defenders of any authentic tradition but the guardians of oppressive colonial forces that have occupied the national territory for the last five centuries.

DIVERS[]S: Curating An Exhibition

The exhibition, and the very idea of carrying out an exhibition on sex-gender diversity in pre-Hispanic Ecuador, arose almost hand-in-hand within our joint projects, "Ethnoarchaeology of Sexual Identities in pre-Hispanic Ecuador" (PUCE) and "Gender and Sexual Identities in the Iconography of Precolumbian Ecuador" (Wenner Gren-Foundation) (Benavides 2017, 2019; Ugalde 2017; Ugalde and Benavides 2018; Ugalde 2019). In addition, the exhibition featured a catalog that synthesizes the main ideas that guided the concept.[1]

The exhibition, as well as the other collaborative projects, attempted to review and offer a re-reading of the material culture from pre-Hispanic

Ecuador. Most specifically, we were interested in the huge set of figurative art—for example, anthropomorphic figurines—produced from around 3500 BC to the arrival of the Spanish Conquistadores in the early 1500s. This five-thousand-year-long productive history of "bodies in clay" offers an exceptional opportunity to assess the ideas projected upon them by the people who produced these objects, particularly in terms of gender dynamics, which curiously have never been analyzed from this perspective before (Ugalde 2021).

For quite a while, the possibility of actually doing the exhibition seemed like a dream, and a crazy and unattainable one at that. When the first conversations with the MuNa took place in 2016, the dream became an almost obsessive goal, but at the same time a kind of running joke stemming from our continuous disbelief (almost like finishing one's doctoral dissertation, a tangible yet distant reality). Would it really be possible to mount an exhibition of this nature, in a city and country as homophobic and transphobic as Ecuador and its capital city, Quito? And, if we were successful, what would happen next? Would we physically and professionally survive it?

In hindsight, however, it was precisely the urban landscape of the capital that allowed us to carry out this archaeological advocacy. For one, the capital is by far the place with the largest number of nongovernmental organizations (NGOs), foundations, and other human rights groups, as well as being the location of foreign embassies. All of these entities make the city the most visible location in Ecuador and open it to a global focus, which allowed for more international visitors to the exhibition than would have been the case in other parts of Ecuador, and it also permitted the exhibition to connect to a larger regional and global conversation about diversity and its place in the ideal of a modern nation.

Against all odds, in May 2019, we were able to see this exhibition become a reality (Figure 7.1). Its opening marks a "before" and an "after," not only in our stories, but in some way in the history of the MuNa as a National Museum, in the team of guides/mediators, and also—and this is truly the most transcendental element—in many of the individuals who found in this space a safe place, even if an ineffable one, for their existence and their ancestral histories.

The project "Ethnoarchaeology of Sexual Identities in pre-Hispanic Ecuador" laid the basis for much of what would come later, given that it was conceived as a cross-sectional experiment. Despite the academic nature of the project, the intention was always for it to be open to other interdisciplinary spaces and above all to other ways of approaching the past; so from the very beginning, we attempted to go beyond (both physically and mentally) the urban academic setting of the university. The experiment, therefore, led us to converse with artists, artisans, and other specialists

Figure 7.1. Museo Nacional del Ecuador Frontside, Av. Patria, Quito, 2019. © María Fernanda Ugalde.

in different urban and rural spaces, all of which enriched the project, but more importantly, enriched us.

In this way, and with the slogan of freeing ourselves from the straitjacket of taxonomic rigor, we looked for knowledge, feelings, and perspectives that would help us in the exercise and practice of looking again, looking at things differently. We also sought a different way of going back because what we were analyzing and trying to understand was a set of well-known archaeological figurines: well-known not only in the imagination of archaeologists, but of most Ecuadorians, as they are constantly used to illustrate school texts, murals of public buildings, and tourism propaganda, and have even been used as a symbol and logo for some of the most important institutions of the state, like the *Banco Central* or the *Ministerio de Cultura*. They also play an important role in the urban imaginary, where they are often found and expressed in varied manners on walls, signs, and vehicles (Figure 7.2). These figurines, in a way, have been described, analyzed, and interpreted *ad nauseam*; yet, particularly with regard to anthropomorphic figures, the project allowed us to assess

Figure 7.2. House in Quito decorated with collage combining motifs inspired by Botticelli's *The Birth of Venus* and a Valdivia "Venus" figurine. March 2021. © María Fernanda Ugalde.

how they had constantly been viewed and studied with a patriarchal, heteronormative, and transphobic historiographic bias.

We saw how archaeology, like traditional readings of ethnohistoric sources, has sought to make invisible the pre-Hispanic sexual diversity to which chroniclers make clear reference (see Benavides 2002; Horswell 2005). In archaeology, too, a biased historiography is evident. Traditional interpretations seem blind to what we recognize as ideological discourses embodied in figurines, the main mass communication medium of the time (Ugalde 2009, 2021; Ugalde and Benavides 2018).

Thus we proposed to "look again and look differently" alongside people and groups not linked to the academy. We brought together artists from different branches who work with a focus on gender issues and craftspeople who specialize in the manufacture of reproductions of pre-Hispanic figurines. We also consulted people who define themselves as nonbinary or transgendered. Together, we looked at the pieces, and imagined their possible meanings and social and cultural implications. We also invited this group to use the figurines as inspiration for their own artistic creations within the framework of a type of creative laboratory titled *Ir tomando cuerpx* (Taking Body) (León and Ugalde 2021).[2]

After about two years from our initial conversations with the MuNa, a coming and going of rejected and amended proposals, long phases of silences and doubts, extensive discussions about what "could and could not be done in a National Museum," and thanks to the generous demeanor of the museum team during this period, we finally achieved a consensual museological concept for the temporary exhibition, organized around three thematic axes:

1. *The beginnings of figurative art—Female representations and rituality in the Formative Period*. This first part explored materials for which the figurative universe was almost exclusively concerned with the depiction of female bodies (Figure 7.3). For almost three thousand years, as expressed in this figurative record, people in coastal Ecuador seem to have used female symbolism as their main expressive component.

2. *Social stratification and patriarchy—Societies of the Regional Development Period*. The second part focused on the shift that occurred around 600 BCE, when many social, economic, religious, and political changes took place on the Ecuadorian coast—changes that are visible in the archaeological and iconographical record. Societies became ranked, hierarchies emerged, and the figurines show a notable contrast between depictions of hieratic women versus active men (Figure 7.4). An ideological discourse laden by a patriarchal structure seems to rule the nature of this iconography (for larger discussions on this specific topic, see Benavides 2019; Ugalde 2021).

3. *Perceptions of gender in the past through the iconographic analysis of the figurines of the Ecuadorian coast*. The third part, focusing on gender diversity, combined archaeological and ethnohistorical evidence. Starting with the description in the early ethnohistoric accounts of same-sex-relations, which were condemned by the Spanish Conquistadores, we presented archaeological objects from all periods showing plausible female and male elements intertwined in the same figurine. These varied combinations appear in many ways, including, for instance, in what today we define in very strict binary terms as male and female sexual organs (Figure 7.5), or sexual organs from one sex combined with the typical clothes or ornaments from another one (for a detailed discussion on this specific topic, see Benavides 2002; Ugalde 2019; Ugalde and Benavides 2018).

The exhibition was a collaborative effort with museum curators, museologists, and educators starting (as mentioned above) from questionings rather than trying to offer answers or solid truths. For example, some of the questions that guided the proposal were: Was gender understood in binary terms in the past? Is there a relationship between gender and power,

Figure 7.3. Part of the exhibition showing some of the displays containing, in the front (*left section*), some of the female figures from the Formative Period. © María Fernanda Ugalde.

Figure 7.4. Part of the exhibition showing some of the displays containing some of the male figures from the Regional Development Formative Period. © María Fernanda Ugalde.

Figure 7.5. Part of the exhibition showing some of the displays containing some of the figures representing possible gender diversity in the past (female couples, female shapes with male dresses, etc.). © María Fernanda Ugalde.

and if so, how is it made evident? How rigid or flexible were gender roles in the past? (Ugalde and Benavides 2019). The national and urban pace of the MuNa allowed these questions to be asked (an achievement in and of itself) and for all participants to be part of the dialogues they created.

Ecuador's National Museum (the MuNa): Historical Narratives at Work

The fact that DIVERS[]S was debated and carried out in a space such as the National Museum in Quito made the challenge to its successful realization even greater. To better understand the magnitude of this challenge, it is important to assess the place of the National Museum within a Latin American country like Ecuador, and also the particular historical moment in which we were debating to make it a reality.

What is now known as the National Museum, or MuNa, developed from a complex history of initially frustrated attempts linked to the desire to reinforce a feeling of pride in the nation-state. Such an undertaking is always a challenging task, even more so, in a country like Ecuador, marked by identity conflicts and a constant search for justification for their self-assessment. As Benavides (2004) has developed elsewhere, Ecuador very much suffers from a failed attempt at being a nation, either because of its initial national belonging as part of Great Colombia, or of its close ties to the Virreynato de Lima during the colonial period. Either way, the very fact that it chose a name that refers to an imaginary line not exclusively unique to the national territory, but rather that circumnavigates the whole world, points to the nation's lack of historical congruity at its very emergence. Precisely due to these historical realities, Ecuador, like all nation-states, has made various museum-based attempts to create meta-historical narratives and, in that regard, archaeological discourses, artifacts, and themes have been central to this enterprise.

According to the National Directory of Museums (MUSEUMS 2019), Ecuador has 175 museums, including public, private, ecclesiastical, and community-based ones. Although the directory is organized by provinces and not by themes, a quick glance allows the browser to recognize that archaeological collections are a constant, and in some way constitute the material base associated with the museums' sense of identity locally, regionally, and nationally.

The first attempt to start a national museum was around 1839, only nine years after the foundation of the nation, as a consequence of a "scientific, pedagogical and civilizational will related to the formation of the modern nation and the consolidation of an early notion of citizenship" (Durán and Armijos 2018). This effort was undertaken within the framework of a regional drive set by examples from the neighboring countries of Colombia and Peru. However, this first attempt would not succeed or last for long, despite the push of the progressively minded president, Vicente Rocafuerte. Nor did, years later, the conservative president Gabriel García Moreno succeed in realizing his desire for a national museum linked to the National Polytechnic School (Kennedy Troya 1992; Zapater 2018). In both cases, the interest seems to have focused on the state becoming the custodian of a collection of objects understood as fine arts that would be open to the public to achieve a kind of national aesthetic education (Zapater 2018, 40).

By the middle of the nineteenth century, several efforts were underway to generate museums with collections of various types, such as the "Museum of machines and instruments used in Arts and Crafts" as well as a "Museum of Natural History" (Kennedy Troya 1992). It was not until 1917, by presidential decree, that the Museum of Archeology and the National Galleries of Painting and Sculpture was founded in Quito and eventually became the first well-established and long-standing national museum of Ecuador (Zapater 2018).

All of these attempts at establishing a national museum must be understood within the nineteenth-century historical context that prompted them. In this context, the attempt to replicate European museums was primary as it was shaped by a supposedly universalist perspective of heritage that, in reality, concealed Western colonial values and logic. It was this colonial mindset that would be reproduced in national museum spaces throughout Latin America (Puebla 2015; Cazar 2018). Of course, behind this logic is the hegemonic construction of an official past in order to "consolidate and reproduce a common imaginary of a national and patriotic nature" (Puebla 2015, 241; see also Benavides 2004).

In 1969, another reformulation took place in the Ecuadorian Central Bank (BCE) Museum created by the Ecuadorian State. As in other countries in the region, the Central Bank—the issuer of the currency and custodian of the state's monetary reserves—was considered the appropriate space in which to safeguard the archaeological, historical, and artistic heritage of the nation. The collection of the Museum of the Central Bank of Ecuador had a strong archaeological foundation, although quickly, it was vastly complemented with collections from other materialities and temporalities. According to Durán and Armijos (2018, 20): "The democratization policy that sustained it was based on the creation of areas destined for cultural diffusion within the BCE and sought the consolidation/exhibition of certain collections from a desire to promote the access of citizenship to national cultural assets through a pedagogical task. Its ultimate goal would be to sediment an idea of a 'national' culture, strengthen a sense of identity and consolidate a shared story about the past." With this objective, and a clearly cultural-historical approach linked to it, the Museum of the Central Bank of Ecuador maintained a fairly uniform discourse over several decades (although there were several temporary exhibitions—some focused on archaeological themes—that frequently highlighted the monumentality or great technological achievements of the original Ecuadorian societies) (Ontaneda 2007). Although there was a temporary exhibition called "Gender and Archeology," its focus was limited to a cultural-historical review of the female presence throughout prehistory (Yépez 2002).

The BCE continued as the custodian of national heritage until the beginning of the twenty-first century, when political and economic processes strongly shook the country and led to significant structural changes. These changes included the dollarization (as the new national currency) of the national economy and therefore the extinction of its old currency, the *sucre*, with very pronounced consequences including mass migration (about one million Ecuadorians left the country in the first decade of this century—around 10 percent of the population) and the restructuring of Ecuadorian families (single parenting household became the norm because of the exodus). With this, the Central Bank lost its main function—that of an issuing entity, and therefore also gradually lost its authority in terms of being the arbiter of patrimonial assets and heritage, which came to be controlled by the Ministry of Culture.

Structural changes at the national level in the post-dollarization era, when the Museum of the Central Bank passed into the hands of the Ministry of Culture, were also reflected in the structuring of cultural institutions and public museums. After extensive debate, workshops, and strong disputes, a new museological concept was imposed. This new concept moved away from the previous linear chronospatial logic to focus on the visitor as the center and end of the museum's cultural action (León 2020). This proposal was implemented through thematic axes that use transversal concepts, based on the idea of social memory and its multivocality rather than on monumentality and a unilinear national discourse.

With this new approach, the MuNa (the new version of the National Museum) opened in 2018, after being closed to the public for more than two years while this new museological concept was being implemented. The transversal concepts it contemplates are gender and interculturality, heritage and memory, knowledge production, participation, and citizenship (López 2018). Each of these axes is approached from museum and curatorial perspectives. Without this new museological approach, not even the idea of an exhibition such as DIVERS[]S would have ever been possible.

Unlike its predecessor this new version of the National Museum (the MuNa) has been a success. According to statistics from the Ministry of Tourism, the National Museum is the most visited museum in Ecuador, and therefore the impact of an exhibition in this space is significant. For example, by the middle of 2019, the National Museum had received around 150,000 visits (León 2020, 5). During DIVERS[]S's tenure, numerous visitors came expressly looking to visit the temporary exhibition, some of them on more than one occasion (Museum guides, personal communication).

By the end of 2019, however, a change of authorities in the Ministry of Culture and at the museum led to a change in the MuNa's conceptual approach. The critical museological model came into question and a return to the cultural-historical vision of the National Museum was proposed. Alongside this change, DIVERS[]S was dismantled overnight, without us or even the guides being notified beforehand. We would find out about the dismantling of the exhibition by sheer chance, as we passed in front of the museum and saw that the large DIVERS[]S advertisement hanging outside the museum had been removed.

Ironically enough, several months later, the same administration that had dismantled the exhibition would reach out to us with some urgency. They were hoping we would quickly put together an exhibition for them, as Global Museum Day was approaching and the theme selected for the year 2020 by the international committee was diversity. They had no qualms at attempting to eliminate the only exhibition highlighting diversity from their midst but found themselves hard pressed by transnational forces to check their own colonial mindset.

In this way, the new National Museum administration attempted to erase all traces of our work from the urban space without attracting attention and without any closing events. In many regards, this silent removal and erasure made sense within Ecuador's traditional homophobic structure. If anything, the fact that we had succeeded in developing DIVERS[]S was the real democratic anomaly. However, although DIVERS[]S vanished overnight from the museum space, the effort, we hope, was not erased from the national imaginary.

The Mediating Process: A Discussion and Concluding Thoughts

The contents of the exhibition, the museum concept, and the selection of pieces were all sources of intense debate and negotiation. However, what we refer to below as the mediation process refers more specifically to the situation once the exhibition was already underway. Its particular characteristics and peculiarities in turn say a lot about how Ecuadorians deal with their history, identity, and sexuality. We owe much in terms of this invaluable information to the generosity of two exceptional museum guides—and now friends—whom we met on this exhibition journey, and who shared with us the experiences they lived from within the museum.

Thus, we know that the process was permanently characterized by "productive tensions" (Hall 1997). As did Hall, we understand tensions as an integral, and not a negative, part of social and political relationships. In this manner, it is also important to highlight that the process was not an easy one nor did it flow in a linear fashion, and that it constituted a challenge, not only for us, but for the museum authorities and for the team in charge of the guides and mediation as well.

We are sure that, as researchers and promoters of the exhibition, there were many issues behind the scenes that we do not know about. But despite the filters, some resistance was very clear throughout the process. Tensions were presented at all levels of participation, from the museum's floor archaeologists, who rejected the type of nontraditional reading that was proposed, to some of the guides, who refused to present the exhibition to visitors and looked for any pretext to evade this task.

We were told that one of the guides/mediators considered it absolutely impossible that homosexuality might have been a normative practice among some of the Indigenous societies of the Ecuadorian coast, as the chronicles written by the first Spaniards show and some pre-Hispanic figurines suggest (Benavides 2002; Ugalde 2017). The very idea, as we were told, produced horror and a near identity crisis for this guide because "his heroes, the warriors of the Jama-Coaque culture, would no longer be proper men."

The association of homosexuality as a naturalized practice with cowardice is already problematic enough, but here it is further problematized in other (temporal) spaces and relationships. It is quite interesting to see, in this case, the link between one's own manhood and an ancestral masculinity reflected in figurines from two thousand years ago. It is curious, in this sense, that although there has been some debate around masculinities in Ecuador from different approaches (Andrade and Herrera 2001), this historical link has not really been addressed. A sort of crisis of virility seems to appear as a latent threat the moment the possibility of some homosexual ancestors is mentioned or comes into view.

Another interesting resistance among the guides/mediators came in relation to the very materiality of the sources that were the core of the investigation. For one of the guides/mediators, trained as a historian, it was impossible to conceive of a narrative that started from material culture as discourse, as she only considered written accounts to be valid discourses, even when none exists for most pre-Hispanic societies. This conservative position is also interesting and surprising, as one would expect a historian to be critical and quite aware of the possible manipulation of written documents themselves and to recognize that every place is an archive (Turkel 2006), therefore accepting that it is impossible to see historical sources as exclusively limited to written texts.

The range of reactions from the public that was reported to us by the guide/mediators was also interesting. An audience focus research project (León 2020) that was carried out inside the museum during the time of the exhibition addressed visitor perceptions of the museum in general, but unfortunately does not refer to the exhibition in particular. Therefore, the information below is from the two guide/mediators mentioned above, who were very much empowered by the project (their words) and excitedly wanted to share their experiences with us.

The reactions from the public, according to them, ranged from rejection and bewilderment to a sense of well-being and identification. The rejection was felt by some, for example, from families with children, where parents turned around and took their children out quickly when they noticed the subject of the exhibition. A sense of perplexity was noted in many people who actually saw the whole exhibition and did not know what to say when asked about it at the end of their visit. Meanwhile, many members of the LGBTQ+ community said they found in the exhibition a place where they could feel safe and show themselves as they are, without fear.

An interactive space was included in the exhibition at the very end of the tour, which proved vital from the museum's perspective. In this space, the public felt much freer to express their thoughts and feelings. They were able to touch replicas of some of the archaeological pieces on display, look at videos and pictures that spoke of the project and, most importantly, share opinions and feelings through simple colored Post-it notes made available for visitors to fill out. The Post-Its filled all the walls of the room and even the ceiling several times over, so they had to be removed every couple of weeks to make room for more. A pending work is the systematization of this material, but we were struck by the number of times the word "LOVE" appeared over and over again.

The City of Quito, like other Ecuadorian and Latin American cities, is highly homo- and transphobic (Asociación Silueta X 2018; Picq and Viteri 2020; Viteri et al. 2021). Violence and crime due to intolerance toward sexual dissidents have been highlighted in both regional studies (Figari 2010) and vivid local testimonies (Cabral 2017). In this context, it is encouraging that DIVERS[]S appears to have constituted, to some small extent, a safe haven. The hopeful testimonies shared by the guide/mediators and others who visited the exhibition, both Ecuadorians and foreigners and especially young people, make us think so.

Many in the public expressed their feeling of being in a place where they could be and show themselves as they are, without fear. Most of these were young people from the urban landscape of Quito: young LGBTQ+ persons who are otherwise afraid to walk as who they are on the streets of the city where they were born and live, who like us decades ago are still growing up feeling out of place and very much accustomed to being a stranger in the place they call home (*sensu* Ahmed 2012, 2).

There is something invaluable in the pride the museum exhibition offered, allowing many an experience in the authoritative manner in which their bodies were in control while visiting the exhibition and museum space. It was a safe space where they could hold hands, be intimate, and even choose the bathroom of their gender preference (something unheard of in the country and which caused a stir among the security guards). The pride was also expressed in the fact that they would bring back their loved ones and family members, repeat the tour with the guides, and show an air of approval to their loved ones of their ancient and recent past, assenting to what the guides were asking about their ancestors and their own contemporary existence.

It is precisely this part of the exhibition—this experience-of-the-exhibition—that best expressed what all of us who were involved were attempting to do. Through the academic knowledge gained and sorting through our own gendered experiences in Ecuador (and abroad), we were hoping to provide less of a lesson on what the past was like than an invitation. This invitation was also very much enabled precisely because of the authoritative museum reputation within the urban landscape of the capital. In this manner, all these elements allowed us to offer DIVERS[]S to be read as an invitation into a performative experience of what our contemporary life could be like if we allowed ourselves to assess the archaeological record in accordance with an empirical methodology not completely determined by racist, sexist, and homophobic neocolonial legacies.

We think this is, in the end, the great challenge of such heritage-related institutions like the National Museum; namely: to do the serious work of diversity. And diversity work, as Ahmed (2012, 173) has pointed out, does not simply generate knowledge about institutions, but rather recognizes that different kinds of knowledge are created in the diversifying process. And hopefully, it is those new-found forms of knowledge that will ultimately make the institutions, and us, more human.

María Fernanda Ugalde is an Ecuadorian archaeologist whose research focuses on the intersection of art and social processes. Her interests include, particularly over the last few years, gender and public archaeology. She is currently professor at Pontificia Universidad Católica del Ecuador.

O. Hugo Benavides is an anthropologist whose research interests include historical and national production, social theory, sexuality, and identity, Latinx and Latin America cultural politics. He is also the author of three books and over sixty articles.

Notes

1. The DIVERS[]S exhibition catalog can be found at https://muna.culturaypatrimonio.gob.ec/index.php/exposiciones/exposiciones-temporales/divers-s-facetas-del-genero-en-el-ecuador-prehispanico.
2. The *Ir Tomando Cuerpx* website can be found at https://arteactual.ec/ir-tomando-cuerpo/.

References

Ahmed, Sara. 2012. *On Being Included. Racism and Diversity in Institutional Life*. Durham, NC: Duke University Press.
Andrade, Xavier, and Gioconda Herrera, eds. 2001. *Masculinidades en Ecuador*. Quito: FLACSO.
Asociación Silueta X. 2018. *Informe 2018. Runa Sipiy Ecuador. Asesinatos Trans-LGBT*. Quito: Asociación Silueta X.
Baldwin, James. 1963. *The Fire Next Time*. London: Michael Joseph.
Benavides, O. Hugo. 2002. "The Representation of Guayaquil's Sexual Past: Historicizing the Enchaquirados." *Journal of Latin American Anthropology* 7 (1): 68–103.
———. 2004. *Making Ecuadorian Histories. Four Centuries of Defining Power*. Austin: Texas University Press.
———. 2006. *The Politics of Sentiment. Imagining and Remembering Guayaquil*. Austin: Texas University Press.
———. 2017. "Transgéneros en la Costa Ecuatoriana: Una Historia del Presente Evanescente." In *Trans. Diversidad de Identidades y Roles de Género*, edited by Andrés Guitérrez Usillos, 119–23. Madrid: Museo de América.
———. 2019. "The Island of Menstruating Men: Queerying Leacock's Introduction to Engel's "Origin of the Family, Private Property, and the State." *Revista Arqueologia Publica* 13 (1[22]): 85–98.
Butler, Judith. 1993. *Bodies that Matter. On the Discursive Limits of Sex*. London: Routledge.
Cabral, Alberto. 2017. *Los fantasmas se cabrearon. Crónicas de la despenalización de la homosexualidad en el Ecuador*. Quito: INREDH.
Cazar, Diego. 2018. "El Museo Nacional, un proyecto desbordado." *Mundo Diners* 431, April 2018.
Conkey, Margaret W., and Janet D. Spector. 1984. "Archaeology and the Study of Gender." *Advances in Archaeological Method and Theory* 7: 1–38.
Durán, Lucía, and Ana María Armijos. 2018. "Pensar una política educativa para el Museo Nacional del Ecuador: trayectorias, enfoques y perspectivas." In *MUNA Guión Académico*, 19–31. Quito: Ministerio de Cultura y Patrimonio.
Figari, Carlos. 2010. "El movimiento LGBT en América Latina: institucionalizaciones oblicuas." In *Movilizaciones, protestas e identidades políticas en la Argentina del Bicentenario*, edited by Astor Masetti, Ernesto Villanueva, and Marcelo Gómez, 225–40. Buenos Aires: Nueva Trilce.
Foucault, Michel. 1991. *Remarks on Marx. Conversations with Duccio Trombadori*. New York City: SEMIOTEXT(E).
Gero, Joan M., and Margaret W. Conkey, eds. 1991. *Engendering Archaeology: Women and Prehistory*. Oxford: Blackwell.
Hall, Stuart, ed. 1997. *Culture, Media and Identities: Representation: Cultural Representations and Signifying Practices*. Los Angeles: Sage Publications.
hooks, bell. 1994. *Teaching to Transgress. Education as the Practice of Freedom*. New York: Routledge.
Horswell, Michael. 2005. *Decolonizing the Sodomite: Queer Tropes of Sexuality in Colonial Andean Culture*. Austin: University of Texas Press.
Kennedy Troya, Alexandra. 1992. "Del Taller a la Academia. Educación artística en el siglo XIX en Ecuador." *Procesos. Revista Ecuatoriana de Historia* 1 (2), 119–34.
León, Milvia. 2020. *MuNa: Estudio cualitativo de públicos. Beca Ibermuseos de Capacitación 2019. Proyecto de Multiplicación*. Quito. http://www.ibermuseos.org/wp-content/uploads/2020/06/estudio-de-publicos-muna-2020-compressed.pdf.
León, Paulina, and María Fernanda Ugalde. 2021. *Ir tomando cuerpx*. Quito: FLACSO.

López, Alejandro. 2018. "Re-pensar el museo: enfoques transversales del Museo Nacional del Ecuador." *MUNA Guión Académico*, 78–81. Quito: Ministerio de Cultura y Patrimonio.
Mogrovejo, Norma. 2020. *Del sexilio al matrimonio: Ciudadania sexual en la era del consumo neoliberal*. Washington, DC: Westphalia Press.
MUSEUMS. 2019. Directorio Red Ecuatoriana de Museos. Quito: Ministerio de Cultura y Patrimonio.
Ontaneda, Santiago. 2007. *Ecuador: Hitos de un pasado precolombino*. Quito: Banco Central del Ecuador.
Picq, Manuela, and María Amelia Viteri. 2020. "Being LGB in Ecuador." In *Worldwide Perspectives on Lesbian, Gays and Bisexuals: Culture, History and Law*, vol. 3, edited by Paula Gerber, Ch. 23, 388–402. Westport, CT: Praeger Press.
Preciado, Paul Beatriz. 2002. *Manifiesto Contrasexual*. Madrid: Anagrama.
Puebla, María Florencia. 2015. "Discursos curatoriales y representación del pasado en museos de América Latina." *Revista del Museo de Antropología* 8 (2): 239–50.
Segato, Rita. 2016. *La Guerra Contra las Mujeres*. Madrid: Traficantes de sueños.
Slocum, Sally. 1975. "Woman the Gatherer: Male Bias in Anthropology." In *Toward an Anthropology of Women*, edited by Rayna R. Reiter, 49. New York: Monthly Review Press.
Turkel, William. 2006. "Every Place is an Archive: Environmental History and the Interpretation of Physical Evidence." *Rethinking History* 10 (2): 259–76.
Ugalde, María Fernanda. 2009. *Iconografía Tolita. Lecturas del discurso ideológico en las representaciones figurativas del Desarrollo Regional*. Wiesebaden: Reichert.
———. 2017. "De siamesas y matrimonios: tras la simbología del género y la identidad sexual en la iconografía de las culturas precolombinas de la costa ecuatoriana." In *Trans. Diversidad de Identidades y Roles de Género*, edited by Andrés Gutiérrez Usillos, 109–14. Madrid: Ministerio de Educación, Cultura, y Deporte.
———. 2019. "Arqueología bajo la lupa queer: una apuesta por la multivocalidad." *Revista de Arqueología Pública* 13 (1): 135–54.
———. 2021. "Clay Embodiments: Materializing Asymmetrical Relations in Pre-Hispanic Figurines from Ecuador." Joseph C. Miller Memorial Lecture Series, vol. 5. Berlin: EB Verlag.
Ugalde, María Fernanda, and O. Hugo Benavides. 2018. "Queer Histories and Identities on the Ecuadorian Coast. The Personal, the Political and the Transnational." *WHATEVER. A Transdisciplinary Journal of Queer Theories and Studies* 1, 157–82.
———. 2019. *DIVERS[]S. Facetas del género en el Ecuador prehispánico*. Exhibition Catalogue. Quito: Ministerio de Cultura y Patrimonio.
Vázquez, Jorge. 1985. *Las Criaturas de la Noche: Cuentos*. Colección Narrativa Ecuatoriana, no. 6. Quito, Ecuador: Planeta.
Villalobos, Álvaro, and Francisco Cabanzo. 2020. "La experiencia como forma de conocimiento. Propuesta metodológica para la creación artística desde el diálogo y la performance." *Index, Revista de Arte Contemporáneo* 10, 94–111.
Viteri, María Amelia, María Fernanda Ugalde, and O. Hugo Benavides. 2021. "Dignifying and Decolonizing Queer Histories in Ecuador." *NACLA Report on the Americas* 53 (2): 187–92.
Wittig, Monique. 2006 (1981). *El Pensamiento Heterosexual*. Barcelona: Egales.
Yépez, Alexandra. 2002. *El Género: Un concepto útil para interpretar la dinámica de las sociedades pasadas*. Quito: Museo del Banco Central del Ecuador.
Zapater, Irving. 2018. "Breves apuntes sobre los museos de la Casa de la Cultura en Quito." In *MUNA Guión Académico*, 39–53. Quito: Ministerio de Cultura y Patrimonio.

Chapter 8

American Apotheosis
Confronting Exceptionalism in the (Re)Production of National Identity

Diane F. George

Introduction

This chapter begins in the present day with an insurrection. On 6 January 2021, the world watched as a violent mob stormed the United States Capitol building trying to prevent certification of the 2020 presidential election results. The insurrectionists styled themselves patriots and revolutionaries,[1] drawing on American Revolutionary War mythology and imagery — a symbolic well tapped by the Tea Party, their movement progenitor, a decade earlier. They carried the Gadsden flag and spoke of the founding fathers.[2] One militia group leader who took part in the attack called it "the shot heard round the world," referencing the beginning of the American Revolution at Lexington and Concord, and proclaimed openly that "the second revolution begins today" (Hennessy-Fiske 2021).[3] A member of Congress went so far as to justify the violence that took place, stating that "our Declaration of Independence ... says to overthrow tyrants" (Blake 2021).

To the majority of Americans, and to much of the world—as evidenced by the reactions of friends, news outlets, and social media from abroad (e.g., Afzhal et al. 2021; Murphy 2021)—the events of January 6 were astounding. As this chapter critiques the idea of American exceptionalism, the irony of my reaction on that day—"it can't happen here"—is not lost on me. But that was my response, one that I heard many echo, and the events

---

Notes for this chapter begin on page 196.

did seem surreal. How did we get here, to the point where an armed and violent mob tried to stop the peaceful transfer of power, buoyed by their conviction that they were true American patriots?

This chapter interrogates a small segment of the genealogy of American national identity in order to challenge the version of America that seems to foster the white patriarchal entitlement behind the insurrection. It uses archaeological evidence from the post–Revolutionary War era to expose the constructedness of this particular narrative. Specifically, the chapter looks at ceramics, mainly British transfer-printed wares produced for the American market, as they were used in social negotiations over national and other intersecting identities. While this is just one piece of a much larger picture of post-Revolutionary national identity formation, it sheds some light on the meanings embedded in the country's framework—ideas that are recognizable in the present day. The goal is to act as an advocate for a more inclusive and equitable nation.

Advocacy for the Nation

While American national identity (like all national identities) has always been subject to power and contestation, in the present moment there is a particular entrenchment and extreme polarization in the United States around and over specific visions of the nation. Those who claim to know the past as an indelible truth ignore that American identity has never been singular: we are and always have been too diverse, too large, too geographically and culturally distinct. The mob that stormed the Capitol on January 6, and a large segment of those who support their goals, nevertheless insist that they alone can define the nation, patriotism, and who gets to be called an American.

The particular national narrative that drove the insurrectionists—and many other supporters of the forty-fifth president—is rooted in the very formation of the United States, in the notion of divine exceptionalism that was woven into the national imaginary from its inception and to which white Americans have turned to justify genocide, slavery, imperialism, and more. This idea provides a sense of entitlement to commit—and justification for—such acts: they are a God-given right and even an obligation. History and archaeology, however, demonstrate that this identity is mythical: that "America" was not the inexorable nation conjectured by the exceptionalism narrative. Rather, the "imagined community" (Anderson 1991) of *America* had to be produced to draw together the many and disparate interests that comprised the new and fragile country.

The past haunts the present in terms not of what was but of what is not and what might be (Derrida 1994; Fisher 2012). For the insurrectionists, holding on to a past that was shaped first and foremost by patriarchy, racism, and the privileging of "whiteness" is resistance to future possibilities of a more equitable and equal society. Their answer to who gets to be an American is reflected in the makeup of the rioters: almost exclusively white (95 percent) and overwhelmingly male (85 percent) (Pape 2021). The reality of America is far different: as reported by the Brookings Institute, census data since 1990 show rapidly increasing diversity in the country and, in 2020, a decline in the white population (Frey 2020). This is precisely the specter that haunts those who have benefited from four hundred years of white patriarchy or who have based their very identities in its structures. In fact, a University of Chicago study recently found that a key unifying factor among those arrested for the Capitol insurrection was not economic precarity or unemployment but residing in counties with the largest declines in the non-Hispanic white population (Pape 2021, 54).

It seems particularly relevant to examine and deconstruct narratives of national identity in these fraught times given that those who seek to hold on to power and privilege, like the insurrectionists, rely so heavily on them. The question is, can archaeology serve an advocacy role by providing for a view of the past that allows space for the potentialities that haunt the nation? As the authors in this volume have discussed, archaeological advocacy can take many forms. One of these is the use of archaeology and the material record for confronting powerful and oppressive narratives, such as the anti-democratic and racist narratives that permeate our discourse (such that it is) on national identity. I have endeavored to challenge the hegemonic concept of America as a divinely ordained, inexorable nation by beginning to expose the genealogies of white, male, capitalist power embedded in the production of the nation. The data suggest a different narrative, one that recognizes the mythological nature of American exceptionalism. By excavating these origins (both literally and figuratively) and adding this dialectical narrative to present-day discourse, we can advocate for a more inclusive and equitable nation. As Margaret Purser's excellent foreword to this volume shows, addressing the present moment as archaeologists is not only necessary but unavoidable. Only by allowing the present to engage with the materiality of the past can we begin to address the future.

"Deep Anxiety": American Identity after the Revolution

Contrary to the national mythology of thirteen united colonies fighting for their independence, the new country emerged from the Revolutionary War to a "world turned upside down."[4] Precariously united against a common enemy during the war, this group of loosely connected and disparate states with significant regional variations had to figure out if and how to come together as a nation. Debates raged over what form and how much power the new federal government should have. Federalists believed that the states should form a cohesive body with a robust central government, while anti-Federalists (later Democratic Republicans) wanted power to be more dispersed among the states. These were serious and potentially fatal divisions, entangled with and inseparable from regional/local interests and identities. "Thoughtful men viewed with alarm the state of anarchy into which the country was rapidly drifting" (Stokes 1915, 375). Even as late as 1796, in his farewell address to the nation, George Washington spoke of his "deep anxiety" (Wood 2009, 206) over the future of the nation, referring to it as an "experiment" and admitting his uncertainty about whether the country with all of its diversity could hold together (see Washington 2004 [1796], 6–13).

European American identity at the time of the war was still largely connected to Britain. In 1768, the well-known pamphleteer John Dickenson wrote: "If we are separated from our mother country . . . where shall we find another Britain to supply our loss? Torn from the body to which we are united by religion, liberty, laws, affections, relations, language, and commerce we must bleed at every vein." Dickinson's graphic language creates a visceral sense of the (white) colonists' embodied Britishness by siting the loss of their connection in figurative bodily imagery. While there were some, such as Thomas Paine, who saw independence as the only alternative to the colonists' complaints, many more tried to resolve their differences with the mother country, even on the eve of revolution. As hostilities turned violent, the Second Continental Congress sent the "Olive Branch Petition" to King George, requesting that he intervene with the British Parliament to resolve their disputes without bloodshed. The language of the petition displays more than an effort to avoid charges of treason, not only reassuring the king that his subjects will remain loyal but extravagantly describing the feelings of the colonists toward Britain: "We beg leave to further assure your Majesty, that notwithstanding the sufferings of your loyal colonists, during the course of the present controversy, *our breasts retain too tender a regard for the kingdom from which we derive our origin*, to request such a reconciliation as might in any manner be inconsistent with her dignity or her welfare [emphasis added]" (National Archives 2021[1775]). Local and regional identities posed perhaps a greater challenge to unification, making it difficult for George Washington even to muster a sufficient and stable army to fight the war (Brown 2000, 189; McDonnell 2001, 5), where militia would "rise briefly to defend their own localities, but . . . were unwilling to travel long distances to fight away from home" (Brown 2000, 189). Colin Woodard (2011, 115, 127) argues that the American Revolution was actually "fought by a loose military alliance of [six] nations, each of which was most concerned with preserving or reasserting control of its respective culture, character, and power structure." Undoubtedly, revolution was not the inevitable or inexorable path for the colonies. "In fact, the revolution divided families and neighborhoods. Benjamin Franklin hated his son William for clinging to loyalty. In New York, Gouverneur Morris was a leading Patriot, but his brother served in the British army. Horatio Gates commanded an American army while his brother-in-law was a British officer. Pennsylvania's chief justice conceded that America 'was not a nation at war with another nation, but a country in a state of civil war'" (Taylor 2016, 211–12). This division continued long after the war. In 1788, James Madison famously wrote that the "spirit of locality" was an "evil" that was destroying "the aggregate interests of the community" (National Archives 2021 [1788]). Combined (and intertwined) with debates on the form of government, these decentralized identities threatened the existence of the young United States.

Without digressing into the practical details of the political debates, it is important to stress that the conflicts were intense and often personal. These were not casual differences amicably discussed but deeply felt beliefs that drove passionate acts. More than two decades after the Declaration of Independence, the presidential election of 1800, which ultimately resulted in the defeat of the Federalist candidate John Adams, led some later historians to speculate that the country had been on the brink of civil war. Defining the national identity in this era was serious and fraught business. The archival record from the period thus demonstrates that the United States was not a nation freed by revolution to fulfill its divine destiny, but a group of people who had to figure out what to do when they realized they had overthrown their king. It was in this context of dissonance that the production of an American national identity became an imperative.

The Apotheosis of Washington: American-Themed Ceramics and the Production of the Nation

After the war, upper- and middle-class Americans became avid consumers of American-themed British ceramics, including jugs (pitchers), plates, punch bowls, tankards, tea wares, and coffee pots. Arman and Arman (1998) and Teitelman et al. (2010) provide extensive catalogs of the vessels that were available for the American market. Ships are one of the most common subjects of these prints, both as naval vessels and merchant ships. "Success to America"—or a modified and perhaps more honest version reading "Success to American Trade"—was a popular slogan, as were other mottos advocating for peace, prosperity, liberty, equality, and supremacy for the new country. Symbols of unity were commonly used, along with messages or slogans urging America to "stand united" or a similar sentiment. These unity symbols include eagles, which evoke the Great Seal of the United States (the thirteen stars and stripes unified on the eagle's escutcheon and above the bird's head symbolizing the joining of the thirteen colonies) and the state chain motif, with thirteen or more links bearing the name of each state. Perhaps the most sought-after designs were of George Washington in both his military and presidential roles, and, after his death in 1799, in memorials and tributes (Nelson 1980, 99; Halfpenny 2010, 36). Other founding fathers and heroes of the revolution such as Franklin, Jefferson, Madison, and Lafayette, as well as famous battles, were also commemorated.

One concept that emerges clearly in a closer examination of British transfer prints is the idea of American exceptionalism, the belief that America is a divinely ordained nation whose existence was inevitable, and which therefore has a responsibility and an entitlement to "shine its light" on the rest of the world. This story is produced on ceramics through the deification of the founders and the mythologizing of the nation's origins. Prints incorporate heavenly imagery (angels, cherubs, trumpets, clouds, rays of light) or direct textual references to God and mythologize the American nation through classical symbolism that connects the United States to the virtuous principles (e.g., liberty) of these societies and to their ancient past. Some prints describe the founding fathers using tropes of the savior and the noble hero-warrior (who himself is somewhat mythical).[5]

Classical elements are prevalent in many of the patterns found on American-themed ceramics, connecting the new country to antiquity and imbuing it with an ancient, even primordial, history. America herself is represented by Columbia, a goddess-like figure draped in a classical garment, as are figures representing Liberty, Peace, and Justice. Other images incorporate laurel leaves, willow trees, urns, and columned ruins, all taken from classical imagery. Latin phrases such as *Vincere Aut Mori* (Conquer or Die) are sometimes found accompanying the prints. Familiarity with the classics was also a sign of education and class status, part of one's expected catalog of knowledge during the Enlightenment. Thus, a print with classical components (now called "neoclassical") could have added an aspect of socioeconomic class to the national identity.[6]

Divine involvement in the creation of the United States is explicit in a print titled "America Declared Independent" (Arman and Arman 1998, 65) (Figure 8.1). An angel and a classically garbed woman appear in the ruins of a Greek temple. The Corinthian columns foreground a pyramid,

Figure 8.1. "America Declared Independent—July 4, 1776." Courtesy of Transferware Collectors Club, Pattern Number 13827.

and a harp and cannon lie at the feet of the seated woman. She holds a tablet or parchment that reads "July 4 1776-America Declared Independent." Both the columns and the pyramid connect the newly independent country to classical antiquity and to the endurance of the cultures they represent. (Egyptian artifacts became part of the neoclassical lexicon after the Napoleonic invasion of that country in 1798 [Dobson and Tonks 2018, 311], and pyramids were incorporated into Western design aesthetics, including on the United States dollar). Values of classical democracy and Republicanism would also have been associated with the declaration of American independence by setting the action in the print against classical Greek ruins. Key here, however, is the angel, who points to the proclamation as if explaining it to the woman. The angel is standing, the teacher instructing the seated female pupil. Here, knowledge and values are explicitly imparted from the divine.

While this print may be one of the most obvious presentations of divine exceptionalism, many others make this connection. One pattern that is largely textual still manages to visually link the names Washington and Adams to that of "God." The text is that of the first and final two stanzas of the poem "Adams and Liberty," written in 1798 by Robert Treat Paine. The three names (Washington, Adams, and God) appear in larger font than the rest of the poem, making them immediately noticeable and drawing a connection between them. Washington is described as superhuman, the defender of "Freedom's temple," standing at its portal to "repulse, with his Breast" the tempest of war. It is unclear how Washington's breast would be weaponized—perhaps bolts of lightning to repel "the thunder." Despite the poem's title, Adams is not presented quite so loftily—more in the realm of mortals—but still as the best of the best: America's pride whose laws shall flourish. Classical antiquity is once again entwined with America in the poem's text, where the poet imparts to the nation "the glory of Rome and the wisdom of Greece." The verse also references Leonidas, the king of Sparta who died along with the three hundred soldiers whom he led against a much larger Persian force at Thermopylae. Greek history and myth are evoked by the use of this name, eliciting both the tremendous bravery of the actual historical figures and their willingness to die for Sparta, and the mythical connection of Leonidas to the superhuman Heracles (or Hercules to the Romans) (see Prakken 1940).

Another print centering on Adams provides an example of the use of imagery to create a sense of divinity, or at least divine-adjacency, among the founders. Titled "John Adams, President of the United States," this print places the second president among mythical and heavenly figures on a large medallion encircled by laurel leaves (Arman and Arman 1998, 61). Sitting in the clouds to Adams's left is the classically garbed figure of Justice with her scales. To his right is Plenty bearing a cornucopia. A cherub hovers above Adams, holding a Phrygian (liberty) cap on a pole and looking down at the president with what might be interpreted as a benevolent or even tender gaze.[7] Arcing above the entire image are rays of light surrounding the figures, which, particularly combined with the clouds, give the viewer a sense of heavenly splendor.

Many other prints too numerous to describe use the same and similar imagery to construct the founders as divine and mythical, including vessels for children (see George 2022). Transfer prints naming Washington warrant further mention as he was the most popular figure in American-themed designs. He appears on ceramics in three contexts: as military leader, as president, and in mourning imagery after his death. The breadth of these depictions constructs a larger-than-life character, one who in all things in both life and death is "a man without example, a patriot without reproach" (as described in Thomas Paine's eulogy). He is called the father of the country and "The Deliverer" (Arman and Arman 1998, 210). A number of prints refer to his "glory"—a word that has divine connotations. Certainly, the word can refer to people or things of great renown or splendor, but it is commonly used in association with the Judeo-Christian God, as a quality of the divine or as something given to honor him (see Cambridge English Dictionary 2022). In the context of other Washington designs, some heavenly association seems likely here; in at least three prints, he is called "immortal."

Many of the mourning prints express deep and overwhelming grief. These sentiments are set among copious neoclassical mourning imagery including willows, urns, and obelisks, and are conveyed by weeping female figures in classical dress as well as Native Americans (who were sometimes used to represent America during the colonial era). The prints are unanimous in their version of American sentiment: America is of one mind in its reverence for Washington and profound sorrow at his death. A number proclaim that Washington is "in glory" and "America in tears" (see Arman and Arman 1998, 205). One shows a Native American weeping over a medallion bearing Washington's portrait. He stands beneath a lush willow tree and the entire oval-shaped image is crowned by an eagle. The print reads "America Lamenting the Death of her Favorite Son" (Arman and Arman 1998, 208). These images use Indigenous bodies to elide Washington's complex and often violent relationship with Native Americans and his culpability for the death and displacement of thousands (Calloway 2019). While doubtless most of the audience for these prints would not have seen this legacy as problematic, it must be viewed in the larger processes of heroicizing and mythologizing the country's most famous leader.

One print stands out among the efforts to deify the founders and to present the United States as an exceptional entity. Taken from an engraving by John James Barralet in 1802 (Nelson 1980, 101) (Figure 8.2), the print is titled "Apotheosis"—literally "deification." It is thick with imagery, beginning with the figures shown mourning Washington's death. Slumped in front of the tomb, Liberty and a Native American figure mourn (Liberty being placed in a superior position to the Indigenous figure). An American eagle holding an escutcheon in the lower left of the image discards its usual stoicism, its head thrown back and beak open as if crying out. Three female figures—possibly Faith, Hope, and Charity—and two cherubs appear at center left. The Metropolitan Museum of Art describes these surrounding figures thusly: "hunched over in mourning and guarding Washington's sarcophagus, they resemble images of sleeping soldiers at Christ's tomb." The tomb itself reads "Sacred to the Memory of Washington" together with his death date and age. "Sacred" invokes the divine and literally means the subject is worthy of veneration or even worship (George 2019, 267). In the center, the focus of the print is Washington himself being lifted from his tomb by two angels, one of whom represents Time or Immortality. One of the angels holds Washington's arm, leading him heavenward toward "rays of glory" (Earle 1902, 264). These rays bathe Washington in heavenly light as, clothed in classical robes, he reclines in

Figure 8.2. *The Apotheosis of Washington*, engraving and etching by John James Barralet, 1800–1802. Painting in the collection of the Metropolitan Museum of Art, Gift of William H. Huntington, 1883, public domain.

a Christlike sacrificial pose in the arms of Immortality. "How can one not believe in [the country's] exceptional nature in the face of such heavenly splendor?" (George 2019, 267).

Success to American Trade: Two Federal-Period Households in Lower Manhattan

Two features from sites in Lower Manhattan containing American-themed ceramics provide case studies of how these ceramics might have been used to produce national identity. Both sites are located on the east side of the island near its southern tip within close proximity (about 0.4 miles) to one another and both are on land that was originally part of the East River and was granted to wealthy and prominent citizens with the condition that it be filled in by the grantees. The first feature, from the Assay site, was likely a public privy at the waterfront: a roughly eleven-foot-by-eight-foot wooden box built at the intersection of two wharves (Louis Berger 1990, IV-100). The second feature, from the Beekman Street site, was a single-episode trash deposit in the corner of a small stone foundation beneath the present-day street (Chrysalis Archaeology 2007, 41).[8] Both date to the later postrevolutionary period: the privy deposit is likely circa 1807 but with a possible range of 1795 to 1807, and the trash deposit dates between 1800 and 1823. The mean ceramic dates are 1799 and 1797, respectively.

The urban context of New York City at the time is part of the milieu of national identity creation at these sites. New York City by the end of the eighteenth century was the country's largest entrepôt (Burrows and Wallace 1998, 333). An infusion of capital after the federal assumption of state debts "bathed" the city in "prosperity" (Burrows and Wallace 1998, 306). Immigrants with "cash, credit, and connections" flocked to New York City (Burrows and Wallace 1998, 302), helping to create a cosmopolitan economic hub. In the final decade of the eighteenth century, the city population exploded, nearly doubling between the first census in 1790 (33,131) and the second in 1800 (60,515) (Stokes 1915, 381). Wealth, specifically highly valued real estate, was concentrated in the East River port area, where the study sites are located (Klein and Willis 1985, 269–70). This was the axis of overseas commerce: the business heart of the city with "several spacious streets crowded with ships, stores, and warehouses of every description" (Stokes 1915, 401). The Beekman Street area in particular was a hub of commercial activity and was advertised as "the best" and "the most desirable" location in the city for doing business (Commercial Advertiser 18 February 1801, 2).

The People

The site occupants associated with the ceramics recovered from these features (or those visible in the archival record) were merchants and businessmen, some with families, who were members of the upper and middle classes. Virtually all were connected in some way to overseas trade. At the Assay site, specifically at 91 Front Street, where the feature was located, the property was occupied and later owned by Coertlandt Van Beuren, whose initials decorate a set of porcelain teawares that are among the ceramics from the privy. Van Beuren was a grocer and was quite wealthy, having extensive land holdings in addition to a successful business. He, his wife, Ann, and several children resided at 91 Front Street between 1801 and 1812, and Coertlandt's storefront occupied the street level until his death in 1820. Van Beuren was a Democratic-Republican who was heavily involved in New York City and State politics. He served as the leader of the Republican Saint Tammany's Society, which counted among its members lawyers and merchants as well as artisans and masters of skilled trades (Burrows and Wallace 1998, 316) who sought to "foster democratic and republican institutions" (Stokes 1915, 374) and opposed the "resurgence" of the "New York aristocracy" (Burrows and Wallace 1998, 316). Van Beuren chaired the Democratic-Republican state nominating committee in 1797 and, in 1804, was nominated himself for state assembly on the Republican ticket with Aaron Burr. (*Greenleaf's New York Journal*, 22 April 1797, 3; *New York Evening Post* [NYEP] 21 April 1804, 3). Van Beuren, then, was plainly concerned with the identity and path of the American nation.

Not much is known about Ann Van Beuren or the Van Beuren children beyond their names, but they likely played an active role in constructing the nation through ceramics. Women were often the purchasers of ceramics, making the choice as to what would be displayed on the family table and at teas (Wall 1994, 135–6). Ann and her elder daughters, Catherine and Ann, would have shopped for ceramics to use in the family home. Ann may have been trying to support her husband's politics while perhaps adding her own ideas to the mix. The three women, and particularly the elder Ann, would have been very aware that the family's bread and butter came from Coertlandt's business and likely would not have wanted to purchase anything that could offend business partners or customers. They may also have shared the view that national unity was necessary to create stability for their family by allowing trade to flourish.

Because the feature was likely a public privy (although located on private property), it is impossible to associate all of the artifacts with the Van Beurens. The neighboring property at 93 Front Street probably contributed at least one set of tea wares: Chinese porcelain with the initials "JE"—likely John Ellsworth, who ran a genteel boarding house here until 1800. Although items may have been deposited over a range of years, several characteristics of the feature suggest a more limited deposition, making their association with the Van Beurens more plausible. The lack of a floor means that tides would have washed many artifacts into the river over time, suggesting a later deposit date. Most ceramics were recovered from only a few contexts with numerous cross mends, and approximately one-third of the vessels were more than 50 percent complete, suggesting a fairly rapid accumulation (Louis Berger 1990, IV62–IV63). This may have been part of the landfill process, when the water lot was ultimately filled in 1807, with both the Van Beuren household and the neighboring boarding house contributing household trash to the deposit.

Identifying the owners of the Beekman Street ceramics is more problematic, as the feature is located between two historic properties and cannot be clearly assigned to one or the other.[9] Both possible properties (286 Pearl Street and 224 Water Street) were owned by extremely wealthy merchants (Robert Crommelin, or his widow, Elizabeth, by the relevant time period, and Peter Schermerhorn, respectively). Elizabeth Crommelin rented the Pearl Street property to several well-to-do merchants, who at times took on lodgers, and in 1801 and 1814, the property is listed as a boarding house in the city directory. Schermerhorn likewise rented his property to the merchant Thomas Carpenter until 1808, the year it became a genteel boarding house, although Schermerhorn appears from tax records to have stored some personal property on the site at least through 1811. The known residents of the Water Street boarding house were merchants and a few artisans.

While it is thus impossible to associate the Beekman Street ceramics with any particular person or family, there are some general similarities in the demographics of the properties' occupants. The majority of those identified through archival records were merchants, some engaged mainly in the West Indian trade and others trading with "East India" and Europe. Some specialized in particular goods, such as the merchants living and working at 286 Pearl Street after 1805, who dealt mainly in umbrellas and other accessories. Others may not have been directly involved in overseas trade but sold items that were manufactured abroad and shipped via this network. All would have been at least middle class. Thomas Carpenter, the merchant who occupied 224 Water Street until 1808, appears to have been successful and fairly wealthy. He owned several ships (e.g., *NYEP* 10 April 1810, 3) and conducted trade with Liverpool (*NYEP* 23 November 1803, 1) and the southern states (*NYEP* 6 December 1803, 1). John Tonnele, who resided and worked at 286 Pearl Street from 1806 until 1815, along with his wife and several children, also appears to have been well-off, possessing extensive property holdings (New York City Liber of Wills 98, 304).

The main occupants of 286 Pearl Street between 1797 and 1815, Claude Fortin, Bruno Comte, and John Tonnele (Fortin preceding Comte and Tonnele) were also connected by their country of birth. All were French nationals and became naturalized US citizens (US Naturalization Records Indexes, 4 May 1803; US Passport Applications, 1795–1925, 17 June 1811; Scott 1983, 280–3) This was not a coincidence. Between 1789 and 1814, a total of eight residents or business owners occupying this property were French born or descended, suggesting a network that immigrants were able to use as social capital to find lodging, homes, and places of business. In fact, Tonnele and Fortin's acquaintance and possibly friendship is documented in Fortin's 4 May 1803 naturalization record, which lists Tonnele as the witness. After 1793, the beginning of the Reign of Terror in France, many French citizens came to the United States to flee the turmoil

(Burrows and Wallace 1998, 313). In 1794, an English traveler wrote that the city was "so full of" the French that they "constitute a considerable part of the population" (Burrows and Wallace 1998, 313). The individuals at 286 Pearl Street may have sought a place to conduct trade without the interruption of war.

The French connection to the Enlightenment ideals of the postrevolutionary period is evident in the country's support of the American Revolution and in the ideals of its own revolution. Tonnele seems to have shared these ideals himself: he was a member of *L'Union Français,* the French Masonic Lodge, which according to the city directory met twice a month, on the first and third Mondays (Jones's New York City Directory 1805, 106). The lodge was the first Masonic delegation to march in Washington's funeral procession and carried as one of its treasured emblems the sword of Lafayette (*L'Union Française* 2009). Tonnele's views were Republican: in 1801, he was involved in a questionable real estate purchase made along with a number of other individuals in order to qualify to vote in city charter elections in a ward where he was not a resident (*NYEP* 15 December 1801, 2). Both Comte and Tonnele financially supported American causes, donating to the Committee of Defence during the War of 1812 (*National Advocate* 22 August 1814, 2).

The Ceramics

The negotiation of political and national identities is evident in the American-themed ceramics found at both the Assay and the Beekman Street sites through overt political messages as well as more subtle communications about national values and characteristics.[10] The Assay site assemblage contains two American-themed transfer prints found on three jugs, a pearlware teapot with a molded figure of Liberty, a felspathic (or Castleford-type) stoneware teapot that likely had molded American motifs, and a printed pearlware plate that, while produced for the British market, may also have had meaning for American identity. This chapter will focus on the possible use of the ceramics by the Van Beuren household, which was the most likely owner.[11]

The items from the assemblage present interesting possibilities for this analysis of national identity formation. The British-themed plate bears a brown printed pattern known alternatively as "Britannia," "Pax" (Magid 2006, 12), or "Peace of Amiens" (Transferware Collectors Club [TCC] Pattern #11108; TCC Classical Ladies #3), with colored enamels or "clobbering" highlighting the transfer print. The focus of the pattern is three classically dressed female figures representing Britain, France (Libertas), and

Peace (Magid 2006, 12). The plate was made to commemorate the signing of the Treaty of Amiens in 1802, which provided a short truce in Britain's decade-old war with France. Although the treaty was not expected to last and was disadvantageous to Britain in many ways, it was widely popular and received with massive celebrations. "London and other towns across Britain were illuminated," and there were "fireworks, feasts, congratulatory addresses, sermons, and poems" (Johnson 2002, 20). A key reason for the celebratory atmosphere, despite the drawbacks of the treaty's terms, was the renewal of commerce. The agreement preserved British supremacy on the seas and safeguarded British trade (Johnson 2002, 23).

The Peace of Amiens pattern appeared on any number of vessels and forms, including coffee and teapots, teacups and saucers, bowls, plates, punch bowls, and serving dishes. While it was manufactured for the British market, its meanings are more complex. The respite and chance for recovery from war provided for open and reinvigorated trade. The popularity of the motif thus transcended Britain and appealed to consumers in America as well. Barbara Magid (2006) writes about this pattern in George Washington's hometown of Alexandria, where archaeological investigations uncovered the motif in two households and a tavern. Magid (2006) suggests that the print was popular in the United States not for its British associations but because it could also be used to celebrate American victory over France in the "Quasi-War" of 1798–1800, a naval conflict that brought an official end to the alliance that had existed with France since 1778. As in the British context, this too was about commerce: the compact signed with France allowed American trade to resume.

Although Republicans like Van Beuren tended to be supportive of France, that country's interference with the Caribbean trade during the Quasi-War would have put him at a disadvantage. He may have procured a commemorative plate (or a set) when they became available in 1802. Van Beuren's status and occupational identity would have been continually reproduced by the display of the plate in the household. Perhaps Ann Van Beuren chose it to affiliate the family with "Pax" or peace, expressing her political beliefs through her role in purchasing decorative household items or ceramic wares for use by the family. She may have also chosen the plate to express broader Enlightenment ideals of Republicanism (the figure representing France, with a Phrygian [liberty] cap and manumitting staff), with the figure of Britannia acknowledging the importance of British trading partners. This would make sense with Coertlandt Van Beuren's active Republicanism, as a way to produce a layered identity incorporating those values while preserving trade alliances.

The two teapots may also be considered American-themed, although the pearlware vessel is the only one with an extant motif: a silhouette of

Liberty surrounded by laurel leaves and stars.[12] These teapots closely resemble others decorated with American themes, comprising an ovular shape with embossed classical figures, usually with an eagle closely resembling the Great Seal of the United States. On most known vessels, the raised embossing is lined in blue or black. One other version found online does not include Liberty but bears a seated figure of Peace on the reverse (Bohanna 2021).

The use of the Great Seal—the official symbol of the United States— would have been seen as a patriotic gesture (in the sense of loyalty and duty to the country). The teapots, however, could have been used in more complex ways to construct their users' identities. The seal was adopted in 1782 after substantial debate and the specific symbolism of each element was quite significant. While the emblem itself would have been immediately recognizable to members of the merchant class and anyone in their social orbit, it is likely that educated and politically aware consumers had at least some understanding of the messages it embodied, given the recency of its adoption. The version used in this teapot pattern is quite similar to the actual seal and may have been chosen deliberately—rather than any of the numerous loosely based variations—so as to reproduce official meanings. As described in a statement by the Secretary of the Continental Congress, Charles Thompson, on 20 June 1782 (Bureau of Public Affairs 2002, 5), the shield and the country's motto *"e pluribus unum"* (out of many, one) represent unity, "the several states all joined in one solid compact"; the eagle clutches an olive branch with thirteen olives in one talon and thirteen arrows in the other, "denot[ing] the power of peace [and] war"; and "the escutcheon is borne on the breast of an American Eagle without any other supporters to denote that the United States of America ought to rely on their own Virtue." The seal loudly proclaims a *united* nation through the escutcheon, motto, and the repeated appearance of objects in sets of thirteen (representing the thirteen colonies), including a constellation of thirteen stars floating above the eagle's head. The creators of the seal saw this unity as coming through Congress (Bureau of Public Affairs 2002, 5) as representatives of the people—an idea that might have been supported by a Democratic Republican such as Van Beuren, who favored diffused central power. As a merchant, he would have wanted to construct a unified identity in order to bring stability to the nation and remove obstacles to commerce. The vessels' users may also have incorporated the messages of strength and self-reliance into their version of the nation, as these qualities might prove useful in business.

Finally, three creamware jugs bear American-themed motifs (one motif appears on two separate jugs). The first jug has motifs on three sides: a ship on the sea with a banner reading "Success to Trade;" an American-

Figure 8.3. Complete versions of two of the prints found on a jug from the Assay site. *Left:* Jefferson quote and American eagle, Metropolitan Museum of Art, "Jug 1800–1830," the Collection, The American Wing (public domain). *Right:* Ship, stock print with American flag, "Success to Trade" banner. Reproduced with permission from Division of Cultural and Community Life, National Museum of American History, Smithsonian Institution, Object ID CE.63.087, Robert H. McCauley.

style eagle with a line from Jefferson's 1801 inaugural address; and the Bakers Arms, the crest and motif of one of the dozens of London trade guilds (Figure 8.3). Most of the ship motif is missing, but the remaining portion is recognizable as the standard print of a ship that was among the most common items to appear on creamware jugs (Garrett 2010, 37). While ships were often personalized with national flags or names, the details of this particular ship are unfortunately lost, but the banner below the waves with the words "Success to Trade" speaks volumes. Trade and commerce were often referenced on American-themed ceramics, always with a hopeful sentiment of success or blessing. These themes wove the idea of commerce into the national psyche, making it inseparable from the success of the nation. For the Van Beurens, who became wealthy from the overseas trade, a merchant ship with the rousing exhortation of "success to trade" would have emphasized the importance of their own identity as upper-class merchants and constructed it as integral to national identity. This is particularly true, as the jug also contains an American eagle with the words "Entangling alliances with none" and "Jefferson. Anno Domini 1802." This line, which is taken from Jefferson's 1801 inaugural address, reads in full: "Peace, *commerce*, and honest friendship with all nations—Entangling alliances with none" [emphasis added]. Jefferson was referring in particular to America's long association with (and obligation to) France. The end to this "entangling alliance" allowed a resumption of unhindered American trade, thus the connection between the words and the first motif on the jug. In fact, Van Beuren could have used the vessel to solidify or reaffirm his Republican identity and commitment to unfettered trade. Jefferson was a Democratic Republican, and the presence of the eagle and the name of the president connect the sentiments on commerce to the national identity.

The final piece of this jug's decoration is more of a mystery. What aspect of the wealthy Van Beurens' identity might be constructed by the display of a trade guild motif? Perhaps the vessel was in the merchant's inventory or served as a display piece, and the children were enchanted by the somewhat playful deer that flank the crest. Possibly Coertlandt or Ann chose it for the two motifs that did speak to their sense of self, particularly as the former at least had very strong Republican affiliations. Maybe they were willing to "put up with" with the Bakers Arms because it was already part of a design that was "mostly" what they wanted even if not exactly (Britt, personal communication). It is also possible that the Democratic-Republican appeal to working people (Burrows and Wallace 1998, 319) was an aspect that Van Beuren wished to incorporate into his own—or the national—identity. Perhaps he simply wished to present the appearance of cross-class solidarity, or possibly he truly believed in these values. If so, the irony of his enrichment through the Triangular Trade and the wealth disparity between himself and tradesmen may have been lost on Van Beuren.[13]

At least two jugs bear the second American-themed image, one that could have been used to produce a national identity of divine exceptionalism (Figure 8.4). A poem paying tribute to Washington is contained in a central oval medallion surrounded by classically based American iconography. The border is composed of laurel leaves. The poem, a stanza from *American Independency* by Edward Rushton, reads:

> As he tills your rich glebe, the old peasant shall tell
> While his bosom with Liberty glows
> How your Warren expired—how Montgomery fell
> And how Washington humbled your foes.

Below the poem is a banner with the word "Independence," and above is a Phrygian cap with the word "Liberty" on a pole and surrounded by a laurel leaf. There is a version of the American flag with an eagle surrounded by a circle of stars on a background of stripes and a banner with stars and two stripes. Below the poem are numerous images, including baskets of fruit, farming implements, a globe, an artist's palette, books,

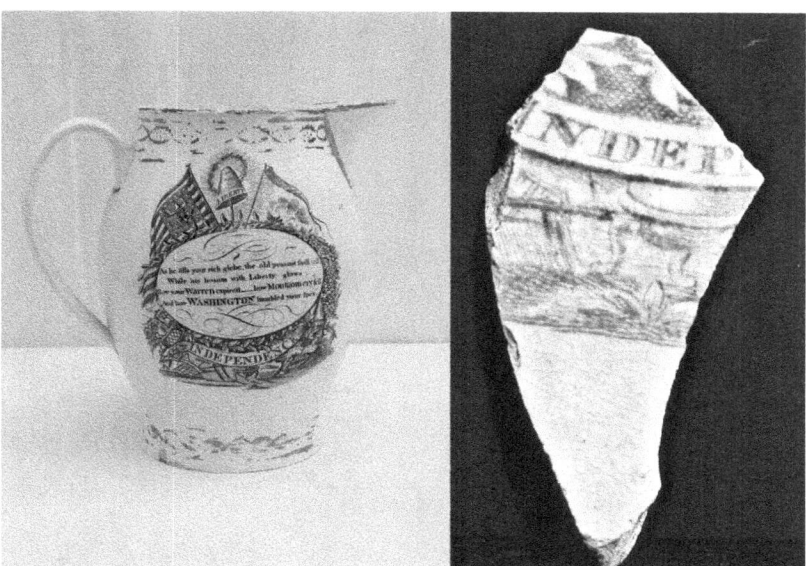

Figure 8.4. *Left:* Jug with stanza from Ruston, American Independency (Division of Cultural and Community Life, National Museum of American History, Smithsonian Institution, Object ID CE.63.080, Robert H. McCauley). *Right:* Sherd from jug with the same print found at the Assay site. © Diane F. George.

and a quill. The neoclassical elements and the actual words of "independence" and "liberty" could have been used to construct a national identity built on Enlightenment values. Here, these explicitly include knowledge and education—the globe, books, and pen. The farming implements and the baskets of fruit may have been used to express pride or belief in the productivity and economic foundation of the nation, enabled by independence, the bounty of harvest being produced in service of the nation's growth: everyone needs to play their part.

Not only the images but also the rousing poem itself calls on the "horizontal comradeship" spoken of by Benedict Anderson (1991, 7): "A nation is imagined as a *community* because regardless of the actual inequality and exploitation that may prevail . . . the nation is always perceived as a deep, horizontal comradeship," for which many will sacrifice their lives. This visceral appeal to an overwhelming national passion elides the fact that the "peasant" is tilling land that he probably does not own and will never be anywhere close—literally or figuratively—to the Van Beurens. Whether part of Van Beuren's inventory (because of the duplicate copies) or a set that adorned their table, the Rushton poem would have been used

Figure 8.5. Shell-edged pearlware soup dish with black overglaze transfer print of Columbia, from the Beekman Street site. © Diane F. George.

by people who likely were never glebe tillers themselves. The words of the poem produce a glorious American history, with valiant leaders who fell in combat and one, whose name is literally larger than the others, who "humbled" the nation's enemies. These heroes of the Revolution can be revered by all, not just those with the means to purchase such a vessel. The use of the jugs may have reassured their consumers that liberty and independence was meant for all, rich and poor. They would have been used to produce—along with a national identity that valued valor, sacrifice, and Enlightenment ideals—the illusion of a classless society, rejecting the entrenched British titled nobility but glossing over the deeper divisions within American society. This is consistent with what we know about Van Beuren's Republican politics.

The second ceramic assemblage, from the Beekman Street site, also contains American-themed ceramics: one British transferware vessel with an American-themed print and at least four Chinese porcelain saucers decorated with American-style eagles. The former is a blue shell-edged pearlware soup dish bearing a black overglaze transfer-printed motif commemorating the death of George Washington (Figure 8.5). The print, which is untitled but sometimes referred to as "Columbia," is rare, and there are no other known examples on shell-edged ware (Arman and Arman 1998, 77; Teitelman et al. 2010, 214). This vessel is personalized, likely with the initials of a husband and wife: "MB" is fully extant on the marly but there are traces of another letter or possibly an ampersand to the left of this monogram. This personalization, along with use wear on the dish, suggest it may have been part of a set.

The Washington plate has multiple layers of symbolism and potential meaning. Almost certainly, it was owned and used by one of the merchants who lived and worked at 286 Pearl Street or 224 Water Street. While class and status vary somewhat among these individuals, all would have moved in overlapping circles because of their connection to the overseas trade. Whether reproducing or attempting to produce an identity of higher social and economic status, their desires in this regard would have been similar: to negotiate a position as a respectable, cosmopolitan businessman who was a worthy trade partner and social peer. The Washington plate could have been used to achieve this, and more.

The print has a classical aesthetic, with a number of recognizable elements. The central focus is a female figure draped in classical garments, meant to represent Columbia (see Arman and Arman 1998, 77; Teitelman et al. 2010, 214). Drawing on the Roman goddess Libertas and her Greek counterpart, Eleuthera, Columbia (from a feminized version of Columbus) was a goddess-like figure commonly used in representations of "America" after the Revolution. She could be found in "paintings, newspapers, journals, broadsides, coins, paper currency, seals, almanacs, punch bowls, flags, wallpaper, architecture, furniture, and fashion" (Winterer 2005, 1264). On the dish, Columbia is foregrounded by an American-style eagle with a stars-and-stripes shield and a banner containing the motto *e pluribus unum*. In the background of the print is a plinth and pyramid-shaped tomb bearing Washington's silhouette and reading "Sacred to the memory of Washington." A willow tree frames the tomb. Much of the imagery is not merely classical but is specifically neoclassical mourning symbolism of the later-eighteenth and early-nineteenth century. Female figures, plinths, tombs, urns, cypresses, willows, angels, and even eagles were incorporated in popular mourning miniatures, jewelry, and other media (Potts 2019). This iconography would have been "a constant decorative reminder of common social bonds—success, reputation, and taste—and of Christian virtues," including civil and spiritual liberty (Schorsh 1979, 48).

Grief over the death of Washington, then, is clearly one of the main messages that could be conveyed by the plate's users, not just in the literal commemoration on the tomb but in the common touchstones of mourning. The eagle and goddess, personifying America and American values, connect the person of Washington to the nation. Thus, the owner was not merely expressing sorrow—particularly as the tomb is pushed to the background of the image—but aspiration and hope for the nation that Washington helped to birth. Specific ideals of national identity may have incorporated Roman connotations of political participation (for citizens) and freedom from despotic government (see Kennedy 2014, 490, 493). This could have stood as an explicit rejection of British monarchical government and the assertion of a new American/non-British identity.

The connection of classical imagery to the French Revolution also adds an interesting layer to the plate's possible meanings. The long history of British and French conflict created strong anti-French associations with Britishness, so using this revolutionary imagery may have been a way of producing a subtle contrast with British identity. "Embracing [the representations on the plate] could have communicated a rejection of Britishness, but perhaps not overtly enough that this message would have insulted British business partners" (George 2019, 267). For the French merchants in particular, these connotations of political participation and freedom standing in contrast to British notions may have carried a distinct weight. Tonnele's membership in *L'Union Française*, a Masonic lodge demonstrably devoted to the first president, strongly suggests he would have made good use of this imagery in producing his identity. It contains elements that would have felt familiar from home but also had meaning in his new place of residence. Both he and Comte were contributors to the Committee for Defence during the War of 1812, indicating that both men had an interest in presenting themselves as dedicated Americans. Either could have used the ceramic to produce their own American identities and to shape the contents of a shared national one.

The print also contains elements alluding to both war and peace: a cannon and cannonballs, a shield laid on the ground, and an olive branch carried by Columbia. The presence of weapons implies war, but their placement on the ground may be more of a statement regarding a desire for peace, backed by a willingness and preparedness to defend the nation. Merchants specifically would have desired peace in order for commerce to prosper. This aspiration is borne out by the focus of Columbia's gaze: a merchant ship on the horizon. The olive branch she bears is raised in greeting or tribute to the ship, a gesture of goodwill and a desire for peaceful commerce. The use of this imagery in a merchant's home would almost certainly have indicated the user's paramount concern and desire to connect commerce to the nation's future, "actively integrating commerce with being American" (George 2019, 267). This linkage of commerce to the health and prosperity of the United States is a theme repeated frequently in ceramics of the Federal period, but here we see it more subtly, insidiously masquerading as a background element when in fact it is the main focus of the print. That Columbia is so central to the design makes us won-

American Apotheosis

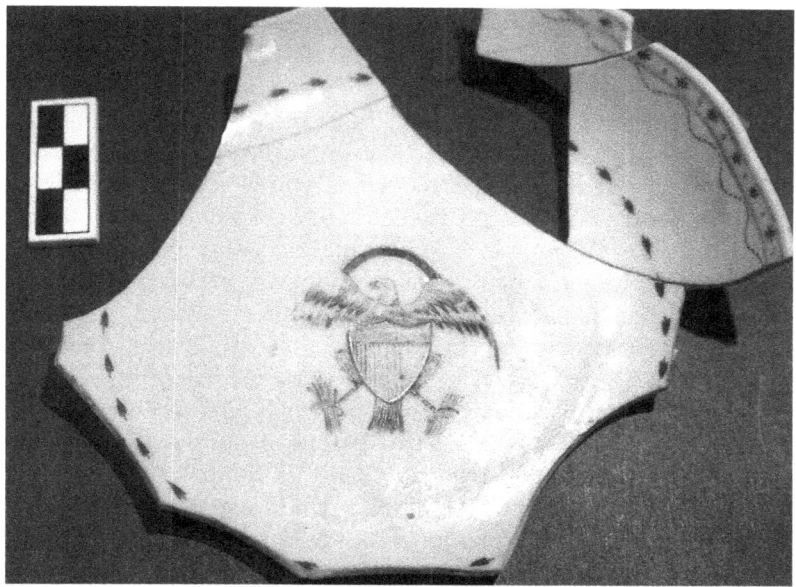

Figure 8.6. Chinese porcelain saucer in overglaze sepia enamel and gilt with American eagle, from the Beekman Street site. © Diane F. George.

der what the object of her reverent gaze is. The viewer's eye is directed toward the ship: the object is commerce!

In addition to the pearlware soup dish, occupants of the Beekman Street property were using a Chinese porcelain tea set with eagles painted in overglaze sepia enamels and embellished with gilt (Figure 8.6). The design on these tewares would have been an overt and clearly recognizable way of constructing an identity of affiliation with the new country and of inserting certain values into that identity. Eagles, as the avian emblem of the United States, were used widely on Chinese export porcelain (see, e.g., Arman and Arman 1998, 161–70; Schiffer and Schiffer 1980, 110). Chinese potters and artists "willingly" made whatever American consumers demanded, and eagles and other "patriotic" motifs were in great demand (Carlson 1945, 33–34). Schiffer and Schiffer (1980, 110) have analyzed the design elements of various Chinese-produced eagle motifs, including various particulars such as wing position, the presence and presentation of stars, and the direction in which the eagle is looking. The authors found a full fifteen variations on the eagle theme (Schiffer and Schiffer 1980, 109–36), suggesting that this motif was produced by more than one Canton artist when it became apparent that there was a market for the imagery. All fifteen versions, however, were variations on the Great Seal. Although "never exactly duplicating it" (Carlson 1945, 34), the various versions would have been clearly recognizable, particularly as they all carried an escutcheon emblazoned with the stars and stripes of the country's flag. As discussed, this design on the eagle's shield represents "the country's unification, the depiction of the eagle as the sole shield bearer expresses American independence and self-reliance, and the (implied) red, white, and blue denote valor, purity, and justice" (George 2019, 265). The eagle and the accompanying accoutrements were thus overt symbols of American identity but also of deeper values associated with a particular understanding of national identity.

Any of the merchants could have used these commonly understood symbols as part of negotiating their participation in an American nation that, while seeking unity, valued the self-reliance that came with commerce.[14] The fact that these emblems appear on Chinese porcelains may also be expressing the "owner's participation in purely American commerce" (George 2019, 265): direct trade with China that only began after independence. Any of the French merchants may have used these teawares to express a long-standing affiliation with the Enlightenment ideals of liberty and individual rights shared by both the American and the French revolutions. The vessels are rich with possible meaning for these individuals and families in constructing their own and the nation's identity.

In the unsettled postwar period of the late-eighteenth and early-nineteenth centuries, many people of widely divergent interests and characteristics created the nation through social acts such as the choice and use of ceramics for various social occasions. Residents of the Assay and Beekman Street sites were a small part of the production of an American nation. As the result of a series of daily decisions and actions in the social practices of a group of people with a vested interest in maintaining unity, an American mythology was constructed. The use of American-themed ceramics was only one of myriad ways this was realized, and New York City was only one of many contexts in which it was done, but the ceramics explored here were consumed beyond this context. The "central political reality of the early Republic" was that "the United States was new, fragile, shaky, and likely to collapse" (Freeman 2004). In this context, choosing to consume ceramics with strong messages of national unity would have been a deliberate and meaningful decision.

The Present Past:
Archaeology and Advocacy in the Realm of the Nation

This chapter has taken a brief look at the production of American national identity after the Revolutionary War through the use of American-themed ceramics generally and through two case studies among New York City's upper and middle classes during the Federal period. National identity, like all identity, is constructed in social arenas through daily practice, the use of material culture, and the negotiation of meaning (e.g., George 2019, 256–8). Analysis of American themes adorning ceramic wares used during the decades following the war shows that the version of American national identity produced by the upper and middle classes was built on a constructed mythology of god-like founding fathers and divine national exceptionalism. The deification of the founders and the connection of the country to the divine in imagery and text on ceramics conjured a narrative of God-given purpose and blessing.

Of course, this particular mythology of the exceptional American Republic is only one aspect, albeit a predominant one, of the plural identities produced by and intersecting with the diverse population of the new country. What is evident from the two small case studies presented in this chapter is that even within a fairly homogeneous group, (national) identities were varied and fluid. While both of the analyzed ceramic collections include at least one transfer print with messages of divine exceptionalism, this idea is interwoven with multiple possible meanings, both in a single print and on other vessels used in the households. The Columbia plate and the Chinese porcelain eagle saucers from Beekman Street and the two transfer prints on creamware jugs at the Assay site (the Jefferson/"Success to Trade" and the "glebe poem" prints) convey the importance of commerce to the nation in overt and more subtle ways. For those involved in the Triangular Trade, the economic foundation of the country, connecting commerce to the health and character of the nation would have been critical. This is all fertile ground for inquiry (see George 2022 for further discussion), but the point for the purposes of this chapter is that complex national identities were being produced and they included and foregrounded, at least among a particular segment of the population, a divine exceptionalism leading to (white and male) entitlement.

The question pertinent to this volume, and to archaeology as a whole if it is to be useful, is what this means in terms of advocacy on those issues implicating this national narrative today. After the September 11 attacks, now twenty years ago, national discourse became hyper-chauvinistic, with "exceptionalism" becoming a household word. This rhetoric was used to justify preemptive war and the country's interventionist role in the world (George and Kurchin 2008). Present-day notions of American exceptionalism, however, are manifest in a seemingly paradoxical way through the withdrawal and alienation of the United States from the international stage and the "Make America Great Again" (MAGA) narrative. In this version, exceptionalism nonetheless remains at the core of American identity, not through its assertion but through its felt loss and the perceived need to regain the country's imagined glory (McMillan 2017). It is not just the idea that we want our nation to be great. It is the idea that we are entitled to be great, and that someone or something (immigrants, liberals, critical race theory, insert villain here) has taken that away. Rather than the aggressive and expansionist George W. Bush version of American chauvinism, the MAGA version is an aggrieved and angry one that carries within it the echoes of a "lost" exceptionalism.

This ideological and populist movement is not new in the Trump era but is the culmination of decades of "culture wars," right-wing media, and, more recently, social media echo chambers, and the increasing visibility of, and gains by, groups that are perceived as a threat to white patriarchal privilege. While it may have had its most visible manifestation in the January 6 insurrection, we have lived with it increasingly in the past several years in intensifying xenophobic and racist rhetoric and policies about immigrants, particularly those crossing the southern border, in continued minimizing of the epidemic of police violence perpetrated on BIPOC (Black, Indigenous, and People of Color) communities, in the rise of anti-Asian violence related to the COVID-19 pandemic, in the national blindness to the effects of COVID-19 on Native American communities, in transphobic discourse and the rise in transphobic violence, in the racist and misogynistic backlash to BLM (Black Lives Matter) and #MeToo. The list goes on. Undergirding all of this is the idea of the divinely exceptional nation and the foundational presence of white and male privilege in the construction of American identity.

Of course, the currents that led to Donald Trump's election and to the events of January 6 are much larger and more complex than one idea. This chapter is not meant to explain—nor would it be possible to fully understand—the intensity or stability of the popular support that the forty-fifth president continues to enjoy. But this idea of exceptionalism, woven into the American Dream, into evangelical religious ideology, and particularly into white male privilege, is an important piece. As the demographics of the country continue to change, globalization and migration increase, and technology and flexible accumulation result in job loss and perceived obsolescence for a large portion of the working class, the entitlement of exceptionalism compounds anger and disillusionment. Political narratives have focused this sentiment on the invented Other: Mexicans, Muslims, undocumented immigrants, and even the media, to name some of the key signifiers. Those who object are fashioned as "libtards" and "snowflakes," and information that contradicts the narrative is labeled "fake news."

Because the idea of exceptionalism is so foundational and pervasive, and props up a sense of privilege and entitlement, understanding its changing role in shaping national identity is critical. Exceptionalism consistently undergirds popular constructions of national identity: the "city on a hill" of John Winthrop, manifest destiny, Lincoln's "last best hope of earth," George W. Bush's "mission from beyond the stars." Make America Great Again is simply the latest iteration (actually a re-iteration from Ronald Reagan), recognizable but inverted from the era of the Bush Doctrine of preemptive military action. The drive to recapture that sense of lost exceptionalism has mobilized millions of people.

In an interview in 2010, Noam Chomsky succinctly captured the invented nature of exceptionalism: "It is not that I am not a fan of American exceptionalism. That is like saying I am not a fan of the moon being made out of green cheese—it does not exist. Powerful states have quite typically considered themselves to be exceptionally magnificent, and the United States is no exception to that. The basis for it is not very substantial to put it politely." When we understand that "America" is not a primordial entity that was inevitable and divinely ordained, we can begin to question the how, what, and why of its formation and character. This discussion of American-themed ceramics is only a small starting point. More work is necessary to add to the counter-hegemonic discourse that can problematize the narratives of exceptionalism, entitlement, and privilege.

Nations, like all identities, are continually re-constructed and re-imagined. "The state . . . is a partnership . . . not only between those who are living, but between those who are living, those who are dead, and those who are to be born" (Burke 2004 [1790], 194–5). All members of the imagined community participate in creating the nation. Even in these times of heightened xenophobia, extreme wealth inequality, hostility toward pluralism, and seemingly unbridgeable polarization, we still have agency and power to become part of the conversation.

Beyond adding to national discourses, knowledge and education are essential components of advocacy. This idea ties directly into the suggestions raised by Martin (this volume, Chapter 5) and Ulgade and Benavides (this volume, Chapter 7). Ulgade and Benavides detail the use of Indigenous figurines in the National Museum in Ecuador for providing alternative national discourses and advocating for a more inclusive gender/sexuality-diverse national identity. Martin argues for changing K–12 pedagogy and incorporating archaeology/material culture as sources for knowledge production. This shift would problematize the present national narratives, reinforced, as Martin argues, by the primacy of document-based "history," and would disrupt powerful anti-democratic and anti-pluralistic discourses. We need to be teaching these ideas in our college and university courses as well, and specifically teaching students to think critically and to incorporate non-traditional sources of knowledge including archaeology. Ulgade and Benavides' idea for a transgressive museum exhibit and the creation of a safe space for those who do not fit into the hegemonic national narrative is another form of education and knowledge-production as well as empowerment. While I cannot claim optimism about using archaeology to reach people who do not believe in facts, I can and do use these ideas in my curriculum. We need a revolution in how we teach and think about the American Revolution and the nation. Archaeology is an indispensable part of that.

Diane F. George is an adjunct instructor of anthropology at Fordham University. She received her PhD from the CUNY Graduate Center and her JD from the University of Pittsburgh. She specializes in historical archaeology, focusing on nationalism, colonialism, and historical memory. She is the co-editor of *Archaeology of Identity and Dissonance*, (University Press of Florida, 2019).

Notes

1. A few of many examples are: "I am incredibly proud to be a patriot today," from an unidentified thirty-seven-year-old male (Pape and Ruby 2021); "Hold the line, patriots," tweeted by Jake Angeli, the "Q-Anon shaman"; "We're walking down the same exact path as the Founding Fathers" and "[We're] pissed-off patriots" from Stewart Rhodes, a member of the right-wing militia group the Oathkeepers (Hennessy-Fiske 2021); and Ivanka Trump's tweet addressed to the "American Patriots" at the Capitol (Graham 2021).
2. The Gadsden flag bears a coiled snake on a yellow background with the words "Don't Tread on Me." Its first-known use was in 1775 by troops during the American Revolution.
3. The speaker was Chris Hill, a former Marine and leader of the militia group the III% Security Force.
4. "The World Turned Upside Down" is the name of a British ballad that was played, according to an apocryphal account, during the surrender of Cornwallis's troops at Yorktown in 1781 (Schwarz 2006). This story was popularized by the musical *Hamilton*.
5. This theme is connected to capitalism and commerce as explored in depth in George (2022), but that is beyond the scope of this chapter.
6. While the term "neoclassical" is usually applied to such decorative elements in art, architecture, furnishings, ceramics, and other material culture—and is sometimes used in this chapter where appropriate—it should be noted that it was not was not coined until the late 1800s (Winterer 2005, 1264).
7. These are the soft, cone-shaped red hats that were symbolic of liberty in the later 1700s and frequently worn during the French Revolution. They derive from ancient Phrygia (in Turkey) and were worn as a sign of freedom for formerly enslaved persons in Rome (Wills 2021).
8. The Assay site was excavated by Greenhouse Consultants with the final report prepared by Louis Berger & Associates in 1990; the Beekman Street site was excavated in 2007 by Chrysalis Archaeology.

9. There is no known to-scale site map that would allow for precise placement of the feature. Further complicating the issue, the modern streetscape was substantially altered in the mid-twentieth century.
10. For details on the full assemblages from both sites, see George 2022.
11. It is much less likely, although still possible, that the vessels come from the boarding house next door given the expense of overglaze transfer-printed ceramic and the felspathic stoneware.
12. The main motifs are not discernible on the felspathic stoneware teapot. Its inclusion here is based on its conformance to this particular teapot design and the presence of the second (pearlware) vessel with an American theme. This is, of course, speculative.
13. Whatever his beliefs, they did not transcend racial categories, as he continued to own captive Africans until his death, as indicated by a manumission paper for an individual named Pompey, aged about twenty-one years, "belonging to" the Van Beuren estate, and signed by the eight Van Beuren children (Estate of Coertlandt Van Beuren 1820).
14. While eagle motifs on Chinese porcelain became relatively common in the late eighteenth century, these were still expensive wares. Such an expense for vessels to use within a boarding house is unlikely.

References

Afzal, Madiha, Ranj Alaaldin, Marsin Alshamary, Célia Belin, Charles T. Call, Vanda Felbab-Brown, Lindsey W. Ford, Ryan Hass, Kemal Kirişci, Suzanne Maloney, Michael E. O'Hanlon, Bruce Riedel, Natan Sachs, and Constanze Stelzenmüller. 2021. "Around the Halls: How Leaders and Publics around the World Are Reacting to Events at the Capitol." Brookings Institute, 8 January. https://www.brookings.edu/blog/order-from-chaos/2021/01/08/around-the-halls-how-leaders-and-publics-around-the-world-are-reacting-to-events-at-the-capitol/.

Anderson, Benedict. 1991. *Imagined Communities. Reflections on the Origin and Spread of Nationalism*. London: Verso.

Arman, David, and Linda Arman. 1998. *Anglo-American Ceramics Part I. Transfer Printed Creamware and Pearlware for the American Market 1760–1860*. Portsmouth, RI: Oakland Press.

Blake, Aaron. 2021. "Marjorie Taylor Greene Says Jan. 6 Riot Was in Line with the Declaration of Independence." *Washington Post*, 26 October 2021. https://www.washingtonpost.com/politics/2021/10/26/marjorie-taylor-greene-says-jan-6-riot-was-line-with-declaration-independence/.

Bohanna, Paul. 2021. "Paul Bohanna Antiques, AP/640 Felspathic Stoneware Teapot." https://www.ceramicsbooks.com/ap640.htm.

Brown, Richard D. 2000. *Major Problems in the Era of the American Revolution, 1760–1791. Documents and Essays*. Boston: Houghton Mifflin.

Bureau of Public Affairs, US Department of State. 2002. "The Great Seal of the United States." https://2009–2017.state.gov/documents/organization/135450.pdf.

Burke, Edmund. 2004 [1790]. *Reflections on the Revolution in France and on the Proceedings in Certain Societies in London Relative to that Event*. J. Dodsley, London. 2004 facsimile ed., edited and with an introduction and notes by Conor Cruise O'Brien. London: Penguin.

Burrows, Edwin G., and Mike Wallace. 1998. *Gotham*. New York: Oxford University Press.

Calloway, Colin G. 2019. *The Indian World of George Washington: The First President, the First Americans, and the Birth of the Nation*. New York: Oxford University Press.

Cambridge English Dictionary. 2022. "Glory." https://dictionary.cambridge.org/us/dictionary/english/glory.

Carlson, Edith F. 1945. "Chinese Export Porcelain." *Bulletin of the City Art Museum of St. Louis* 30 (3), 32–35.

Chomsky, Noam. 2010. "Noam Chomsky on American Foreign Policy and US Politics." Interview by Cenk Uygur, the Young Turks podcast, 26 October 2010. Transcription by Ken Levy. https://chomsky.info/20101026/.

Chrysalis Archaeological Consultants. 2007. *Wall Street Water Mains Project, New York, New York*. Monitoring and Limited Phase IA Documentary Report. Submitted to New York City Landmarks Preservation Commission, Project No. MED-583A. http://s-media.nyc.gov/agencies/lpc/arch_reports/979.pdf.

Commercial Advertiser. 1801. "Advertisement for Real Estate Sale." *Commercial Advertiser (New York)*. 8 February 1801, 2.

Derrida, Jacques. 1994. *Specters of Marx. The State of the Debt, the Work of Mourning, and the New International*. New York: Routledge.

Dobson, Eleanor, and Nichola Tonks. 2018. "Introduction: Ancient Egypt in Nineteenth-Century Culture." *Nineteenth-Century Contexts* 40 (4): 311–15.

Earle, Alice Morse. 1902. *China Collecting in America*. New York: Charles Scribner's Sons.

Fisher, Mark. 2012. "What is Hauntology?" *Film Quarterly* 66 (1), 16–24.

Foucault, Michel. 1994. "The Subject and Power." In *Power. The Essential Works of Foucault 1954–1984*, vol. 3, edited by James D. Faubion, 326–48. New York: New Press.

Freeman, Joanne B. 2004. "The Presidential Election of 1800: A Story of Crisis, Controversy, and Change." *History Now* 1. https://ap.gilderlehrman.org/essay/presidential-election-1800-story-crisis-controversy-and-change.

Frey, William H. 2020. "The Nation is Diversifying Even Faster than Predicted, According to New Census Data." https://www.brookings.edu/research/new-census-data-shows-the-nation-is-diversifying-even-faster-than-predicted/.

Garrett, Wendell D. 2010. "The Rising Glory of America." In *Success to America. Creamware for the American Market*, edited by S. Robert Teitelman, Patricia A. Halfpenny, and Ronald W. Fuchs II, 15–29. China: Antique Collectors Club.

George, Diane F. 2019. "'Sacred to the Memory of Washington': National Identity Formation in Post-Revolutionary New York City." In *Archaeology of Identity and Dissonance. Contexts for a Brave New World*, edited by Diane F. George and Bernice Kurchin, 251–76. Gainesville: University Press of Florida.

———. 2022. "American Apotheosis: Ceramics and the Production of National Identity in Post-Revolutionary New York City." PhD Diss., the City University of New York, The Graduate School and University Center.

George, Diane F., and Bernice Kurchin. 2008. "Spinning Then, Spinning Now." Paper presented at the Annual Meeting of the Society for Historical Archaeology, Albuquerque, New Mexico.

Graham, Jennifer. 2021. "Why Even the Term 'Patriot' is Polarizing These Days." *Deseret News*, 13 January 2021. https://www.deseret.com/indepth/2021/1/13/22225243/patriot-american-flag-capitol-riot-new-england-patriots-bill-belichick-donald-trump-medal-of-freedom.

Greenleaf's New York Journal. 1797. "Report on nominations to the state assembly by the Republican Citizens." *Greenleaf's New York Journal*, 22 April, 3.

Halfpenny, Patricia A. 2010. "Creamware and the Staffordshire Potteries." In *Success to America. Creamware for the American Market*, edited by S. Robert Teitelman, Patricia A. Halfpenny, and Ronald W. Fuchs II, 30–39. China: Antique Collectors Club.

Hennessy-Fiske, Molly. 2021. "'Second Revolution Begins': Armed Right-wing Groups Celebrate Capitol Attack." *Los Angeles Times*, 6 January 2021. https://www.latimes.com/

world-nation/story/2021-01-06/the-second-revolution-begins-today-armed-right-wing-groups-celebrate-attack-on-capitol.

Johnson, David. 2002. "Amiens 1802: The Phony Peace." *History Today* 52 (9), 20–26.

Kennedy, Geoff. 2014. "Cicero, Roman Republicanism, and the Contested Meaning of 'Libertas.'" *Political Studies* 62, 488–501.

Klein, Herbert S., and Edmund P. Willis. 1985. "The Distribution of Wealth in Late Eighteenth-Century New York City." *Histoire Social-Social History* 18 (36), 259–83.

Louis Berger and Associates, Inc. (Louis Berger). 1990. *The Assay Site. Historical and Archaeological Investigations of the New York City Waterfront*. New York City Landmarks Preservation Commission. http://s-media.nyc.gov/agencies/lpc/arch_reports/485.pdf.

Magid, Barbara. 2006. "Commemorative Wares in George Washington's Hometown." In *Ceramics in America*, edited by Robert Hunter, 2–39. Milwaukee, WI: Chipstone.

McDonnell, Michael. 2001. "National Identity and the American War for Independence Reconsidered." *Australasian Journal of American Studies* 20, 3–17.

McMillan, Chris. 2017. "#MakeAmericaGreatAgain: Ideological Fantasy, American Exceptionalism and Donald Trump." *Subjectivity* 10 (2). https://www.academia.edu/39717099/MakeAmericaGreatAgain_Ideological_fantasy_American_exceptionalism_and_Donald_Trump.

Murphy, Glen. 2021. "'Insurrection': How the World's Media Covered the Storming of the US Capitol by Trump Supporters." *Irish Times*, 7 January 2021. https://www.irishtimes.com/news/world/us/insurrection-how-the-world-s-media-covered-the-storming-of-the-us-capitol-by-trump-supporters-1.4452334.

National Advocate. 1814. "Details of contributions for defence." *National Advocate (New York)*, 22 August 1814, 2.

National Archives. 2021[1775]. "Second Petition from Congress to the King, 8 July 1775." *Founders Online*. https://founders.archives.gov/documents/Jefferson/01-01-02-0114. [Original source: *The Papers of Thomas Jefferson, vol. 1, 1760–1776*, edited by Julian P. Boyd, 219–23. Princeton, NJ: Princeton University Press, 1950.]

———. 2021[1788]. "Observations on Jefferson's Draft of a Constitution for Virginia, [ca. 15 October] 1788." *Founders Online*. https://founders.archives.gov/documents/Madison/01-11-02-0216. [Original source: *The Papers of James Madison, vol. 11, 7 March 1788–1 March 1789*, edited by Robert A. Rutland and Charles F. Hobson, 281–95. Charlottesville: University Press of Virginia, 1977.]

Nelson, Christina H. 1980. "Transfer-printed Creamware and Pearlware for the American Market." *Winterthur Portfolio* 15 (2), 93–115.

New York Evening Post (*NYEP*). 1801. "Statement on the Election of Charter Officers for the Fourth and Fifth Wards of the City." *New York Evening Post*. 15 December, 2.

———. 1803. "Advertisement placed by Thomas Carpenter." *New York Evening Post*, 23 November 1803, 1.

———. 1803. "Advertisement placed by Thomas Carpenter." *New York Evening Post*, 6 December 1803, 1.

———. 1804. "Meeting of Republican electors of New York." *New York Evening Post*, 21 April 1804, 3.

———. 1810 "Advertisement placed by Carpenter & Fowler." *New York Evening Post*, 10 April 1810, 3.

Pape, Robert A. 2021. "Understanding American Domestic Terrorism. Mobilization Potential and Risk Factors of a New Threat Trajectory." Research findings presented at A Conversation on American Radicalism, Political Violence, and National Security to the Friends of the Truman Foundation and the University of Chicago Project on Security & Threats (Zoom), 6 April 2021. https://d3qi0qp55mx5f5.cloudfront.net/cpost/i/docs/americas_insurrectionists_online_2021_04_06.pdf?mtime=1617807009.

Pape, Robert A., and Kevin Ruby. 2021. "The Capitol Rioters Aren't Like Other Extremists." *Atlantic*, 2 February 2021. https://www.theatlantic.com/ideas/archive/2021/02/the-capitol-rioters-arent-like-other-extremists/617895/.

Potts, Elizabeth. 2019. "Breaking Down the Symbols in a Neoclassical Miniature." *The Art of Mourning*. https://artofmourning.com/2019/12/06/breaking-down-the-symbols-in-a-neoclassical-miniature/.

Prakken, D.W. 1940. "Herodotus and the Spartan King Lists." *Transactions and Proceedings of the American Philological Association* 71, 460–72.

Schiffer, Herbert Peter, and Nancy Schiffer. 1980. *China for America: Export Porcelain of the 18th and 19th Centuries*. Exton, PA: Schiffer.

Schorsh, Anita. 1979. "A Key to the Kingdom: The Iconography of a Mourning Picture." *Winterthur Portfolio* 14 (1): 41–71.

Schwarz, Frederic D. 2006. "The World Turned Upside Down." *American Heritage* 57 (5). https://www.americanheritage.com/world-turned-upside-down.

Scott, Kenneth. 1983. "New York City Naturalizations, 1795–1799." *National Genealogical Society Quarterly* 71, 280–83.

Stokes, I. N. Phelps. 1915. *The Iconography of Manhattan Island, 1498–1909*, vol. 1. New York: Robert H. Dodd.

Taylor, Alan. 2016. *American Revolutions: A Continental History, 1750–1804*. New York: W.W. Norton.

Teitelman, S. Robert, Patricia A. Halfpenny, and Ronald W. Fuchs II. 2010. *Success to America. Creamware for the American Market*. China: Antique Collectors Club.

L'Union Française. 2009. "History of Our Lodge." http://www.unionfrancaise.org/.

Wall, Diana diZerega. 1994. *The Archaeology of Gender. Separating the Spheres in Urban America*. New York: Plenum Press.

Washington, George. 2004 [1796]. Washington's farewell address to the people of the United States. 108th Congress 2nd Session, Senate Publication No. 108–21, Washington, Government Printing Office. https://www.google.com/books/edition/Washington_s_farewell_address_to_the_peo/La2Q9WHptokC?hl=en&gbpv=1&printsec=frontcover.

Wills, Matthew. 2021. "The Rise and Fall of the Liberty Cap." *JSTOR Daily*. https://daily.jstor.org/the-rise-and-fall-of-the-liberty-cap/.

Winterer, Caroline. 2005. "From Royal to Republican: The Classical Image in Early America." *Journal of American History* 91 (4), 1264–90.

Wood, Gordan S. 2009. *Empire of Liberty: A History of the Early Republic, 1789–1815*. New York: Oxford University Press.

Woodard, Colin. 2011. *American Nations. The History of the Eleven Rival Regional Cultures of North America*. New York: Penguin Books.

Afterword

Christopher N. Matthews

Introductory Comments

Advocacy in archaeology requires paying close attention to what archaeology is, what it does, and what it can do. As archaeologists, we all want our work to reflect the capacity of archaeology to document, inform, educate, preserve, engage, and challenge the social and material worlds we encounter. Archaeology is primed for these tasks because its focus is unearthing and exposing what was demolished, replaced, and buried in the process of creating our world. Like other social research fields, archaeology expands what we know about ourselves but it also highlights that knowing who we are is always based on partial knowledge that is itself constantly subject to change. For one, archaeology reminds us that we stand on foundations that many have helped to build. But also, metaphorically, archaeology exposes the hidden places in our world so that we may better understand the fabrications that give it structure. Archaeology can be a platform for advocacy where these exposures challenge the legitimacy of the present, which is not often the sort of news people want to hear.

This collection of papers brings this understanding of archaeology to a wide range of advocacy and issues. To explore and comment on these chapters, I want first to discuss what advocacy is and why archaeologists become advocates. This involves exploring who advocates for what and what it takes to be an advocate. These are vital questions that we need to answer so that we may feel confident that the advocacy we pursue is productive and effective. I then turn to discuss the chapters in more detail to show how they realize the potential for an archaeological advocacy useful in modern urban societies.

What Is Advocacy?

As defined in this volume, advocacy is any work involving archaeological resources or praxis that aims to make the world a more just place. Yet, it is important to understand that injustice is the result of its own forms of advocacy. Some are acts and policies intentionally designed to harm, but the majority of injustice is caused by inaction or a passive form of advocacy for the world as it already is. Active forms of advocacy seek to change the world through direct actions or indirectly by making people aware of issues and problems that can be addressed to bring about change. Activism is focused on organizing, educating, collaborating, and building coalitions for the purpose of exposing, unsettling, and changing the world.

By its very nature, archaeology exposes buried histories that upset the solid base most people rely on to reproduce the world as it is. That said, most archaeologists exhibit a way to do advocacy without themselves being activists. I believe this reflects the way archaeology is understood—in both academic and cultural resource management (CRM) settings—as outside of politics. In the contemporary world, archaeologists have the privilege of doing research for the sake of preservation, documentation, and a general sense of broadening our understanding of humanity through the study of sites and material culture. This privilege, however, exists in large part because archaeology's voice is constrained by the power of cultural structures. Take for example the well-documented conflicts over the excavation of human remains at the New York African Burial Ground (ABG) site (discussed by many of the authors in this collection) and the debates surrounding the return of Indigenous remains and objects to tribes and nations as a result of Native American Graves Protection and Repatriation Act (NAGPRA). These conflicts were not focused on archaeological practice but on larger concerns with restorative, social, and racial justice that most archaeologists were unaware of and thus entirely unprepared for when they faced activists' critiques. Given their primary interest was the preservation of archaeological materials and access to collections for their research, archaeologists and archaeological professional societies were exposed as supporters of the status quo. Some archaeologists learned from these events that their research came at the expense of others who were not informed or consulted before work commenced (e.g., Zimmerman 1989; LaRoche and Blakey 1997; Colwell-Chanthaphonh and Ferguson 2008; Atalay 2012). However, this neglect caused injury and reproduced centuries of racism and related violence perpetrated to benefit the mainstream settler culture where archaeology was born and, for the most part, still resides.

The New York African Burial Ground and NAGPRA were watershed events in the history of American archaeology. Since then, many archaeologists have shifted the way they approach their work by making efforts to consult with descendant and local communities, updating professional training and education so archaeologists can be sensitive to the political and social meanings of archaeology among diverse communities. For a new generation, these troubled moments led to greater interest in recognition and understanding of the social impact of their professional work, and many, like those represented in this book, turned to develop archaeology into new forms of advocacy.

The turn to advocacy has found many expressions, but the most common have been of two sorts. The first is the advocacy for social justice, such that archaeological research is used explicitly to document and recover histories of marginalized, vulnerable, and oppressed groups. This sort of advocacy is based on the recognition that mainstream narratives intentionally rely on one version of history that neglects poor, outcast, and supposedly insignificant people so that the resulting story is favorable to those in power. Displacing established voices with those from the margins allows for the emergence of a richer and more complicated narrative filled with negotiation, violence, and conflict. Advocates argue that we benefit by learning these difficult histories because doing so fosters a better understanding of the unequal paths traveled by different groups to reach the present.

The second common form of advocacy is, in the words of Margaret Purser in her foreword, an "advocacy for the resource." Here we see archaeologists fighting for the preservation and care of the sites, objects, and remains that make up the archaeological record itself. There is no archaeology without the materials that make up the data that sustain meaningful archaeological interpretations and engagements with the past. Yet, this effort has grown beyond the confines of advocating for site preservation so that archaeologists may conduct effective research. A broader and more inclusive approach has emerged in which sites are documented and preserved so that they are known to exist regardless of any active research interests or development plans. Establishing the presence of significant archaeological sites changes the landscape in areas where they were not previously known. This becomes, in essence (and as illustrated by Elizabeth D. Meade and Douglas Mooney), an advocacy for the dead. That Meade and Mooney focus on abandoned urban cemeteries makes the presence of the dead quite real; but human remains are not the only materials that represent the dead in our world. Every artifact, including mundane items such as rusted nails, shattered window glass, and broken crockery, represent human lives that are relevant to understanding the world we inherit and inhabit. Recognizing the continuing presence of these lives is a powerful counter-narrative about the past that humanizes us by building connections to those who came before.

The Gift of Second Sight

So far, I have explained what advocacy is and why archaeologists might pursue advocacy in their work. This leads to the question of how someone gains the capacity to advocate for social justice and the archaeological resource as I have described. To explore this question, I want to consider W. E. B. Du Bois's notion of "second sight." This concept is often tied with Du Bois's (1903) well-known notion of "double-consciousness" articulated in the first chapter of his famous book *The Souls of Black Folk*: "After the Egyptian and Indian, the Greek and Roman, the Teuton and Mongolian, the Negro is a sort of seventh son, born with a veil, and *gifted with second-sight* in this American world,—a world which yields him no true self-consciousness, but only lets him see himself through the revelation of the other world" (3; emphasis added). Du Bois depicts here the struggle of African Americans in American society, where they are cast as "Negros," people within but not part of America. Double-consciousness is how Du Bois described the experience of being both Black and American. It is implicitly opposed to the single consciousness of white Americans who do not suffer from a disjointed social being because, in their minds, an American is by definition white. Du Bois uses the concept of second sight to further explain this situation. Second sight is what allows the "Negro" to "see himself through the revelation of the other world." In this case, it is the way African Americans see the world through their own eyes and also through the eyes of whites. This double sight provides African Americans with critical knowledge of the people and the systems that oppress them, a requirement if they are to survive. Du Bois calls second sight a gift as it permits African Americans to see the world twice, providing them, in addition to strength, a sort of clairvoyance about the world not shared with their oppressors.

The capacity to advocate as an archaeologist requires recognition of this sense of second sight. An advocate needs to speak from the standpoint of someone or some cause, not necessarily of themselves. For those advocating for "the resource," this effort is potentially less of a struggle since the presence of the past in the form of surviving archaeological materials is not inherently an engagement with the voices of the dead. Advocates for justice, however, must center the politics of standpoint and perspective and work to promote empathy for a diversity of experience and interpretation. To advocate for the marginalized and injured, for example, archaeologists must know the histories that formed the subaltern consciousness. How were people and communities marginalized? What harms were caused? What is the traumatic legacy of these injuries? Who is responsible? Advocacy here is based on understanding the way the world is known to those who have suffered and who want the suffering to stop.

Critiques of archaeological practice that were voiced at the ABG and because of NAGPRA allowed this consciousness to become visible to those outside these injured communities. At the same time, this was also the moment when several members of these marginalized communities decided to enter the field to start doing archaeology themselves. We see this in the demand by New York's African American community that the African Burial Ground research be placed under the direction of African American scholars. The development of Indigenous archaeology has pursued the same goal (e.g., Watkins 2001; Atalay 2012; Gonzalez et al. 2018) as has the Society for Black Archaeologists, an organization founded in 2011. Because of these efforts, there is an increasing number of Black and Indigenous archaeologists—though increasing diversity in the field, while essential, is not a final goal. The larger strategy must include developing an archaeology that can support the advocacy these communities require to protect their cultural resources and give voice to the histories their ancestors created and endured.

A powerful expression of this strategy is Alexandra Jones's call for a shift in the agenda of advocates from being allies in ongoing struggles to becoming accomplices within them (Archaeology in the time of Black Lives Matter 2020). To be an accomplice, an advocate must have something at stake, stick their neck out, and be willing to suffer the consequences when those with power push back. This work demands that antiracist advocacy be adopted as a central platform in the field so that those who follow do not have to fight just to exist (Flewellen et al. 2021). These unyielding efforts to change the way archaeology works represent a form of advocacy we should expect to see as members of marginal communities increasingly take control of the narratives constructed about their pasts.

Another form of advocacy from the margins aims to change narratives by emphasizing and advocating for diverse ways of knowing the world. These approaches typically embrace a critique of the primacy of Western rationality in scientific study by de-emphasizing the duality of subject-object and the detachment of the researcher. A powerful movement for such critical viewpoints in archaeology is found at the core of Indigenous archaeology and the promotion of traditional Indigenous knowledge. Margaret Bruchac (2014, 3815) defines Indigenous knowledge as "a network of knowledges, beliefs, and traditions intended to preserve, communicate, and contextualize Indigenous relationships with culture and landscape over time." Such knowledge is kept by elders and passed along to new generations, effectively creating "ancient continuities" between past and present. It is based in "the survival tactics Indigenous people perfected [and] preserved in collective memory and community teachings" (Bruchac 2014, 3816). As Bruchac shows, knowledge-keepers are afforded great respect in their home communities but "have not gained the same degree of status afforded to scientific knowledge-keepers" by outsiders (Bruchac 2014, 3816). They are instead regarded as "public scientific property" and "objectified subjects rather than participatory colleagues" (Bruchac 2014, 3818–19).

Advocacy for Indigenous knowledge is rooted in the question of sovereignty of Indigenous people and their capacity to know and engage the world through their own frames of reference and understanding. Bruchac (2014, 3821–22) notes that the United Nations recognized such Indigenous sovereignty in the Declaration on the Rights of Indigenous Peoples in 2007, which states in Article 31 that "Indigenous peoples have the right to maintain, control, and protect their cultural heritage, traditional knowledge and traditional cultural expressions." Advocacy for Indigenous knowledge in archaeology needs to embrace research defined in partnership with Indigenous people in which the resources of archaeology work in service to Indigenous interests and in conversation with Indigenous understandings of archaeological questions and findings.

Concepts of Advocacy in the Chapters

This essay has thus far traced a genealogy in archaeological advocacy from an advocacy based in the preservation of archaeological resources to an advocacy framed more directly by social justice and sovereignty that have redefined center and margin in the contemporary world. It is heartening to observe these developments. Archaeology attracts a great deal of attention because of its glorious and inglorious histories. Thus, we are in a position not only to advocate for the materiality and well-being of others but also to share with a broad interested public what we know, how we know it, and what happens when we learn to think about and respect differences in historical experience and worldview. This is no longer just an opportunity, it is a responsibility. Turning to discuss the several chapters in this collection, I want to illustrate how they inspired these thoughts, and provide guideposts for advocacy in archaeology and heritage work.

I see three main themes of advocacy in this collection. These include work that can be framed as advocacy for the dead, projects that aim to demonstrate the complexities of commemoration, and, finally, the intersections of education and social justice in advocacy work.

Advocacy for the dead is expressed in two ways in this collection. For one, there is the work of the preservation of archaeological sites so that the materials they contain can be recovered by professionals trained not only in excavation techniques but also in the methods required to read meaning and narrative from artifacts, features, and sites. The Professional Archaeologists of New York City (PANYC) stands out as one of the most important organizations to take on this work in the United States. As Joan Geismar recounts in Chapter 2, when the founders of PANYC convened in 1980, they faced a "mind-bending" task of convincing New Yorkers that there even was an archaeological record in the city. Few places were and are as committed to embracing progress and looking toward the future as New York City; yet, as we are aware, the past plays a role in the future. We need to know where we have come from in order to know where we are going. This was the motivation of PANYC and why it committed its energy to working against the grain of local practices and politics in the metropolis. As Geismar writes, "PANYC does not 'do' archaeology, instead, we make sure that archaeology is done." While this is indeed a form of advocacy for archaeology itself, it should be seen as a recognition that we need this foundational work to support advocacy hoping to preserve sacred spaces as well as develop counter-narratives to those that dominate urban life. That developers now support archaeological research and archaeological exhibits is a way for the past to have life in urban space, lending a sense of precedent, humanity, and complexity to our understanding of how cities work.

Certainly, nothing is a clearer example of advocacy for the dead than in work shared here on cemeteries whose history and presence is poorly understood. Meredith B. Linn, Nan A. Rothschild, and Diana diZerega Wall make a clear case that advocacy for the dead requires respect for the act of burial. Knowing that the Seneca Village community included cemeteries that are no longer marked, they employed noninvasive geophysical techniques to identify the locations of burial sites so that they could avoid any chance of disturbing them. They then shared this information with the Central Park Conservancy so that they too could be expected to respect the wishes of those long-since passed.

Similarly, Meade and Mooney have undertaken impressive projects to document and preserve historic cemeteries in New York City and Philadelphia. Both cities house hundreds of cemeteries within their borders, many of which are unmarked and unknown. Before their efforts, it was not uncommon for cemeteries to be discovered by the blades of backhoes cutting through graves, effectively ending the permanent rest that loved ones counted on generations before. The creation of the Philadelphia Archaeological Forum's Historic Philadelphia Burial Places Map and Database and Meade's database of New York City's cemeteries created as part of her PhD dissertation give the evidence of past care and sacredness associated with burial a continuing presence in the modern world. Their work is already proving useful. As they report, unmarked cemeteries in Philadelphia in the PAF database have been identified and the remains properly protected and preserved. In one case, the database led to the discovery of the oldest known Black burial site in West Philadelphia.

Ana Edwards and Matthew R. Laird discuss projects in Richmond that have involved advocating for the preservation and consideration of African Americans whose lives passed in that city. Their powerful chapter recounts the effort to document three sites associated with slavery whose presence was unknown before community advocates voiced their concerns. They highlight that this work substantiates "what Black people have long understood about themselves . . . but struggled to make palatable to a society infected with (or tolerant of) racial hatred and white supremacism—that they know themselves, their roles in and contributions to American society, and have affected its landscapes accordingly." This is a very clear statement that stories and sites of enslavement play a role in the way African Americans tell their story. Edwards and Laird task archaeologists and other heritage advocates to embrace this reality to ensure that this history is not erased. I was especially impressed with the effort to address the mistreatment of the remains of fifty-three people recovered from a nineteenth-century well formerly associated with a medical school. The care and concern put behind the recovery of the remains housed at the Smithsonian for more than a decade and the celebration of their reburial allowed the wider public to be made aware of a positive turn in this disheartening story but also to see the value placed on ensuring that the lives of the deceased are remembered with dignity.

Of course, connected to the memory of our predecessors and ancestors in the places we live is the role of commemoration in the work of heritage and historical archaeology. Since the discovery of the New York African Burial Ground in the 1990s, historical archaeologists in particular have become sensitive to the complexity of commemoration. Advocates for respectful and inclusive forms of commemoration from both within and outside the discipline have been impactful in the way sites are approached, studied, and interpreted. Perhaps the most succinctly powerful statement in this collection is found in the chapter by Linn, Rothschild, and Wall, in which they credit their colleague Herbert Seignoret for sharing Chimamanda Ngozi Adichie's notion of "the danger of a single story." To think that one story can serve everyone is naïve and, following Adichie, dehumanizing since the simplification of human experience to one story necessarily silences those who are not included in the standpoint presented. Historic sites and artifacts, perhaps more than texts, are rich nodes of meaning because they *can* hold so many stories about people who engaged with them in both the past and present. Children and adults, men and women, rich and poor, as well as members of diverse communities, can be read through objects from among these many lives.

Edwards and Laird introduce one of the means through which single stories develop at heritage sites. As they write, "the Lumpkin's Slave Jail site ... embodies how Richmond's post-Civil War 'progress' too often involved burying those places the dominant culture chose to forget, while simultaneously erecting monuments to a more comfortably imagined past." In this case, as well as many others, including the New York African Burial Ground and Seneca Village in New York City, seen in Linn et al.'s work in Chapter 4, erasure of the past involved not only the demolition and burial of sites but also the replacement of these with monuments and narratives that covered over even their possible existence. In these cases, the replacing narrative was tied to white supremacy and the way anti-Black racism fostered the erasure of African Americans and their historical experience in early America. Certainly, stories of slavery, racism, and the resilience of Black people despite these conditions complicate simple stories.

We learn more about commemoration from Diane F. George who bravely takes on the master narrative of the American nation: exceptionalism. Tracing this idea to the Federal era in the decades following the American Revolution and the founding of the nation, she shows how easily mainstream Americans adopted a sense that their country was somehow unique and blessed. From "American themes adorning ceramic wares" recovered from excavations in New York City, she documents "a constructed mythology of god-like founding fathers and divine national exceptionalism." Moments of nation-building like this typically call for ways that citizens and others might understand the identity of the new nation as an imagined community, but the embrace of a divine origin calls for a uniformity that has not served Americans well. George sees the perpetuation of a belief in American exceptionalism stretching into the present where it was found again among those involved in the 6 January 2021 uprising at the United States Capitol. She cites Edmund Burke who wrote in 1790 that "The state ... is a partnership ... not only between those who are living, but between those who are living, those who are dead, and those who are to be born." From this, she encourages us to reflect on our responsibilities and the possibility of reimagining the nation across such historical eras. What we need are spaces in which alternative communities and futures can be imagined and constructed.

Opportunities for such reimagining, in fact, can be found throughout this collection. The key is how authors work to connect their research and project goals with communities in a way that combines education about sites and archaeological pasts with the goals of social justice. A straightforward example is the understanding expressed by Linn et al. that training routines in archaeology are deeply unjust. As they write, the traditional tuition-bearing field school "devalues the work of students, privileges those who can afford to work for free and/or pay field school fees, and creates insurmountable barriers for students from economically disadvantaged backgrounds, who, because of structural racism are more likely to be members of minority communities." In a reversal of the pay-to-play system, they compensated their students for assisting in the research on Seneca Village and ensured that they not only acquired skills to do effective fieldwork but would be able to translate these skills in fields outside of archaeology. I also find their support for the role of artistic license in the interpretation of Seneca Village to be inspiring. While some artists may stray from the hard facts of history and archaeology, I agree fully with the authors that "artists and writers, who specialize in imagination, and especially those who themselves come from Black communities, can reveal aspects of and questions about the experiences of Seneca Villagers—deeper layers of truth—that cannot be found by digging in either the ground or the archives. Their work can also connect powerfully to the truths in our present and provoke meaningful feelings and discussion about injustice and how to overcome it." We need not only many stories but multiple storytellers if we hope to reach broad and diverse audiences and create reimagined communities.

As Elizabeth Martin cogently explains, some of the most difficult limitations that reimagined community futures face come from school curricula where most Americans learn the nation's history. Martin focuses on the prized role of document-based learning in social studies education which has the ill effects of marginalizing diverse learning capacities and approaches as well as non-native English language speakers. Moreover, centering and prioritizing written sources reproduces the inequalities of the past that were based in the higher status, presumed superiority, and power of literate people over others. Martin argues that historical archaeology, which places focus on objects and tactile learning, is an untapped resource in social studies education. As an archaeologist, I am easily swayed by this argument but I want to amplify the point. As often as we hear that the success of American democracy requires an educated citizenry, we also hear that American youth are not being educated successfully. Perhaps methods that recognize and embrace different educational approaches and strengths, including learning through the materiality of archaeology and artifact analyses, could be useful?

The tactile basis of archaeological knowledge has a parallel with the value of experience as presented by María Fernanda Ugalde and O. Hugo Benavides: specifically the experience-of-the-exhibition they curated at the National Museum in Quito, Ecuador. The exhibit's focus on gender and sexual diversity in the pre-Hispanic era of the nation was transformative for visitors who found a means for exploring unasked questions about the past and for engaging and challenging structures they faced in the present. Ugalde and Benavides follow a lead proposed by Foucault to describe that we learn by doing and acting in the world. To expect the world to be set up for our consumption is to give away the power we have as conscious and knowledgeable agents. They show instead that archaeologists and heritage workers have an opportunity to create and share spaces and places where we can consider what we know, how we know it, and what happens when we learn to think about and respect differences in historical experience and worldview. In this case study, Ugalde and Benavides clearly show that normative and conservative gender and sexuality biases have restricted most readings of pre-Hispanic material culture. Layered over these biases are that these have been harmful practices aimed at reinforcing state power and colonial oppression at the expense of those who fail to conform. Ugalde and Benavides explain by following the lead of bell hooks to use their "gained academic knowledge to answer why it is often so painful to be who we are." Here is where they find that the exhibit they created was a space where advocacy for sexual diversity and nonbinary gender identity in Ecuador could be defined, engaged, and advanced. Seeing how spaces such as those provided by this exhibit are opportunities for collective learning and action is essential.

Kelly M. Britt picks up this same challenge in her exploration of the right to the city. The concept of the right to the city comes from Marxist geographer David Harvey, but Britt takes the idea to the streets where African American communities and heritage struggle to survive. Inspired by her work and experiences, Britt suggests a novel explanatory framework of abolitionist heritage. Like Ugalde and Benavides, Britt sees a conservative underpinning to heritage preservation that needs to be exposed. This traditional framing places a higher value on buildings than the people and social networks that built, use, and now consider the importance of historic sites. Abolitionist heritage, inspired by Ruth Gilmore's notion of abolitionist geography, seeks to shift the focus of preservation to the humanity of history and provide mechanisms for people and communities to engage this humanity at historic sites and places. Built into its name, abolitionist heritage is at root a form of resistance to and transformation of the way heritage is typically designed and delivered. Rather than heritage as a thing to be discovered and consumed, an abolitionist approach prioritizes the agency of those who create and engage with heritage such that it is a means to an end, not an end itself. Heritage is also what the people did, and importantly what they passed along for us to pick up. Heritage is a means to engage with human actions and intentions, therefore we have to play our role and converse with it. This is the advocacy Britt promotes. As she describes it, this work is "advocacy *for the people* associated with the [historic] resource . . . archaeology becomes translational, using the advocacy for the resource to advocate for the community associated with the resource." People and history become entwined in abolitionist heritage. We are among those people and thus have responsibilities to engage with heritage as people, community members, and hopefully advocates for the goals of those who are asking for our support.

Concluding Thoughts

To see the world through another's eyes has long been the goal of archaeology. The academic and theoretical work of the discipline has tried for decades to develop methods that can turn seemingly mute objects into data about the social worlds and cultural perspectives of past people who can no longer speak to us directly. Much of this work has focused on developing methods of data collection and analysis that have truly made a difference in the capacity of archaeologists to understand the past. Unfortunately, there has not been as intense or rigorous an effort put into the human side of archaeological knowledge production. This collection reflects this alternative. Seeing the purpose of archaeology as a form of advocacy that puts the agency of archaeologists in the present with the capacity to serve communities brings value to our work through the value it creates for others. It is not radical to assert that engaging in the politics of race, gender, sexuality, nation, class, and educational opportunity should be our primary purpose. It always has been. If there is anything radical here, it is the acknowledgment in these chapters that we can be successful while at the same time being respectful, open to dialogue, and sharing the cultural resources we have to benefit the whole.

Christopher (Chris) N. Matthews is a historical archaeologist and professor of anthropology at Montclair State University. He teaches courses on the anthropology of race, Native North Americans as well as historical and public archaeology. His research is focused on the archaeology and history of marginalized and racialized communities in North America with a focus on the mid-Atlantic region. He is also a specialist in community-engaged research and teaching. Matthews is the author and editor of several books including *The Archaeology of American Capitalism* and *The Archaeology of Race in the Northeast*. His most recent book, *A Struggle for Heritage: Archaeology and Civil Rights in a Long Island Community*, examines how conflicting histories reinforce social and racial inequalities in both local communities as well as in professional heritage work.

References

"Archaeology in the Time of Black Lives Matter." 2020. Video of panel on "Archaeology in the time of Black Lives Matter." Columbia Center for Archaeology, 27 June 2020. https://archaeology.columbia.edu/2020/06/27/video-of-panel-on-archaeology-in-the-time-of-black-lives-matter/.

Atalay, Sonya. 2012.*Community-Based Archaeology: Research with, by, and for Indigenous and Local Communities*. Berkeley: University of California Press.

Bruchac, Margaret. 2014. "Indigenous Knowledge and Traditional Knowledge." In *Encyclopedia of Global Archaeology*, edited by Claire Smith, 2069–77. New York: Springer.

Colwell-Chanthaphonh, Chip, and T. J. Ferguson, eds. 2008. *Collaboration in Archaeological Practice: Engaging Descendant Communities*. Lanham, MD: AltaMira Press.

Du Bois. W. E. B. (Wiliam Edward Burghardt). 1903. *The Souls of Black Folks: Essays and Sketches*. Chicago: A.C. McClurg & Co. Reprint, New York: Johnson Reprint Corp., 1968.

Flewellen, Ayana Omilade, Justin P. Dunnavant, Alicia Odewale, Alexandra Jones, Tsione Wolde-Michael, Zoë Crossland, and Maria Franklin. 2021. "'The Future of Archaeology Is Antiracist': Archaeology in the Time of Black Lives Matter." *American Antiquity* 86 (2), 224–43.

Gonzalez, Sara L., Ian Kretzler, and Briece Edwards. 2018. "Imagining Indigenous and Archaeological Futures: Building Capacity with the Confederated Tribes of Grand Ronde." *Archaeologies: Journal of the World Archaeological Congress* 14 (1), 85–114.

LaRoche, Cheryl J. and Michael L. Blakey. 1997. "Seizing Intellectual Power: The Dialogue at the New York African Burial Ground." *Historical Archaeology* 31 (3): 84–106.

Watkins, Joe. 2001. *Indigenous Archaeology: American Indian Values and Scientific Practice*. Lanham, MD: AltaMira Press, Lanham.

Zimmerman, Larry J. 1989. "Made Radical by My Own: An Archaeologist Learns to Accept Reburial." In *Conflict in the Archaeology of Living Traditions*, edited by Robert Layton, 60–67. London: Routledge.

Index

175 Water Street, 6, 8, 181, 189
227 Duffield Street, 116–118, 122

A Man Kicked to Death. *See* Palacio, Pablo
abolitionist geography, 101, 115, 121, 211
Adams, John, 51, 173, 176
Adichie, Chimamanda Ngozi, 84, 208
advocacy for social justice, 203
advocacy for the dead, 203, 206–207
advocacy for the resource, xv, 104, 203, 212
advocacy, definition, xxxi, xxxii
African Burial Ground (Richmond, Virginia), xxviii, xxix, xxx, 38, 47–49, 53, 63–66
African Burial Grounds (New York City), xxviii-xxx, xxxii, 6–7, 12, 19, 36–37, 39, 46–50, 73–75, 81, 85, 93, 105, 108, 115, 122, 138, 142, 202, 205, 208–209
African diaspora, 19, 90, 104–105, 115
African Friends to Harmony Cemetery, 32–33
African Methodist Episcopal (AME) Zion Church, 32–33, 74–75, 78
African Union Church, 78
Afrofuturism, 90
AKRF (Allee, King, Rosen, and Fleming), 36, 39
All Angels' Church, 74–75, 78, 89, 94
American Independency (Rushton, Edward), 175, 186, 188, 192–193
Apotheosis of Washington (Barralet, John James) xix, 169, 173, 177–178
Appadurai, Arjun, 138
archaeological perspective, xix, xxii, xxiii
archaeology
    activist, xxx, 49, 120, 202

    community-based, xvi, xvii, xx, 98, 101, 103–104, 122–123
    engaged, xxxii, 49
    participatory, xxviii, 101, 103
    as platform for dialogue, vxiii, xxiii, xxiv, 201
    whiteness problem, 85
Assay site, 178–179, 182, 185, 187, 193, 196
Atlantic Garden, 11
authority, xvii, xx, xxiii, 18, 20, 23, 28, 32, 73, 121, 162

Baker, Christopher, 60
Barnard College, 82, 92–94
Beekman Street site, 179–182, 188, 191–193, 196
Black and white binary, 70
Black Lives Matter, xiv, xxx, 47, 69, 71, 118, 142, 194, 205
boarding house, 55, 180–181, 197
Broad Street site, 8, 48, 56, 60
Bruchac, Margaret, 205–206
buenas costumbres, 151–152
Bunch, Lonnie, xxiv, xxv
burial disturbances. *See* cemetery disturbances
Burial Places Database, 26, 28, 32–33, 38, 207
burial sites. *See* cemetery sites
Burns, Anthony, 56

cemetery disturbances, 24
cemetery sites, xxvii, 14, 16–19, 23–29, 31–39, 207
    redeveloped, 17–19, 21, 27, 31, 34–35, 38, 112
Central Bank Museum (Ecuador), 161–162

Central Park, 5, 68–69, 78–79, 81, 83, 207
 Conservancy, 79–80, 82–83, 89, 92, 94, 207
 conservation during excavation, 80
 description, 79
Charlie Rose Show, 65
Chinese porcelain, 180, 188, 191, 193, 197
City College, 3, 78, 82, 84, 92–94
City Environmental Quality Review (CEQR), 4, 40
College-Ready Skills, 130
Columbia, 153, 175, 188–190, 193
Colver, Nathaniel, Reverend, 56
commerce, 54, 172, 179, 183–186, 190–193, 196
Common Core Learning Standards (CCLS), 128, 130
Comte, Bruno, 181–182, 190
conservative gender agenda, 211
Consortium. *See* New York Performance Standards Consortium and Center for Inquiry
constructivism, 130, 137
contested narratives, xxiv
Conyers, Larry, 79, 94
Copeland, Cynthia, 74–75, 78, 84, 90
COVID-19. *See* pandemic
Crommelin, Elizabeth, 181
Crommelin, Robert, 181
Cultural Resource Management (CRM), xxviii, 39, 65, 119, 202

Democratic Republicans, 172
Department of Education (DOE), 128, 133, 139
Department of Parks and Recreation (Parks), 8, 75, 82, 92–93
Derrida, Jacques, xxxi, 170
Descendant Community, xxvii, 37, 39, 46, 50, 61, 64, 73–74
Devil's Half Acre, 47–48, 53, 55, 58
Dewey, John, 130
Dickenson, John, 172
digital projects, 85, 87
Dinkins, David, Mayor, xxvii, xxviii, 49
displacement, 71, 84, 101, 103, 108–113, 120–121, 177
document-based questions (DBQs), 129, 131, 133–135
document-based research, primacy of, 121, 129, 195

eagle motifs, Chinese porcelain, 191, 197

East Marshall Street Well, 47–48, 60–61
Ecuadorian State, 145–147, 150–155, 157, 159–164, 166, 195, 210–211
education, four types of learners, 130
Edwards, Ana, xviii, 45–46, 62, 65, 85, 104, 208
Edwards, Cornell, 75, 92
Ellis Island, 6–7, 92, 142
eminent domain, 68, 84, 90
Enlightenment, the, 49, 174, 182–183, 187–188, 192
environmental review, 8, 14, 18, 20, 23, 35, 37–38, 115
erasure, xiii, xvii, xviii, 69–71, 81, 84, 101–102, 108, 117, 163, 209
exceptionalism, xxx, 169–171, 174–175, 186, 193–195, 209

Federalists, 173
figurines, 146, 154–157, 164, 195
First Baptist Church Cemetery, 16, 27, 34
Floyd, George, 64, 118
Fort Gibson. *See* Ellis Island
Fortin, Claude, 181
Franklin, Benjamin, 15, 173
French citizens (in New York City), 181
Friends of the Tents, 102, 121, 122
future-oriented pasts, xxi, xxv

General Services Administration (GSA), xxvii, xxviii, 6–7, 49, 73
gentrification, xvi, xxxii, 71, 84, 101, 105, 109, 110–111, 113, 115, 120–123
geographical imagination, 114
Gilmore, Ruth Wilson, 101, 115, 121–122, 211
glebe poem. *See American Independency*
Great Seal (US), 174, 184, 191
ground-penetrating radar (GPR), 75, 79, 94
guides, museum, 145, 149, 162–165

Hanover Square site, 6, 8, 93
Harlem African Burial Ground, 36
Harvey, David, 60, 101, 105–107, 114, 121–122, 211
haunting, xxxi
heritage management, 101, 103, 114, 121
heritage, xiv, xviii, xx, xxiii, xxv, 4, 10, 19, 24, 59, 63, 91, 100–101, 103–104, 108, 114–115, 118, 120–121, 148, 161–162, 166, 206, 208–209, 211–212
high school, xix, 131, 143
Historic Districts Council, 114

Index 217

historical archaeology, xii, xv, xvi, xxi, xxxii, 68, 91, 137, 141
Hunter Research, Inc., 6–7, 80, 94

imagined community, xix, 170, 195, 209
immigrant exodus (Ecuador), 151, 162
Indigenous archaeology, 205
Indigenous knowledge, 205–206
Institute for the Exploration of Seneca Village History (IESVH), 69, 72–73, 76, 79–83, 87–90, 94
interstate slave trade, 54, 56

Jacobs, Jane, 104, 110, 121
James River Institute for Archaeology, Inc. (JRIA), 65
January 6th insurrection, 169–170, 194
Johnson, David, 183
Johnson, Paul, 75
Jones, Alexandra, 205
Jones, Celedonia (Cal), 75, 82–83, 90

Kambourian, Elizabeth Cann, 51–52
knowledge construction, xx, xxii, xxiii

L'Union Français, 182
Landmarks Preservation Commission (LPC) (New York City), 4, 6, 8, 10, 20, 31, 36, 40, 78, 89, 103, 116–119
Lefebvre, Henri, 101, 107–108, 121
LGBTQ+, 149–152, 165
Liberty/Libertas, 182, 189
literacy, 131, 141
Lumpkin, Mary, 55–56
Lumpkin, Robert, 55, 57, 63
Lumpkin's Slave Jail, 52, 55–56, 58–59, 62–63, 65, 209

MacLean, Jessica Striebel, 76
Madison, James, 173
Make America Great Again (MAGA), xxx, 193–195
masks, xii
material culture studies, xxv, 142
materiality, xiii, xiv, xxii, 15, 102, 123, 164, 171, 206, 210
Maynard, Joan, 84
Medical College of Virginia, 60, 63
Meet Me in the Bottom (film). *See* Utsey, Shawn
merchants, 8, 173, 179–181, 184–186, 189–190, 192

Metropolitan Atlanta Rapid Transit Authority Project, xxviii
migrants, xxiii
Miller, Daniel, 138
Ministry of Culture (Ecuador), 162
mobility, xx, xxiii, 51, 115
monuments, xiv, xxv, 21, 59, 209
Morrison, Toni, 65
Mouer, L. Daniel, 61
museological models, 157, 162

National Historic Preservation Act (NHPA), xxvii, 6, 18, 40
National Museum of Ecuador (MuNa), xix, 145–146, 150, 152, 154, 157, 159, 162
National Register of Historic Places (NRHP), 18, 21, 81, 84, 102, 116
 erasure of Black Americans, 81–82, 84, 116
 free Black communities, 81, 102
Native American Graves Protection and Repatriation Act (NAGPRA), 18–19, 39, 202, 205
neoclassical mourning imagery, 174, 176–177, 189
neoliberalism/neoliberal (planning) policies, xxxi, 103, 111, 121
New York City Archaeological Repository (Repository), 77–78
New York Performance Standards Consortium and Center for Inquiry (Consortium), 136, 166
New York State Education Department (NYSED), 130
New York State Office of Parks, Recreation, and Historic Preservation (OPRHP), 31, 40
New-York Historical Society (N-YHS), 68, 75
Ng, Olivia, 75

Obama, Barack, 64
Olive Branch Petition, 172
Orphans' Court, Pennsylvania, 28, 33–34, 41

Pagano, Daniel, xxviii
Paine, Thomas, 135, 172, 176
Palacio, Pablo, 150
pandemic, xii, xxx, xxxi, xxxiii, 5, 87, 105, 118, 128, 135, 194
PANYC public program, 9
Participatory Action Research (PAR), 101, 103–104

Paterson, David, xxvii
Peace of Amiens, 182–183
Pearl Street, 181–182, 189
performance-based assessment tasks (PBAT), 136, 143
Peters, Marcus-David, 64
Philadelphia Archaeological Forum, 10, 17, 27, 35, 41, 207
Piaget, Jean, 130
placemaking, xiv, xvii, xxiii, 101, 104, 106, 115, 118, 121–122
plurality, xix, xx, xxii
praxis, xvi, xviii, xix, xxiii, xxx, xxxi, xxxii, 148, 202
Professional Archaeologists of New York City (PANYC), xvii, 1–13, 36, 114, 207
project-based learning (PBL), 130–131
public archaeology, xxviii, 103, 108, 119, 166, 212
public education, 19, 47

quarantine, xii, xiv
Quito, 145–146, 151–152, 154–156, 159–160, 165, 210

redlining, 112–113
Regents (test/exam), 129--131, 133, 136, 143
revitalization projects, 113
Richmond City Council's Slave Trail Commission, 57
Robert Lumpkin slave trading complex. *See* Devil's Half Acre
Rothschild, Nan A., xviii, 3–4, 8, 12, 68, 72, 74–75, 77, 82, 85–87, 92–93, 207–208

Sacred Ground Historical Reclamation Project, 51, 65
safe space, 165, 195
Salwen, Bert, 3
Savage, Gus, xxvii, 50
Schermerhorn, Peter, 181
Schwarz, Philip, 52, 55, 196
second sight, 204
Section 106. *See* National Historic Preservation Act
Seignoret, Herbert, 75, 84, 94, 208
Seneca Village
    artists' interpretations, 89–90
    Barnard College exhibition, 82
    burial grounds, 78–79
    City College exhibition, 82

    commemoration, 72, 81–82, 84–85
    curry comb, 77–78
    digital Project, 89
    metal sheets, 76
    Metropolitan Museum, *Before Yesterday We Could Fly* exhibit, 90
    Project, xviii, 69, 72, 74, 85–87, 91–92
    Project Advisory Board, 72, 74–75, 90, 92
    student contributions, 86–87
    Teen Thinkers Program, 87–88
sexiles, 152
Shockoe Bottom, 45, 48, 53, 57, 63, 65, 85
Shockoe Creek, 52, 54–56, 58
Shockoe Hill African Burying Ground, 51
Slave Trail Commission, 52, 57
"slavery sites," 64
social studies, 127–129, 133, 136, 139, 210
Society for Black Archaeologists (SBA), 205
Solecki, Ralph, 3–4
spatial consciousness. *See* geographical imagination
Stadt Huys site, 4, 8
stakeholders, 17–18, 36–37, 46, 73–74, 93
Stanford History Education Group, 127, 133–134
Stein, Samuel, 101, 109–110, 113

tangible history, 137
Telco site, 6, 8
Thinking Like a Historian curriculum, 129, 132
Tonnele, John, 181–182, 190
transfer prints
    Bakers Arms, 185–186
    Jefferson inaugural address, 185
    ships, 173
    "Success to Trade," 184–185, 193
Trump, Donald, 64
Turner, Grady, 75

Until the Well Runs Dry (film), see Utsey, Shawn
urban contexts, xii, xiii, xvi, xviii, xx, xxi, xxiii, 179
urban planning, 101, 103–105, 109, 114, 121
Utsey, Shawn, 60–61

Van Beuren, Coertlandt/family, 179–180, 182–184, 186–188, 197
Virginia Union University, 57, 59

Index

Vygotsky, Lev, 130

W. E. B. Du Bois, 81, 98, 204
Wall, Diana, xviii, 3–4, 93
Washington, George, 172, 174, 183, 188
Washington Square Park, 9, 114
"We Dig New York" exhibit, 6
Weeksville, 81, 84, 114, 116, 118–120, 122, 138, 142

Weeksville Heritage Center, 114, 116, 118–120, 122
white supremacy, 65, 209
Wilkins, Sharon, 5, 75
Williams, Andrew, 82–83
Williams, Ariel, 82–83
Wilson house, 75–77
Wilson, William Godfrey, 75

www.ingramcontent.com/pod-product-compliance
Lightning Source LLC
Chambersburg PA
CBHW051536020426
42333CB00016B/1956